The Antislavery Appeal AMERICAN

ABOLITIONISM

AFTER 1830

Ronald G. Walters

 W · W · NORTON & COMPANY

New York · London

For

R.G.W., A.F.W., C.A.W.

First published as a Norton paperback 1984
by arrangement with The Johns Hopkins University Press

Library of Congress Cataloging in Publication Data
Walters, Ronald G.
    The antislavery appeal.
    Bibliography: p.
    Includes index.
    1. Slavery—United States—Anti–Slavery movements.
I. Title.
[E449.W2   1984]   322.4′4′0973   84–1625
ISBN 0-393-95444-7

W. W. Norton & Company, Inc., 500 Fifth Avenue, New York, N. Y. 10110
W. W. Norton & Company Ltd., 37 Great Russell Street, London WC1B 3NU

1 2 3 4 5 6 7 8 9 0

CONTENTS

PREFACE

R. G. COLLINGWOOD fashioned the most appropriate symbol for an historical interpretation: a web. Collingwood applied the analogy to the relationship between evidence and argument, but it was more apt than he realized. Webs are made of criss-crossing strands fastened at points that sometimes shift. Webs are also likely to be buffeted by prevailing breezes. And webs trap things.

In the case of an historical interpretation, it is the spinner who stands the best chance of being caught. The interpretation of American abolitionism that follows began to be woven in 1967, product of my desire to discover what drove a group of whites to work for more just race relations in America (a matter of concern in 1967). Intervening years have bent and deflected portions of the original impulse; some aspects of it have proven shallow or naïve. Other writers, meanwhile, developed in different fashion themes that had begun to emerge in my understanding of antislavery. But the interpretation continued to be spun. Although tempted to move it as the times moved or in response to the newest publication on antebellum America, I have found that the web has its own resilience and that only minor adjustments for public and academic events could be made without pulling the pattern itself unrecognizably out of shape—and with an interpretation the pattern itself is what counts. I hope any reader interested in such things can place the following pages in their context; and I hope I have sufficiently acknowledged contributions of contemporaries and predecessors. More important, I hope this book fulfills its original purpose of demonstrating how social and cultural forces converged in the lives of complex individuals to produce the emotional urgency that was abolitionism.

There are debts that cannot be repaid through footnotes. Robert Abzug, Lawrence Friedman, Lewis Perry, and Bertram Wyatt-Brown, although working on similar topics, generously and constructively criticized drafts of this work or have otherwise shared their knowledge of antislavery with me. Colleagues and former colleagues at The Johns Hopkins University have similarly given invaluable assistance. William Freehling, Louis P. Galambos, and John Higham, in particular, helped shape my thinking about the form this manuscript should ultimately take. David Donald closely scrutinized a paper, surviving fragments of which appear in the middle chapters. Professor Donald, with extraordinary kindness, also outlined for me a synthesis of his own recent researches in antebellum culture. My obligations to the earliest readers —Winthrop Jordan, Tom Leonard, and Leon Litwack—are both professional and personal; each has given much beyond his customary good counsel. The Jordan and Litwack families, Tom and Carol Leonard, and David and Joan Hollinger have been immensely helpful and supportive through the years.

This manuscript also benefited from the generosity of institutions. While working on it I received support from the University of California, Berkeley, The Johns Hopkins University, and the National Endowment for the Humanities. A different version of chapter 5 appeared in the *American Quarterly* and received helpful editorial attention from that journal's staff.

Those who have made the greatest sacrifices for this book are acknowledged, imperfectly, in the dedication.

INTRODUCTION

Definitions and
Implications

OPPOSITION to slavery in North America did not suddenly begin on January 1, 1831, the day William Lloyd Garrison first published his flamboyant, pioneering abolitionist newspaper, the *Liberator*. Yet during the 1830s the *Liberator* and similar instruments of propaganda changed abolitionism so dramatically as virtually to make it new: fervent, intransigent, and sectional where it had formerly been genteel, moderate, and strong in the upper South as well as in the North. In the hands of people like Garrison, post-1830 antislavery rejected the old colonizationist ideas that slavery could end gradually and that freed slaves—all black people—must leave North America, a position many abolitionists held before the 1830s.

After 1830 antislavery rallied around "immediate emancipation," a slogan interpreted differently by different people at different times. Ambiguous though it might be, immediate emancipation was a call to repudiate earlier, ineffective abolitionism and to unite men and women in a vigorous, uncompromising movement. Acknowledging that hardly anything remained of numerous abolition societies organized just after the American Revolution, James G. Birney argued that their decline "may be ascribed to this defect,—they did not inflexibly ask for *immediate* emancipation."[1] Any less drastic program tolerated sin, encouraged procrastination, and lulled the conscience to sleep; any more specific program set people to quarreling about details. As Birney recognized, immediatism's explicit break with previous antislavery sentiment justifies examining abolitionism after 1830 with little reference to what preceded it, even though prior antislavery activities undeniably influenced post-1830 abolitionists and abolitionism.

Here is the most vexing problem connected with abolitionism. The evil of slavery had been with Americans for generations, and the idea of immediate emancipation had been implicit for decades.[2] Yet immediatism did not assume prominence until after 1830. This matter of timing—why 1830?—haunts everything written on the subject. Most historians begin with the abolitionists themselves, with their religious convictions or their roles in society, moving from there to generalizations about motivation. Thus, we are told, abolitionists attacked slavery while under the influence of religious doctrines arising in the 1820s; or abolitionists acted out, through their crusade against slavery, social goals and frustrations stemming from their place in the America of the 1820s and 1830s. Such interpretations have merit but often lose sight of antislavery itself, of what men and women perceived in slavery and why their opposition to it took certain forms rather than others. Such interpretations, moreover, spend too much time chasing after motivation, after what made abolitionists rather than what made abolitionism. We may never learn precisely why people became abolitionists, and the fact is we do not need to know what brings individuals to a movement in order to understand the movement itself. We can suspend the question of motivation and ask, instead, what there was in a social and cultural situation that gave a reform its style, its particular set of concerns and solutions. I have taken that approach and attempted to find the resonance between the most persistent themes in antislavery literature and conditions in antebellum America.

A new kind of abolitionism may have begun in 1831, but slavery itself did not die until 1865. To examine such a lengthy period exhaustively would require dealing with an impossible mass of material and would mean tracing several generations of abolitionists, including individuals who entered the movement quite late and with motives differing from those of the men and women of the 1830s.[3] Historians customarily resolve that difficulty simply by not treating antislavery after the first decade and a half of its existence, arguing that its outlines were clear by then.[4] The oldest abolitionists likewise often assumed not much had changed after the early 1840s. Joshua Leavitt, writing to James G. Birney in 1855, remarked that "the studies which you and others employed upon the subject of slavery and freedom [have] long since reached a point as far advanced as this generation is likely to go." William Lloyd Garrison, who changed as much as any man in the course of his long career, could still, in 1857, present antislavery just as abolitionists had for a quarter of a century—as a working out of Christianity and of the principles of the Declaration of Independence.[5]

In reality abolitionists did discover new applications for the basic beliefs that impelled them against slavery. Not only was this true of a seeker like Garrison or those who followed him into such reforms as woman's rights, anti-sabbatarianism, and ultimately to Christian anarchism; it was also true of the sober men who broke with Garrison in 1840 and went into the Liberty Party and presumably more conventional means of reform (their multiple revelations are recounted in the first chapters). The point here is that while antislavery principles may have remained fixed after a decade or so, antislavery men and women did not. As a consequence, this study could not end with the 1840s and still deal with the relationship between antislavery and the external world.

And yet no chronology suits my purpose. I have not wanted to write an account of a crusade and how it progressed from year to year. I am, instead, interested in the constants that lie behind changes in antislavery, in the maze of assumptions abolitionists brought to their world and in the equally complicated forces society and culture brought to bear upon them. In order to get at those I have had to weave back and forth in time, even to ignore time altogether. In the account that follows, antislavery is a structure of perception. Its history ends not at a precise date but with the pattern set, tested and bent by fire, and resting on the edge of the Civil War.

There remains the matter of deciding who really was part of the movement. It was possible to be against slavery and still not to be an abolitionist, since abolitionists separated themselves from the American Colonization Society, members of which dreamed of exiling blacks from the United States. Another large body of men and women was profoundly disturbed by slavery but could not endorse immediate emancipation or abolitionist tactics. The rise of the Free Soil Party in 1848 demonstrated that much popular opposition to slavery stemmed from belief that new territory should be kept free for whites. Many abolitionists rejected such a position as a distasteful expression of prejudice and not true antislavery. The definition of an abolitionist, therefore, must include adherence to the doctrine of immediate emancipation, a willingness to devote time to expressing that doctrine publicly, and commitment to the creation of a society in which blacks would have civil equality with whites.[6] This definition does not ignore racism in the antislavery movement—abolitionists were men and women of their time and culture. More striking was their attempt to regard blacks as "men and brothers," an essential part of antislavery although never perfectly achieved. Without it, immediate emancipation would have been far less different from colonization and Free Soil than it actually was.[7]

Black abolitionists, nonetheless, are largely omitted here because this is an essay on perception: my interests are primarily in the cultural components of antislavery—in how men and women firmly imbedded in a particular culture could turn against a well-entrenched institution.[8] It takes little imagination to recognize that Frederick Douglass, an escaped slave, and Lewis Tappan, a white New York merchant of New England stock, might well see slavery differently and have different reasons for hating it. The issues of slavery and freedom, discrimination and equality, were brutally and directly thrust upon Douglass as they were not forced upon whites. Douglass had to be against slavery: his race, past, and human dignity allowed him no choice. Tappan could have ignored slavery. More clearly than their black colleagues, white abolitionists serve as a way of getting at the relationship between antislavery and general American society in the three decades preceding the Civil War.

I frequently use the term "abolitionists" as if all members of the movement were interchangeable. Although my early chapters argue that real differences between abolitionists were fewer than commonly imagined, there were sharp disagreements among them on a number of matters. For many purposes abolitionists can be sorted into various camps: political abolitionists, evangelical abolitionists, radical abolitionists, and so on. It is, however, too cumbersome to note differences on each and every issue, particularly when my task is to trace the institutional, cultural, and social parameters of abolitionism, not to write a history of the antislavery movement. The core of abolitionism is fully as fascinating as its fissure-ridden exterior.

I also do not systematically examine relationships between abolitionists and other reformers, and between abolitionists and non-abolitionists. Clearly there is a problem here, since I argue that abolitionism worked within the terms of nineteenth-century American culture and reflected a desire to impose moral order upon broad economic and social change. Forces and attitudes of the sort I emphasize affected many Americans who did not become abolitionists. That, however, is no reason to dismiss such forces and attitudes as preconditions of antislavery. Diverse human beings frequently do find varied forms to satisfy similar impulses; these forms are partly provided by culture, partly limited by class, region, and even by accident. A Southerner disturbed about the direction American society was taking would be far more likely to find his scapegoat in Northern capitalism than in slavery, where abolitionists found theirs. A wealthy or middle-class person of evangelical Protestant upbringing likewise had alternatives to antislavery, most of them far less risky. Such a person might engage in genteel reforms like missionary societies or might do as human beings commonly do—submerge himself or herself in career or family, fretting occasionally about the state of things but doing little to alter it. Abolitionists were less unusual in the nature of their basic concern than in the outlet they found for it. The problem is not to isolate abolitionists from their peers but to find out what it was in antebellum America that made their crusade possible.

We are accustomed to think of antislavery literature and similar kinds of propaganda as something a few people created in order to manipulate other people. True enough—but there is more to be said. Persuasive literature also reveals a great deal about the forces and desires propelling the men and women who make it. Propaganda, furthermore, involves an audience. Those who read, hear, or see it are not simply passive. They interpret its symbols and determine its meaning. For propaganda to move them it must speak a language of public discourse; it must express itself in the terms of a widely shared culture. There are secret messages and hidden compulsions to propaganda, and careful analysis of them will lead one far beyond what the propaganda says overtly. It leads, in fact, to the social and cultural context that makes some long-standing issues assume special prominence at particular historical moments. For all its repetitiveness, shallowness, and occasional inconsistency, antislavery literature is a door opening on to a wide range of concerns in nineteenth-century America. The following is an attempt to pass through that door, to map the "inner history" of abolitionism—to find the source of its power.[9]

An "inner history" need not be an interior one, written solely from within the consciousness of an individual or group. My interest, instead, has been in the interplay between personality, culture, and environment. I attempt to get at that through an analysis of perception—of what it was abolitionists saw in slavery and of how what they saw reverberated with their own social situation. Perception is an important matter because people do not always see what is *there*. They see what their values, attitudes, and preconceptions prepare them to see. When a new view of an old institution arises (as happened with slavery after 1830), it marks social and cultural shifts of great significance. To take such a new perception as one's starting point is to engage in a kind of historical anthropology treating the modes of communication, the rituals, symbols, interactions, and social compulsions of past groups and subgroups.[10] To do that in the following pages, I work from the forms of antislavery (its outer trappings) to the more basic level of meaning behind abolitionist rhetoric, and, finally, outward to the social conditions that gave power and validity to antislavery propaganda. My guiding impulse was not to argue with history as it has been written or with social science as it is practiced. It was to fashion a particular kind of history and, above all, to comprehend why abolitionists perceived slavery as they did after 1830.

Any analysis of abolitionism becomes tangled with moral judgments about slavery and the Civil War. There exists a feeling that virtuous behavior does not need explanation, that a stand against injustice is insulted if social, cultural, or psychological forces are found to shape it. But the majority of antebellum Americans did not take strong public moral stands and did not suffer for principles. Critics of abolitionists are correct in pointing out that it was not "normal" in the 1830s to be an abolitionist. There need be no judgment against the antislavery movement on this point—at times it is admirable to stand in opposition to society; some forms of abnormality, even "insanity," are noble.

In terms of present-day morality, the "disturbed" individuals were not abolitionists but the respectable men who reacted emotionally and violently against them. Still, commitment to immediate emancipation was the exception, not the norm, and it does not demean a moral statement to ask why people were able to make it.

This may seem a devious way to revive the tired controversy over whether or not the Civil War was brought on by irresponsible agitators and fanatics, as abolitionists were once labelled. In truth, the most irresponsible men were those who fanatically refused to take the issue of slavery seriously, the politicians who ignored it whenever possible and compromised it when it could not be ignored. Northern abolitionists and Southern fire-eaters did not make something out of thin air; slavery existed and created differences that had to be settled. Yet antislavery propaganda did help foster a general cast of mind in the North that accepted disruption of the government, even war, as a means of ending an evil institution white Americans had tolerated for generations. Abolitionism's contribution was to provide the Northern public with a way of interpreting events that became more and more credible in the 1840s and 1850s as the South increased its demands. Phrases and insights from the antislavery movement, absorbed through years of repetition, passed into the Free Soil and the Republican parties, and from there into political relevance.

The influence of antislavery, indirect though it often was, did not cease with the Civil War. I am fully convinced that the debate over slavery affected policies and intellectual developments after the war, well past the specific problems of Reconstruction where abolitionism obviously made itself felt. The admiration Garrison and others had for economic growth, for example, provided moral sanction for reformers to reach an entente with late nineteenth-century industrialism. Abolitionists like Henry C. Wright similarly embodied a transition from antebellum religious perfectionism to physical perfectionism, from health reform to post-Civil War hereditarian thought.[11]

Here is the ultimate importance of the antislavery movement: it constructed a series of images and explanations capable of touching non-abolitionists and extending into the post-war world. In this there was to be a bitter irony. Attitudes that helped men and women respond to the evils of slavery finally blended into Darwinism and laissez-faire economics, which were to serve as props for late nineteenth-century racism. Despite such unforseen consequences, antislavery deserves respect for the structure of thought and feeling abolitionists created out of traditional materials, general social concerns, the culture around them, and psychological necessity. That the structure was faulty and ramshackle does not lessen its significance.

I

FORMS

Society and culture provide only a limited number of forms and roles through which men and women can express discontent with the way things are. These are the outer shell of reform, without which the impulses beneath reform commitments would remain amorphous, chaotic, and unarticulated.

1
DIVISIONS
Antislavery Unity
and Disunity

THE STEAMBOAT *Rhode Island* wallowed its way from Providence to New York in the second week of May 1840. One of those aboard, a Boston editor named William Lloyd Garrison, meditated on an "American flag flying in the breeze," mournfully noting that so long as slavery existed it was not "the flag of LIBERTY." With Garrison on this journey were men and women of like sentiments, knit in anxious fellowship. They were going to a convention in New York in order to save "our heaven-approved association"—the American Anti-Slavery Society—"from dissolution, and our broad platform from being destroyed." Garrison regarded his companions as "the moral and religious *elite* of New England abolitionism" and he exalted in the atmosphere prevailing among them. "It was truly a great and joyful meeting," he wrote, "united together by a common bond, and partaking of the *one great spirit of humanity*." Even the weather seemed to be under divine guidance. "The northeasterly storm which had lasted for several days previous," Garrison noted, "cleared up finely just as we left Providence, and a glorious sunset and a bright moonlight evening followed. All was tranquil, all happy."[1]

The voyage was more promising than the arrival. In 1840 organized abolitionism shattered, broke into pieces that themselves splintered and re-formed throughout the next two decades. Thanks to the large number of convention delegates they jammed aboard the *Rhode Island*, Garrison and his followers gained control of the American Anti-Slavery Society. Under their direction it would be the noisiest and most extreme national abolition organization, but small and ill-supported in comparison with the major benevolent enterprises of the day. Put off by Garrisonians and by years of squabbling, many faithful abolitionists simply left the American Anti-Slavery Society in May 1840. Among them were all but one member of its old executive committee. Some of those who departed went into the newly formed American and Foreign Anti-Slavery Society, a small, less heretical, and uninspiring alternative; some devoted themselves primarily to political activity; and others stayed clear of national organizations, preferring to work independently or through local societies.

So spectacularly bitter was the division of 1840 that it bewitched the participants and the historians who followed them. More than any single event, it dominated the way abolitionists regarded one another after 1840. For historians it has symbolized what they have seen as characteristics of abolitionists and abolitionism.[2] The lessons commonly drawn from the schism of 1840 deserve close attention, particularly because they are largely false. Worse than false, they are plausible enough to be misleading. To concentrate on 1840 is to be drawn away from the essential puzzle of abolitionism, the matter of discovering what forces in antebellum America had the power to bring together for any period of time men and women as contentious as the abolitionists were. But the schism did occur and it dominates the landscape of abolitionism. And so it is with 1840 and the lessons mistakenly drawn from it that I will begin.

If the schism had not taken place, Garrison asserted seventeen years afterward, abolitionism might well have changed public sentiment enough to "have settled the question before the present time, and emancipated every slave in the land." Garrison was attacking his "enemies," whom he blamed for walking out of the American Anti-Slavery Society in 1840, but his point was plausible. The division did weaken the society and put to an end a period of rapid growth in its operations. Founded in 1833, it had 225 auxiliaries a scant two years later; by 1837 it embraced over 1,600 auxiliaries and had sponsored hundreds of thousands of pieces of propaganda. By 1838 the society had put numerous agents in the field and collected more than 400,000 signatures on petitions imploring Congress to take action against slavery. Never again would it be able to mount operations on that scale. Surely Garrison was correct to believe that if the American Anti-Slavery Society had not fragmented it could have done more to free the slave.

How much more is open to question. A severe financial panic in 1837 and a subsequent depression dried up funds for benevolent enterprises for several years. Dependable sources of money such as Arthur and Lewis Tappan provided the American Anti-Slavery Society with essential support in its first critical years, and the Tappans' departure in 1840 deprived it of wealth and organizational ability. That loss, however, meant a great deal less in 1840 than it would have in 1835. Some time would pass before men like the Tappans could contribute as much to reform as they had prior to 1837. The schism did cause the American Anti-Slavery Society to curtail operations more than it would have, but even a reform entrepreneur of the calibre of Lewis Tappan could not have kept abolition activities at the high level of the mid-1830s.

More important, abolitionism did not require any strong national organization after 1840. The American Anti-Slavery Society had done its best work by then and was becoming a victim of one of its chief successes. Shortly after its formation the society had commissioned agents to travel about and speak against the sin of slavery. These earnest young men preached with evangelical fervor and left behind them a trail of hostile mobs and newly formed abolition organizations. The agency system could only have been carried out under central direction, and it was a great accomplishment of the society's first few years. Its effect, however, was to create local centers of abolitionism, most of them soon capable of sustaining themselves without the help of the parent society. These local enclaves had only the most remote of connections with the American Anti-Slavery Society and felt—probably correctly— that they knew best how to proceed against the slaveholding spirit in their own areas. "Ideas of state rights and state independence," Gamaliel Bailey wrote in 1839, "determine the character of even our benevolent operations." A year later Bailey himself encouraged the Ohio Anti-Slavery Society to sever its relationship with the American Anti-Slavery Society.[3] In its six years of existence the society had performed its task well enough to make itself largely irrelevant to Bailey, his Ohio friends, and the thousands of abolitionists who had no great interest in whatever Boston or New York faction happened to control the national organization.

The division did increase the variety of abolition societies, and to Garrison and his partisans that meant antislavery energies had been hopelessly diffused. After 1840 there was no unified vanguard, marching under the banner of the American Anti-Slavery Society. There were rag-tag regiments of Garrisonians, American and Foreign Anti-Slavery Society members, Liberty Party men, and a motley collection of stragglers following the flags of religious sects and local societies or simply listening to the drum-beat of their own consciences. Garrison to the contrary, this institutional disarray did no harm. Rather than discouraging abolitionists, the very diversity of antislavery after 1840 probably encouraged\the maximum number of people to enlist in the cause. It insured that the focus of organizational activities would be in the villages, cities, counties, and states of the North. It made access to leadership positions relatively easy in local societies and it produced organizations to serve every shade of opinion.

Of all abolitionist commentators on the schism of 1840, William Goodell was the most sensible. "Abolitionism, before the division," he remarked, "was a powerful elixir, in the phial of one anti-slavery organization, corked up tight, and carried about for exhibition. By the division the phial was broken and the contents spilled over the whole surface of society, where it has been working as a leaven, ever since, till the mass is beginning to upheave."[4] Goodell was one of the few to see that in a nation as diverse and spacious as America reform movements required central direction only at some moments in time and for some limited purposes. The division did not weaken abolitionism by weakening the largest national organization. It proved a large national organization was not essential.

Besides helping to break up their own organization in 1840, many abolitionists disassociated themselves from virtually every other kind of social institution—from churches, political parties, and the government. Such behavior appalls historians who believe America's social and political structure is sound and that responsible reformers have an obligation to work within it.[5] One of their number has tagged the abolitionists with the stubborn epithet "anti-institutionalism."

In some respects it is easy to refute the charge of anti-institutionalism. Abolitionist renunciation of religious denominations and the old political parties came after frustrating attempts to get those organizations to fight slavery; abolitionists hardly deserve blame for rejecting institutions that rejected them. Some abolitionists, moreover, felt that reformers best move society by standing apart from it and beckoning it onward to higher ethics. This is not anti-institutionalism but a faith that institutions function in a Christian fashion only if a few people have enough moral independence to denounce their failings. When churches and political parties did support antislavery, abolitionists were the first to applaud. And when the Civil War removed slavery as an issue, they had little trouble endorsing the Republican Party and the American political process.

Justifications of abolitionist conduct, however, beg the question of whether reformers can work comfortably through any institutional structure, even one they create. Here events of 1840 are of considerable significance—not as the supreme example of anti-institutionalism but as the most obvious clue to a tension inherent in antebellum reform, perhaps in American reform generally.

No doubt about it, abolitionists had a marvelous ability to fight one another and to disrupt their own organizations. They did that before 1840 and they continued to do it afterward. In the mid-1840s the American Anti-Slavery Society lost still more members over its call to dissolve the union between Northern and Southern states. Even then the society was to have acrimonious and disorderly debates for the next quarter century. Its guiding force, Garrison, was as abrasive to colleagues as to slaveholders. One of his admirers, looking back on the movement, had no trouble compiling a long list of able co-workers he had alienated.[6] Garrison himself left the American Anti-Slavery Society in 1865 after a dispute with his friend, Wendell Phillips.

Non-Garrisonians were only slightly less contentious. The American and Foreign Anti-Slavery Society was too lethargic to have any notable schisms, although in 1848 James G. Birney did angrily decline reelection to office in it. Antislavery political organizations, however, suffered feuds and defections throughout the 1840s and 1850s. The Liberty Party had schisms in 1847 and 1848. In the latter year most of its stalwarts deserted for the less principled and more popular Free Soil Party. Beginning in January 1853, William Goodell and Lysander Spooner carried on a lengthy, unseemly correspondence in which each accused the other of stealing ideas about the constitutional status of slavery.[7] Few of these quarrels and schisms stemmed from "anti-institutionalism." Some were over serious tactical questions; some were sheer personality conflicts. Antislavery contentiousness, nonetheless, far exceeded the real issues involved and went well beyond normal irascibility. It had its own special logic.

Bickering helped abolitionists define who they were. Cut off from traditional social institutions, they had little to sustain them besides their sense of personal moral integrity. To keep that in the face of a hostile public required continual scrutiny of one's self and one's colleagues: there was no outside authority to reassure the purest that they were still pure. Through intramural conflict abolitionists were able to set their own exacting standards for belonging to the group. Take, for example, the rhetoric Garrison directed toward his opponents within the movement. It was ripe with terms like "traitor," "apostate," "false friend," and "recreancy to the cause." Such language was harsh —it hurt; and, more important, Garrison's words left no room for doubt, or self-doubt, over who was with the cause and who was against it.

Guarding the righteousness of the movement could be done in ways more subtle than Garrison's invective. One method was to make statements of principles to which morally suspect colleagues could not subscribe. James G. Birney, Henry B. Stanton, and other politically minded abolitionists did precisely that in 1838, when they insisted antislavery men had an obligation to vote and then to vote only for friends of the slave. Birney's and Stanton's proposal would have cast out two important factions: Christian anarchists like Garrison (since they refused to vote at all) and abolitionists who preferred working within the Whig or Democratic parties, even at the cost of voting for imperfect candidates. Garrisonians denounced Birney and Stanton for this narrow definition of antislavery loyalty and prided themselves on keeping their platform open to anyone who advocated immediate emancipation, no matter what his or her other beliefs might be. In practice, though, Garrisonians found means of closing the open platform. In 1843 societies under their control began to pass resolutions asserting that "no abolitionist can consistently swear to support the Constitution [of the United States]." Garrison argued that these statements were nothing more than expressions of majority opinion and that dissenters could remain in the societies. Some did, but their consistency—their sincerity—was under a shadow.[8]

The behavior of Garrisonians and political abolitionists alike was priggish and self-righteous, but it had an intuitive rationality to it. Censoriousness and tests of loyalty made the boundaries of their groups clear and strengthened members with the thought that they were part of a moral vanguard, no matter what the rest of antislavery and the rest of America said. Having no other source of approval besides their consciences and their comrades-in-arms, they measured their own righteousness against the falseness of others, including other abolitionists.

Feuding among abolitionists also stemmed from an inevitable conflict between the character of groups and the character of reform commitments. Groups cannot exist without rules regulating interaction among members and between members and non-members. Belonging to the group inevitably prescribes what a person can and cannot do without risking excommunication. Yet listening to conscience, not obeying external authority, has been the essence of American reformers. Unsure, hesitant men and women never set themselves against society. Abolitionists in particular could not have endured the intense hostility they faced without a strong moral certainty—without a belief within each member of the movement that his or her conscience was a reliable guide to good and evil. That toughness of conscience (self-righteousness, if you prefer) made abolitionists ever alert to the ways institutions and social pressures compel people to sacrifice principles. So it is with most American radicals and reformers and so it was especially in the antebellum period, when political culture and evangelical Protestantism alike stressed individual autonomy. As much or more than American reformers generally, abolitionists were the sort of people who could not live within formal structures. They preferred being right to compromising differences for the sake of unity.

Had abolitionists truly been anti-institutional there would have been no problem. They never would have created the institutions they destroyed. They would have worked (as some did) without organizational affiliation or through ad hoc committees put together for limited purposes. The latter device was well used in the 1840s and 1850s to protest recapture of escaped slaves and to agitate against pro-slavery legislation. But abolitionists took their long-term organizations quite seriously, and for good reason. Institutions have their practical advantages, especially in the resources and the influence they possess. More than that, it was lonely for abolitionists to be in opposition to society and natural for them to crave a community of like-minded persons. In the antebellum period a similar yearning for moral comradeship helped produce actual communities, the hundreds of utopian societies that dotted the landscape of American reform. In a less obvious manner abolitionists likewise came together in quest of brotherhood and fellowship. Their societies and conventions, when not spoiled by fights, were spiritual communions of believers who gathered out of the sinful world they were trying to change. Those moments of harmony were profoundly moving and deeply cherished, and they occurred most commonly within formal institutional structures.

The tension came here: whether abolitionists should bend their consciences to preserve the comradeship and effective action that organizations provided or should separate from organizations since these had rules and boundaries that deprived individuals of autonomy. In their relations with each other, with their own organizations, and with larger American institutions, abolitionists were condemned to suffer bursts of attraction and repulsion. Far from manifesting pure and simple anti-institutionalism, abolitionists wanted institutions for personal as well as practical reasons—but they also wanted the individual conscience to be the basic moral unit of society. Those desires were ever-present, ever-incompatible, and fatal to antislavery harmony when matters came to a head in 1840.

The usual interpretation of the division of 1840, given by abolitionists and historians alike, is that it derived from fundamental ideological differences. The schism, so the story goes, was primarily between Garrisonians and evangelical Protestants. The former were theologically unorthodox, given to radical social doctrines, and violent in their rhetoric. The latter were committed to evangelical orthodoxy, not particularly radical on issues other than slavery, and temperate in their propaganda. A third faction was closely interwoven with the evangelicals. It consisted of men who could not abide Garrison's rejection of direct political action against slavery: their vehicle between 1840 and 1848 was the Liberty Party. According to the common view of 1840, conflict was irreconcilable between Garrisonian radicalism and the cautious moderation of evangelical and political abolitionists. The division was an inevitable parting of the ways.[9]

The implications of such an interpretation are considerable. If the schism of 1840 truly was ideological in origin then abolitionism would have to be treated as a collection of world-views, each with its own peculiar history. If, on the other hand, cleavages within the movement were neither especially ideological nor especially extreme, the important thing would be the basic pattern of abolitionism: the assumptions abolitionists shared and the relationship between those assumptions and conditions in antebellum America. The final problem of 1840 is to determine whether what antislavery men and women held in common was more significant than what they argued about.

The "woman question" precipitated the schism. Abby Kelley's election to the previously all-male business committee gave evangelicals and political abolitionists their excuse to abandon the American Anti-Slavery Society. Miss Kelley's triumph was both a Garrisonian victory and the climax of a long controversy over the place of females in the organization. Women had been present at the Society's creation in 1833 and some had spoken to the original meetings, a bold act for the day. No one, however, was bold enough to assert that women could sign the society's charter, its Declaration of Sentiments, and for the first four years women worked within separate female auxiliaries similar to those of other antebellum reform movements. Yet the Declaration accidentally left the door ajar for women to participate equally with male abolitionists. Membership was opened to "persons" rather than explicitly confined to men, an inadvertent wording eventually used to support the claim Miss Kelley and her backers exercised in 1840.[10]

In 1837 abolitionists were forced to reconsider the role of women. That year two notable converts, Sarah and Angelina Grimké, began a lecture tour of New England. The Grimké sisters came from a prominent South Carolina family, and they spoke against slavery with an authority few Northern-born abolitionists could muster. Curiosity about these eloquent ladies drove a few men to sneak into their talks, which had been intended for women only. It was a terrible affront to Victorian decorum for females to address "promiscuous assemblies" —audiences of men and women—and New England clergymen were appalled at the Grimkés' indelicacy. In June 1837 the General Association of Congregational Ministers of Massachusetts produced a Pastoral Letter informing women that their "appropriate duties and influence" were to be found in subordination to men, not in public work for reform. In August a "Clerical Appeal" circulated, likewise critical of the Grimkés' course and signed by two ministers with respectable antislavery credentials. In the meantime William Lloyd Garrison poured his invective on the sisters' enemies, whether they were stiff-necked parsons or fellow abolitionists or both. Spurred on by controversy over the Grimkés, he and many of his colleagues were beginning an examination of sexual injustices that would lead them into a movement for woman's rights. They came as close to being sexual egalitarians as was possible in antebellum America, and from 1837 onward participation of women in all kinds of general antislavery work became a fixed principle for them.

That does not mean the woman question was fought on principle. Those uneasy with Garrison's position included Theodore Dwight Weld (who married Angelina Grimké), Gerrit Smith, Alvan Stewart, and Henry B. Stanton, each of whom more or less had Garrisonian attitudes toward women but who were convinced antislavery would destroy its effectiveness by waging an unpopular battle against sexual prejudices. Garrison's abolitionist opponents hoped that the Protestant sects would become powerful weapons against slavery, and they feared alienating the clergy as Garrison had done by ill-tempered responses to the Pastoral Letter and Clerical Appeal and by his other polemics against ministers. Preserving peace with organized religion required keeping quiet about radical social doctrines, especially ones like woman's rights that challenged patterns of authority in home and church. Besides worrying about the clergy, some critics of the Garrisonians looked forward to taking political action against slavery, possibly including formation of a separate party. That would call for appealing to an all-male electorate likely to be put off by heresies such as sexual equality. As far as evangelical and political abolitionists were concerned, the tactical disadvantages of agitating woman's rights were overwhelming.

In principles, however, even the most traditionally-minded abolitionists often were closer to Garrison than to the strident antifeminism of the Pastoral Letter. Few were stodgier than Lewis Tappan, who stalked out of the American Anti-Slavery Society upon Abby Kelley's election, declaring it immoral for women to be in closed meetings with men. The constitution he wrote for the American and Foreign Anti-Slavery Society explicitly prohibited women from voting. Yet he did not altogether discourage feminine participation in reform work. The women of his family engaged in abolitionism and other causes, as health and domestic duties permitted. Moreover, in a remark he made defending the schism, he conceded much to Garrisonian egalitarianism: "Women have equal rights with men," he told Weld, somewhat guiltily, "and therefore they have a right to form societies of women only. Men have the same right. *Men* formed the Amer. Anti-S. Society."[11] By 1849 Tappan was emancipated enough to argue in favor of permitting a woman to address a missionary association.

The woman question, one anti-Garrisonian declared in 1840, was "a false issue."[12] He was right. If irreconcilable differences of principle had been involved, Tappan and his followers would have left the American Anti-Slavery Society earlier than they did. In 1839 the organization's Annual Convention granted female delegates the same privileges as male delegates, a more drastic step than it took in 1840. Garrisonian advocacy of sexual equality did create tactical problems and it did offend the sensibilities of men like Tappan. But as much as anything the woman question affected distribution of power within the antislavery movement. A majority of female delegates to the American Anti-Slavery Society aligned themselves with Garrison and their votes shifted control from New York City abolitionists, led by Tappan, to a New England clique dominated by Garrison. The ideology of woman's rights troubled seceders less than the thought of what Garrison might do to the society when he took charge of it.

Garrison's behavior from mid-1837 onward gave his orthodox brethren good reason to worry. He flailed his critics within the movement so harshly it seemed to some as if he was more interested in assaulting fellow abolitionists than in attacking slavery. "His guns are all turned inward," Elizur Wright commented sadly in the fall of 1837.[13] Garrison, moreover, had plunged into a great thicket of heresies that threatened to discredit antislavery in the eyes of conservative men and women. Besides endorsing woman's rights, he had become convinced that Sunday had no special claim to be the Sabbath, since all days should be holy (a position that did not endear him to clergymen). He also adopted an extreme form of perfectionism—the doctrine that man's nature is not inherently depraved and that human beings can become free from sin while on earth. Garrison consistently tried to keep these and other interests separate from antislavery; but no matter what he said the public tended to assume all abolitionists shared his peculiar beliefs, particularly since they appeared in the *Liberator*, the most notorious antislavery newspaper. To their embarassment and irritation, political and evangelical abolitionists found themselves between two fires. Garrison castigated them for their supposed failings and public opinion held them responsible for Garrison's heresies.

That situation was awkward enough, but one of Garrison's heresies made it unbearable. In addition to everything else, the Boston editor had taken up nonresistance, a form of Christian anarchism. The "no-human-government" theory, as detractors called it, asserted that man-made political systems were innately evil and ought to be renounced. Human beings, nonresistants argued, should be ruled directly by God's law and not by earthly legislators.[14] Most antislavery men and women, however, were as committed as other Americans to the idea of orderly government. They found abhorrent the nonresistant proposition that it was sinful to use force to uphold human laws. Such a notion appeared to them to grant license to people to do whatever they pleased, stripping away the social restraints necessary for civilized society.

Besides raising the fearsome spectre of anarchy, nonresistance created a disagreement over tactics that had more to do with the schism than any other single factor. Shortly after Garrison made his turn to Christian anarchism, a group of men clustered around James G. Birney, Alvan Stewart, and Henry B. Stanton began to argue that abolitionists should take advantage of all promising means to fight slavery, including direct involvement in politics. They formed their own organization, the Liberty Party, in time to run Birney for the presidency in 1840. Nonresistants steadfastly believed it was wrong for abolitionists to become enmeshed in the political process (a view likewise held by many who were not Christian anarchists). Political abolitionists were equally convinced of the sinfulness of not using the political process to free the slave. From 1838 onward relations deteriorated between the factions, with each accusing the other of plunging antislavery toward ruin.

Antithetical though they were in terms of tactics, nonresistance and political abolitionism need not have broken apart the American Anti-Slavery Society in 1840. The two coexisted peacefully in Ohio for a time after the schism (when a division occurred in Ohio, it was so friendly that Garrisonians actually elected a Liberty man as president of their state organization). Even the strongholds of Christian anarchism, Garrisonian abolition societies, never had nonresistant majorities and always comprehended men and women of virtually every political and antipolitical persuasion. But more significant than cooperation between nonresistants and political abolitionists was a largely unacknowledged consensus in assumptions underpinning each position. Here, as on the woman question, antagonists were closer in principles than they allowed themselves to admit.

Nonresistants accepted the Liberty Party contention that some political action against slavery was valuable. "I have always expected, I still expect, to see abolition at the ballot box," Garrison remarked in 1839. Although critical of the Liberty Party, he and his nonresistant comrades praised Whig or Democratic politicians who stood up to the South. After 1848 they cheered on the Free Soil and Republican parties, recognizing that neither was truly antislavery but feeling both showed promise of taking more elevated stands in the future. In 1856 Garrison declared "if there were no moral barrier to our voting, and we had a million votes to bestow, we should cast them all for the Republican candidate [John C. Frémont]."[15] Frémont's impressive showing in that election seemed to Garrison a sign of the moral growth of the American people since 1830. Yet Garrisonians never relented in their assaults against fellow abolitionists who participated directly in politics. In truth, some of the ill-will was personal: Garrison could not forgive founders of the Liberty Party for what he regarded as their traitorous course toward him and the American Anti-Slavery Society between 1838 and 1840. Still, Garrisonians had a clear tactical and ethical rationale for praising politicians who moved against slavery and damning abolitionists who delved into politics.

Garrisonians frequently criticized abolitionist political action on practical grounds. They believed reformers were most effective when working through public opinion. "Let us aim to abolitionize the consciences and hearts of the people," Garrison declared, "and we may trust them at the ballot-box, or anywhere else."[16] Until abolitionists converted a sizable part of the electorate, independent nominations weakened the movement's political impact: the major parties, the Whigs and Democrats, could ignore the paltry number of antislavery votes, secure in knowledge they would go to a futile Liberty Party candidate. Garrisonians argued that a tiny minority like the abolitionists must concentrate on building itself into a majority through propaganda; in the meantime it ought to play established political organizations off against each other and encourage them to bid for its ballots in close elections. Even nonresistants among the Garrisonians developed this strategy with sophistication and pointed proudly to cases, particularly in Ohio and Massachusetts, where blocs of antislavery voters were able to defeat pro-slavery candidates and to force concessions from Whigs and Democrats. Garrisonians felt it was more productive to stir antislavery winds and give credit to politicians who bent to them than it was to go down to noble defeats, as Liberty men did.

Garrisonians also saw moral dangers in the Liberty Party and other forms of direct political involvement. They thought the essence of American politicking was lust for office—principles, conscience, everything of spiritual value gave way to the basest sort of demogoguery. (Garrison once compared campaign tactics in presidential elections to "the Asiatic Cholera," with cholera having the advantage since it "spreads no moral contaminations.") For Garrison, Christian anarchism was a protest against the corruptions of Jacksonian politics. By remaining aloof from electioneering and by talking of a time when morality would not depend on laws, nonresistants proclaimed nobler standards than were to be found in the antebellum political system: nonresistance was a way of saying that things did not have to be as they were. Nonresistants accepted the fact that their ideal lay a long time in the future and that for the present men would continue to vote, no matter how vile the candidates and platforms. But Garrisonians could never believe men might engage in partisan warfare and still remain morally pure. Abolitionists, they felt, should encourage voters and politicians to rise to their level instead of sinking to the level of politics.

Liberty men approached electioneering with many of the same apprehensions expressed by Garrisonians. Though favorable to independent nominations, the Ohio Anti-Slavery Society's executive committee warned that "Political parties, in the nature of things, are under strong temptation to compromise principle for the sake of success." The Liberty Party, it added, "must not expect to be free from this tendency." The party's two-time presidential nominee, James G. Birney, did his best to still those fears. Far from becoming an office-crazed politico, as Garrisonian rhetoric predicted, he spent a large part of his first run for the presidency in England attending an anti-slavery meeting. He issued defiantly uninspiring campaign statements and informed the electorate he doubted its ability to govern itself intelligently. Rather than abandoning Birney for his tactlessness, supporters took it as evidence of his fine character. One of his political managers congratulated him for saving "our struggle from degenerating into a mere scramble for office, or from sacrificing our ultimate object to present expediency."[17] When expediency beckoned in 1848, a portion of the Liberty men did depart into the Free Soil coalition, even at the cost of endorsing an old enemy, Martin Van Buren, and abandoning the purely antislavery stand they had taken up to then. But the most adamant Liberty men declined to be tempted by success and continued to lose elections as Radical Political Abolitionists. The only one of their number to win office, Gerrit Smith, was so appalled by what he found in Washington that he resigned before his term was up—he valued his integrity more than his seat in Congress. In common with Garrisonians, abolitionists like Smith were acutely sensitive to conflict between their moral principles and the antebellum political system. What Garrisonians failed to acknowledge was that political abolitionists, no less than themselves, usually came down on the side of principle.

Political abolitionists also shared the Garrisonian belief that a reformer's basic task was to influence public sentiment. An important figure in Ohio Liberty Party affairs, Gamaliel Bailey, declared, "we have no faith in any political action against unconstitutional slavery which is not grounded on a deeply-rooted hostility to all slavery, constitutional or unconstitutional." The "moral aspects" of antislavery, he wrote, "are of paramount importance." For Garrisonians that reasoning implied staying out of politics and concentrating on written or spoken propaganda; for Bailey and fellow Liberty men political agitation was itself a significant form of propaganda. "It is as an educational party, mainly, that we stand before the country," declared one of Gerrit Smith's colleagues while nominating him for governor of New York. Smith used his acceptance speech to predict defeat and to state succinctly what made him run. "Our nomination," he said, "is to serve the purpose of honoring our principles and giving wider publicity to them."[18] Smith was less interested in becoming governor than in taking the abolitionist case to the public. Electioneering—the great American sport of the day—was a means to do so. It was another weapon in the antislavery arsenal and not, as Garrisonians claimed, a renunciation of moral suasion.

In addition to being a tactic, political antislavery was an ethical statement. It permitted abolitionists to withdraw from the corruptions of the major parties and, simultaneously, to show the public a superior alternative, a party based on principle rather than expediency. In that respect, the Liberty Party served much the same function for political abolitionists as nonresistance did for Garrisonians: each reversed the image of the system as it operated; each presented a program rooted in morality rather than in the greed, corruption, and compromise that defined antebellum politics. Differences between political abolitionism and nonresistance dwindled into ideological insignificance when Liberty man Beriah Green announced his concept of electoral politics. "To offer (vote) office or accept of office on any other ground and for any other purpose, than to furnish a true *medium,* thro' which the throne of the Messiah may be reflected," Green wrote, "is exceedingly absurd and immeasurably wicked." He, no less than the Garrisonians, disdained any party "which refused to act upon the principles of Divine Government."[19] Voting for an abolitionist candidate, like becoming a nonresistant, was a gesture of protest against imperfections in American political life.

Like the Garrisonians, Liberty men came to see abolitionism as part of a broad crusade to create a just world. In 1844 the party's platform resolved that slaveholding was merely "the grossest form and most revolting manifestation of Despotism" and that Liberty men must "carry out the principles of Equal Rights, into all their practical consequences and applications, and support every just measure conducive to individual and social freedom." The party came to oppose the tariff, favor hard money, and advocate the right of human beings to possess property earned by their labor. Such a stance was a partial repudiation of the principles of the Whig Party, from which most abolitionists had originally come, and an acceptance of a laissez-faire, individualistic, and localistic definition of freedom that aligned Liberty men with radical Jacksonian Democrats.[20] This emphasis also brought the party nearer to the nonresistants, who, in exaggerated fashion, were likewise fearful of governmental power and who agreed that liberty consisted of the right of men and women to act as independent moral and economic agents, unhindered by society.

Similarities between Garrisonians and political abolitionists became more obvious as years passed. By the mid-1840s Garrisonians had become more politically conscious than they were in 1840. Four years after the schism they renounced the federal union because it involved Northerners in complicity with Southern slavery, an extreme act that, as we shall see, had political calculations behind it. They also established cordial relationships with friendly office-holders and, of course, followed happily the rise of Free Soil sentiment after 1848. A number of their stalwarts went so far as to criticize Garrison for his intransigence toward the Liberty Party, and a few of them flirted with ideas of independent political action.[21] For their part, Liberty men by 1848 either drifted toward the Free Soil movement and on into the mainstream of political life—the course of Gamaliel Bailey and Salmon P. Chase—or else clung to the stern antislavery faith of the mid-1840s, as did James G. Birney, Gerrit Smith, and William Goodell. In the decades following the division Liberty men and Garrisonians alike revealed by their behavior that they were of a divided mind about the political process. Each faction was alternately drawn to it and repulsed from it by the moral compromises it demanded of

successful candidates. Each faction was entranced by a vision of a more perfect society and neither one was quite certain whether the American political system was capable of bringing it about.

"There never was any but an imaginary chasm between us," an old Liberty man told William Lloyd Garrison in 1862.[22] He exaggerated a bit. It was a serious matter for abolitionists to disagree over whether women should participate equally with men in antislavery work and over whether to engage in direct political action. Yet Garrison's correspondent was more right than wrong. Abolitionist quarrels were not between competing ideologies: they took place within a parameter of assumptions. In terms of antebellum political culture, abolitionists possessed a Whig sense of responsibility for national affairs; but they grafted it onto the Democratic ideal of a state free from coercion. In religion, abolitionists drew from Protestant traditions, with their stress on individual conscience, and fused those with 1820s revivalism and its millennialistic faith that mankind could become perfect, or nearly so, while on earth. There was more within the parameter—and we shall deal with that in time—but when conflict arose it generally was because some abolitionist (Garrison most notably) went to the outer reaches of the parameter's egalitarian, anarchistic, and perfectionistic logic, farther than others cared to go. Even at those moments abolitionists were bound together by beliefs and perceptions that went deeper than the issues they argued about.

The division occurred for a simple reason: there was nothing to prevent it. Localism, personality conflicts, hard times, tension between group needs and individual conscience, and differences over tactics limited the American Anti-Slavery Society's effectiveness. By 1840 abolitionists could accomplish more without a single national organization and were better off going their separate ways.

The sad thing is that antislavery men and women, and historians following their lead, made the parting seem more serious than it was. It did not hurt antislavery; it did not demonstrate "anti-instutionalism"; and it did not derive from strong ideological differences. Negative though they are, those points have to be made. If they were not, the division would continue to bewitch and mislead, as it has since 1840. The real problem is to learn what abolitionists *shared*—otherwise we cannot understand what produced a particular style of antislavery in the 1830s and sustained its emotional power for three decades.

MEANS
Abolitionism as Career
and Community

DIVISIONS among abolitionists were so frequent and so noisy that they obscured patterns of expression and social interaction that took place outside institutions and in everyday situations.[1] Such patterns are an important kind of human behavior: they have deep meanings not apparent to a casual observer. We grasp their significance best when we are outsiders, looking at an alien culture rather than at our ancestors or our contemporaries. Through intellect and imagination, for instance, we can tell that power, domination, family, obligation, tradition, and affection have unspoken parts when non-western peoples pay deference to one another. All humans—corporation executives as well as tribesmen—similarly express themselves and interact with one another on several levels simultaneously, governed by rules imbedded in culture.

It is time to turn to such a network of assumptions and coded meanings hidden beneath the surface of words, gestures, and deeds in antislavery. The place to begin is with three matters that were interconnected, although not obviously so: the social role of the reformer in antebellum America; the rituals and artifacts of antislavery; and abolitionist advocacy of violence. These fall into a pattern of their own and it is one that tells much about what antislavery meant to abolitionists.

Wendell Phillips came as close as any abolitionist to being a theoretician of propaganda and of the reformer's place in American society. According to Phillips, a democracy functions morally only if it has agitators who devote themselves to stirring public opinion. Once the public moves, politicians follow eagerly. Phillips argued that effectiveness and fidelity to principles required reformers to take extreme positions, ones unlikely to be accepted by the mass of mankind. Only by being shocking, insistent, and intransigent can an agitator overcome public apathy and inertia, which always favor the status quo. For Phillips this was both an article of faith and something proven by experience. "Our reckless course, our empty rant, our fanaticism," he boasted, "has made Abolitionists of some of the best and ablest men in the land."[2] Such triumphs were temporary. Phillips maintained that it was the reformer's fate never to be found among the majority but eternally to be ahead of the rest of humanity, beckoning it to a higher moral ground.

Phillips' interpretation is attractive in its simplicity. It especially appeals to a cautious or disillusioned liberal sensibility because it assumes reformers have a permanent place in society but that extreme rhetoric results in nothing more than moderate change.[3] Phillips, nonetheless, scarcely described, let alone analyzed, all that abolitionists did.

He was misleading when he claimed reformers worked primarily through public attitudes. That glossed over numerous ways in which abolitionists tried to coerce slaveholders. Some abolitionists hoped to put economic pressure on the South by operating stores selling nothing made by slave labor. David Child even planted sugar beets in Massachusetts in order to show Northerners they could sweeten their diet with "free" sugar. Phillips himself was interested in a project to grow cheap cotton in India to bring down Southern slavery by making it unprofitable. In the 1850s he urged slaves to run away or to rebel.[4] These tactics were very different from the "moral suasion" Phillips glorified in his theoretical statements.

There were more subtle omissions and ambiguities in Phillips' pronouncements on agitation. He and fellow abolitionists argued that moral suasion was a matter of appealing to men and women as responsible beings and convincing them of the justice of immediate emancipation. Yet reformers suspected that most humans were not moral, and they believed that the godly individual's conscience was a surer guide to virtue than was the voice of society. Beriah Green captured the tension perfectly. Although he was a Liberty man and presumably interested in attracting voters to the cause, he felt "a greater delusion was never hatched from a cocaktrice's egg, than what is commonly boasted of as the *Democratic principle*." He wanted "the control of Wisdom" rather than the control of universal suffrage. Phillips similarly refused to indulge in admiration for "the people." "The masses are governed more by impulse than conviction," he said in 1853, in tones appropriate for a Calvinistic Boston Brahmin. The problem was that abolitionists had to appeal to those masses or cease to be agitators in a democratic society. Phillips' response was an uneasy balance of moral elitism and democratic clichés. He argued that the agitator's function was to educate the populace and to lead public opinion to redemption. "The people always mean right, and in the end they will have the right," he insisted, conceding it required a monumental amount of work to bring them to that point.[5]

Phillips' remarks reveal most by their incompleteness. They reflect a general abolitionist disinterest in pursuing abstract questions of tactics. With the great exception of their debate over the Liberty Party and political action, abolitionists did not even make much effort to weigh the relative effectiveness of various propaganda devices—surprising in a movement having to make the most of limited resources. When abolitionists did bring themselves to assess the means they used, they did so with casualness and diversity of opinion. "The press," R. G. Williams thought, "has probably made seven-eights of all the abolitionists in the country." Thomas Wentworth Higginson dated his conversion from reading an antislavery book, but he added that "the eloquence of public meetings was a more exciting stimulus."[6]

It was just as well that abolitionists settled for random statements like those of Williams and Higginson and the engaging generalities of Wendell Phillips. Lack of theorizing about tactics freed abolitionists to pursue various alternatives without the agonizing introspection that that occasionally paralyzes the American left.[7] No one in the movement had to feel guilt over working in the manner he or she found most comfortable, whether through prose, lecturing, or as an organizer of meetings and events. Even within propaganda forms there was a broad spectrum of tolerable styles—as there might not have

been had abolitionists attempted to develop coherent theories of moral suasion. At one extreme were closely reasoned political analyses of slavery; at the other were bitter and emotional polemics; somewhere in between were more or less factual treatises giving examples from the laws and unguarded writings of slaveholders themselves. That diversity of forms and styles let abolitionists have the best of all worlds. They could play to a rational and legalistic audience; they could pummel opponents and waverers with harsh language; they could manipulate sentimental conventions with tearful accounts of black families separated by cruel masters; and they could attack sentimental conventions when the "fastidious decorum of the age" stood in their way.

Whatever its effects, the failure of abolitionists to create a well-defined conception of agitation was indication that the crusade fit comfortably into a pre-existing set of roles, expectations, and techniques. William Goodell saw things accurately in retrospect. He recalled how a "new spirit of moral enterprise and inquiry" had been loose in the land in the 1820s and 1830s and how many future abolitionists had imbibed that spirit long before turning to antislavery. Phillips and his colleagues could avoid systematic self-scrutiny because nearly every kind of activity they engaged in (independent political action again being the exception) was familiar to them and had already proven its worth in earlier benevolent enterprises.

In reality Phillips' agitator was a new kind of profession that derived from several antebellum refinements in techniques of agitation. Some of these were secular adaptations of older Protestant forms. Goodell, the most astute student of the process, remarked upon a proliferation of "voluntary lecturers and agents of societies" and of "promiscuous conventions" attacking diverse evils. The former were the reform equivalent of itinerant clergymen, long a fixture of American religion; the latter were analogous to revivals and camp meetings. Other improvements in propaganda techniques came from innovations in transportation and printing. These reduced the cost of distributing information to a level where individuals and tiny groups could afford to put unconventional ideas before a mass audience.[8]

What neither Phillips nor Goodell quite grasped was that a combination of these factors—some religious, some scientific, and some social—conspired to make reform a viable occupation in antebellum America. To be sure, a few men and women in previous decades had devoted much of their lives to social improvement, but these were figures like John Woolman, a gentle eighteenth-century Quaker, who worked primarily within religious frameworks. The more common type of eighteenth-century reformer had been a man or woman of civic virtue, a Benjamin Franklin engaged in many worthy activities but not defining his or her life in terms of one or two reform commitments. Even in the antebellum period such gentleman-reformers persisted. The distinguished sponsors of the American Colonization Society fit that description well: they were statesmen, lawyers, or planters for whom colonization was a peripheral matter. Phillips' agitator was different. His existence depended on engagement in reform. His income might derive from reform work or he might use income from other sources to support reform activities, but in either instance he was first and foremost a reformer. The significance of Phillips' musings on agitators was not in his sense of how they functioned but rather in the fact he could assume that in antebellum America men and women could make secular reform a career.

Once reform became a profession, professional considerations began to influence what reformers did—reinforcing a social role was as fully a part of some abolitionist enterprises as increasing support for the cause. Abolitionists themselves implied as much when they rejected "expediency." Immediate effectiveness mattered less, most of them insisted, than whether tactics represented adherence to the highest moral standard. Without that uncompromising commitment, abolitionists were in danger of losing the integrity and firmness of conviction that set reformers off from the unregenerate masses. Naturally enough abolitionists did at times choose expediency and they did occasionally fall into manipulating their audiences for effect (a bit cynically once in a while). Those lapses aside, antislavery most frequently entwined a desire to persuade others with a drive to preserve the distinctiveness of the group.

Even many ostensibly public events served to identify and strengthen true-hearted reformers rather than to reach unbelievers. A large number of antislavery meetings, for instance, were essentially private rituals to celebrate dates of significance only to abolitionists. Twenty years after, Boston antislavery men and women marked the anniversary of a violent mobbing they had suffered. New York abolitionists annually commemorated the successful rescue of a fugitive slave named Jerry. In New England, at Oberlin, and probably elsewhere, abolitionists held mournful picnics on the Fourth of July (reminders that democratic America did not give freedom to all) and joyous picnics on the first of August, the date of emancipation in the British West Indies.[9] These were seasons of brotherhood, affirmations of a beleaguered conviction amidst a sinful society, celebrations of a victory yet to come.

In the same category were antislavery fairs or bazaars, held most successfully in Boston and Philadelphia, but also appearing in small towns throughout the free states. Unlike picnics and ritual celebrations, fairs did have their practical side. They were wonderfully profit-making ventures, the Philadelphia one netting around $28,000 through the years while the Boston fair put several thousand dollars annually into antislavery coffers. There was even some thought that bazaars brought new friends to the cause. "Those who shun the lecture room," a correspondent told the *Liberator*, "cannot help receiving the anti-slavery impress from the Fair." She may have been correct but money and converts were not what fairs were all about. Maria Weston Chapman said of the women who helped her organize the Boston bazaar: "It is the moral power, springing from the exertion to raise it [the money]; this increase of light, and energy, and skill, and persever-ance, and christian fellowship, and devotedness to our holy enter-prise,—and spiritual strength and comfort,—that we value far more than the largest sum." Mary Grew recalled fairs as "Passover Festivals, whither 'our tribes went up' with gladness, and found refreshment and strength."[10] Like so many antislavery gatherings, fairs were the rites of a community.

The community itself might be small and faction-ridden, but social criteria for membership in it were unusually generous. Unlike most careers in antebellum America, reform was not the monopoly of adult, white males—the politically important segment of the population. Abolitionists also drew in black people, women, and children, a strik-ingly unpolitical approach to social change, one directed as much at the disfranchised as at the men who presumably made decisions with their ballots. The drive of the reformer was to bring into fellowship the moral part of the nation, which was not at all the same as the po-litical part.

A way to accomplish that end was to hold meetings—fairs, picnics, and conventions—in which all ages, sexes, and races could join. An-other way was to mingle abolitionist commitment with day-to-day spontaneous interaction among family and friends. Fairs did so by turning purchase of Christmas presents and mundane household items into a moral act (simple iron holders at one fair were promoted as "anti-slave *holders*"). Other endeavors likewise brought abolitionism into private situations. There were Ladies' Anti-Slavery Sewing Soci-eties, the one in New York bragging that "with their needles and pen-cils they can reach the heart through the eye." These ladies produced such items as antislavery handkerchiefs for children ("operating upon many a little heart") and samplers for the walls of reform parlors, bearing mottoes like "May the points of our needles prick the slave-holders' consciences." Truly committed men and women could pur-chase antislavery earthenware so that they might "silently preach abolitionism to their guests, and train up their children in sound principles, by the simple process of furnishing their tables." If that were not enough, abolitionists could write on specially printed antislavery stationery and seal these letters with "wafers" telling of slavery's manifold evils.[11]

Trivial as wafers, stationery, earthenware, samplers, and handkerchiefs seem, they were social signs of great importance. Like fairs, picnics, and ritual celebrations, they were evidence that when commitment came it was total. Antislavery was not something to be casually added to a person's previous beliefs and activities. It was acceptance of an image of one's self, admission to a community, and adoption of a way of life having its own peculiar badges of loyalty.

The abolitionists' conception of their role hinged on moral suasion. They saw themselves as teachers, preachers, and prophets of a better society. Yet crucial as moral suasion was, it was compromised by an undercurrent of violence in antislavery rhetoric. At first this appeared as nothing more than an ambivalence toward insurrections, but by the 1850s it became, for some, virtually a loss of faith in moral suasion as a tactic. Like the mundane emblems of antislavery sentiment, this growing fascination with violence was a function of the life-changing hold antislavery took on its converts.

From the beginning there was a strong sense among abolitionists that slavery might end in bloodshed, probably in a slave revolt. Nat Turner's Rebellion, most terrifying of all North American uprisings, occurred in 1831, less than a year after Garrison began publication of the *Liberator*, and it seemed an omen of worse things to come. "There is now about as much certainty that God will destroy the slave states by a series of calamities as that the sun will rise tomorrow," Garrison warned in Turner's aftermath. William Jay, writing about the same time, concluded that "the slaves will either receive their freedom as a boon, or they will wrest it by force from their masters."[12] Abolitionists like Garrison and Jay took care to point out that they did not endorse insurrection but they also did not equivocate: if the white South failed to emancipate its slaves it was doomed.

Clearly abolitionists had practical reasons for talking about slave revolts. Critics frequently charged them with stirring insurrection or else claimed that emancipation led inevitably to race war. As a consequence abolitionists had to spend inordinate amounts of time at such tasks as explaining that the famous uprising on St. Domingo had not come from granting freedom but from French attempts to reimpose slavery.[13] The unfortunate conjunction of Nat Turner's Revolt with the early months of the *Liberator* made it even more imperative for abolitionists to disassociate themselves from black rebellion. By presenting their work as the only alternative to insurrection they denied complicity in slave violence and turned fear of it into a reason for supporting their cause.

In yet another way abolitionists consciously took advantage of white uneasiness about slave revolts. Garrisonians played upon such apprehensions in the 1840s and 1850s when they advocated breaking the federal union between free and slave states. Often mistakenly seen as merely an attempt to preserve personal moral purity, this "disunion" strategy impressed Garrisonians as an effective tactic to scare the South into ending slavery. The terror for Southerners came because the thrust of disunionism, Garrison once explained, "is to withdraw from the masters all those resources and instrumentalities now furnished to them by the North, without which they are powerless." Chief among those instrumentalities was a promise of armed force to put down slave revolts. Disunionism offered the white South a Devil's choice: either emancipation and preservation of the Union or dissolution of the Union and more Nat Turners.[14]

Opponents as well as proponents recognized that disunionism rested upon a logic of violence. Long before the strategy took shape William Jay (hardly a Garrisonian) argued that if the Union collapsed, "a civil war ensues—the moral means heretofore used by abolitionists give place to the confused noise of the warrior, and to garments rolled in blood; servile insurrection necessarily follows in the train of civil war, and if slavery perish it will perish only in a deluge of BLOOD." The *Radical Abolitionist,* reviewing Wendell Phillips' arguments in 1857, gave its mock summation: "And so the 'dissolution of the Union' doctrine has dwindled down, at last, to this—an expedient for settling the slavery question by a masterly inactivity at the North—'*Hands Off! Let the two races fight it out!*'" Yet political abolitionists were as willing as Garrisonians to use hints of disunionism to play upon fears of insurrection. The Liberty Party's 1844 platform resolved that it was not the duty of the government "to maintain slavery by military force." This put the party on record in favor of withdrawal of Northern aid in case of a slave revolt. In a passage ominous to white Southerners the platform asserted "when freemen unsheath the sword it should be to strike for *Liberty,* not for despotism."[15]

Such predictions of violence aside, pacifism was deeply ingrained in early antislavery thought, and genuine concern over the possibility of insurrection may have helped push some of the pioneer abolitionists to advocate immediate emancipation. When first declaring her antislavery commitment, Angelina Grimké portrayed abolitionism as the only way to prevent a catastrophe far worse than Nat Turner's Rebellion. "At one time," she wrote,

I thought this system would be overthrown in blood, with the confused noise of the warrior; but a hope gleams across my mind, that *our* blood will be spilt, instead of the slaveholders, our *lives* will be taken and theirs spared. . . . I say a *hope,* for of all things I desire to be spared the anguish of seeing our beloved country desolated with the horrors of a servile war.[16]

That was the heart-felt language of a Southern-born woman who foresaw bloody atonement unless national repentance came rapidly.

Abolitionists spoke of slave revolts in situations that likewise indicate real apprehensions were at work, not just calculations of propaganda advantage. In a private letter to a fellow Northerner, Maria Weston Chapman in December 1850 predicted "an insurrection within a month." Alvan Stewart's speeches contained references to the horror of Turner's Revolt well after the event, and he justified the Liberty Party by asking if "the avenging sword, the midnight flame, the forlorn shriek of despair" were to be the only remedy for slavery. "God forbid," he exclaimed, "that the fair plains of the South should be delivered over to the vandalism of such a terrible necessity."[17] Stewart knew that his party had no audience in the South and that his words had power only because they expressed the anxieties of himself and his fellow Liberty men.

There is further evidence that abolitionist distaste for violence was genuine. In 1837 an Illinois antislavery editor, Elijah Lovejoy, died at the hands of an angry mob. Abolitionists exploited his martyrdom to generate revulsion against enemies of the cause; but Lovejoy had taken up firearms to defend his press and that fact dampened enthusiasm for him among abolitionists and made their propaganda about his death less effective than it might have been. There were other instances when abolitionists created difficulties for themselves by reproving comrades for endorsing violent means. In 1843 Maria Weston Chapman took Henry Highland Garnet, a black abolitionist, to task for preaching revolt. Garnet felt the rebuke was presumptuous from a white and the dispute between the two assumed ugly racial overtones. These obscured the fact that black Garrisonians likewise disavowed Garnet and that Mrs. Chapman, a month earlier, had criticized her fellow white Garrisonian, Stephen Foster, for not clearly condemning slave uprisings.[18] That kind of bickering would not have occurred if abolitionists had not taken their nonviolence very seriously.

Even after attitudes had begun to change in the 1850s, abolitionists who felt they had little else in common nonetheless paid tribute to each other's lingering pacifism. The *National Era* gave rare praise to Garrison in 1857, calling him "a man who . . . has constantly written and acted against the policy of force, against all physical violence, against the shedding of blood." Two and a half years later the paper was similarly satisfied with his first remarks on John Brown's raid, being "pleased to observe that even Mr. Garrison has been true to his peace principles on this occasion."[19]

It is possible that abolitionist pacifism was a mechanism for denying, on the conscious level, subconscious fantasies of violence. Certainly it took lurid imaginations to create the more gruesome antislavery descriptions of insurrections and of Southern brutality. Whatever its psychological components, nonviolence did have an ambivalence that was easily brought to the surface by events, by frustration, and by taunts of anti-abolitionists.

Antislavery men and women found themselves occasionally having to extol acts of violence in order to refute racist charges that blacks were innately docile and fit only to be bondsmen. The Worcester County North Division Anti-Slavery Society neatly captured the problem in a resolution passed in 1842. The society decided "that while we would deprecate a resort to arms for the emancipation of the enslaved population of the south, yet we rejoice in the fact proved, by the recent strike for freedom of the slaves of the Creole, that slaves are not indifferent, as our opponents have often declared, to the inestimable blessings of civil liberty." Wendell Phillips announced in 1858 that "the Slave who does not write his own merit in the catalogue of insurrections hardly deserves freedom." Driving the matter home, he asserted "no slave proves his manhood, except those who rise and at least try to cut their masters' throat."[20]

Vindications of slave violence also gave abolitionists a chance to reproach Americans for moral inconsistency. Every Fourth of July Americans celebrated resistance to oppression, a principle whites refused to grant to blacks. Mocking patriotic defenders of slavery, James G. Birney claimed, "those who approve of the conduct of our fathers in the American Revolution, must agree that the slaves have at least as good a natural right to vindicate their rights by physical force." Henry C. Wright made the same point. "Is there an 'apology' for *any* one who 'brandishes deadly weapons' in self-defence?" he asked. "For Warren? For Washington? For Nat Turner? There is as much apology for the one as the other."[21] If anything, nonresistants like Wright were under more compulsion than Birney to make that kind of argument. They could twist it to discredit both defenders of slavery and the use of force itself. Such reasoning, however, put nonresistants in the treacherous position of maintaining that rebellions were justified by the principles of the American Revolution (as well as by natural right) and yet of insisting that they personally could not endorse rebellions.

Although abolitionist nonviolence rested upon a firmly Christian base, Protestantism contained countercurrents that helped reformers, as they lost faith in pacifism, to explain and even anticipate violence. Pessimism over the progress of antislavery became a brooding sense that God would chastize His wayward people, as He had done in biblical times. Protestant imagery of a blood sacrifice in expiation of sin and of a final battle between good and evil was, for abolitionists, a guarantee of imminent destruction.

Despair and predictions of godly retribution gathered strength from political developments after 1845. Annexation of Texas that year and a subsequent war with Mexico raised again the spectre of further expansion of slavery. The most provoking of all political events, however, was the Fugitive Slave Act of 1850, which gave Northerners responsibility to help slaveholders capture runaways. Black abolitionists were particularly willing to use force to block masters from retaking their former chattel. Frederick Douglass, who in 1843 blasted Henry Highland Garnet's call for insurrection, now urged blacks to resist enforcement of the act by all possible means. Some whites were no less warlike and over the next several years there was a series of bloody episodes in which ex-slaves and their Northern allies battled would-be slave catchers, sometimes with fatal results.

In the mid-1850s violence on a still larger scale broke out in Kansas —open and savage warfare over whether that territory would be slave or free. A number of abolitionists actively supported the free state forces, and all antislavery factions followed events in Kansas with intense interest. Ironically, some abolitionists in the 1850s were beginning to believe that the political system was responding to their propaganda; but the response seemed too slow, slaveholders too strong, and the times too violent. By 1856 James G. Birney, once chief of the political abolitionists, told Thomas Wentworth Higginson, "I regret that a civil war should rage [in Kansas] but if slavery cannot be exterminated without one—& I don't see how it can be—I say let it come." Lysander Spooner, who had tried to convince Americans that slavery was unconstitutional, lost his faith in the power of law and logic and became entranced with the idea of insurrection.[22]

Among political abolitionists the most interesting pilgrim on the journey away from pacifism was Gerrit Smith, a wealthy New York state landlord who at the time of the division in 1840 declared himself leaning toward nonresistance. He nevertheless broke with the Garrisonians and worked for the Liberty Party. A frequent candidate under the antislavery banner, Smith won a term in the House of Representatives during the Kansas-Nebraska debates. By that time he questioned both non-resistance and the democratic process in America. ". . . I went to Congress with very little hope of the peaceful termina-

tion of American slavery," he told Frederick Douglass. "I have re-
turned with less." Four years later, in August 1859, Smith claimed that
the failure of all parties, from the Liberty through to the Republican,
to do anything for slaves had led "intelligent black men . . . [to] see
no hope for their race in the practice and policy of white men. No
wonder they are brought to the conclusion that no resource is left to
them but God and insurrections." "For insurrection then," he predicted, "we may look any year, any month, any day." Within months
his involvement with John Brown became public knowledge.[23]

The Garrisonians, with their strong nonresistant minority, had been
the faction most committed to pacifism, but even their faith wavered
in the 1850s. It was increasingly difficult for them to condemn all violence when some of it, such as that of the free state forces in Kansas,
seemed nobly directed against slavery. The Massachusetts Anti-
Slavery Society, where nonresistants were strongest, heeded the prod-
ding of Henry C. Wright in 1857 and adopted resolutions pledging
support in "every effort of the slave to obtain his freedom, whether
by flight or insurrection," and asserting "those who hold to the right
of armed resistance to oppression ought to recognize this right on the
part of the slaves against their tyrant masters, and assist them to
achieve their complete enfranchisement." Wright looked forward to
the day "when an insurrection of slaves against the tyrants that crush
them will be most welcome news" to the North. To a critic who felt
Wright and Garrison had abandoned nonresistance, Garrison replied,
"we are taking the American people on their own ground, and judging
of them by their own standard." Wright agreed. "My object," he said,
"is to test this nation by its own acknowledged rule of action."[24] That
rule was violence. By the mid-1850s nonresistants could no longer ask
slaves to live by the principles of peace in a world that was not
peaceful.

More than any other episode in a bloody decade, John Brown's raid
brought abolitionists to open admiration of violent means. Brown was
a stubborn and magnetic man, a religious zealot allied with no anti-
slavery organization but loosely acquainted with some eastern abolitionists. The path of Brown's twisted life took him through failed business ventures, a career of guerilla warfare in Kansas, and, on October
16, 1859, into a poorly planned assault on the Federal Arsenal at Harper's Ferry, Virginia. The raid was doomed, and Brown was never
entirely clear or candid about what he had wished to accomplish. It
was apparent, however, that he and his men, who included blacks as
well as whites, saw their act as a first blow against slavery, most probably as the inspiration for a slave uprising they hoped would spread
throughout the South.

Garrisonians could not endorse Brown's Raid when measuring it by their principles. But falling back on the formula pronounced by Garrison and Wright, they found Brown's actions magnificent when judged by the morality of a society based on force—far more magnificent than they had found Lovejoy's death fighting in self-defense twenty years earlier. The American Anti-Slavery Society devoted its *Annual Report* for 1859 to "the memory of the noble hero-martyr" John Brown, concluding unconvincingly that the raid's failure "confirmed us in the choice we made, at the beginning, of spiritual instead of carnal weapons." Wendell Phillips did not bother to make even that perfunctory bow toward pacifism. "The lesson of the hour is insurrection," he gloated, going on to hint that the antislavery crusade bore responsibility for Brown. "Insurrection of thought," he declared, "always precedes the insurrection of action."[25]

Not all abolitionists were as quick as Phillips to take credit for Brown. The raid was so shocking and so morally ambiguous that at first it stunned and confused abolitionists (indeed, the whole nation). But the moral ambiguities for abolitionists largely disappeared with Brown's trial and his execution by the state of Virginia on December 2, 1859. Brown, who had done few things well in his life, behaved with dignity and spoke with biblical cadences when faced with death. He was hatred of slavery incarnate, a magnificent and ferocious avenging angel brought to earth. Virginia obligingly gave Brown the chance to be a martyr, and he played the part superbly.

But there was more to Brown's appeal to abolitionists than his gallows eloquence. Though Brown's actions were contrary to antislavery pacifism, they resonated with something inherent to the reformer's

role. If reform was to be a career, if there was no ground for compromise, if one's life took meaning from hatred of slavery, then John Brown was a kinsman, less an aberration than a culmination. Brown himself recognized the kinship, as well as the unwillingness of other abolitionists to take their principles as far, when he dismissed Wendell Phillips for only *talking* about fighting.[26] Brown grasped a flaw in Phillips' conception of the agitator that Phillips barely sensed. What if society refused to listen to moral suasion? Give up? Settle for half a loaf? How long could the agitator beckon onward a nation that ignored virtue? Was there not a time when evil became so overwhelming that the only recourse was to strike at it, the Devil's weapons in hand?

War did not follow hard upon Brown's raid, as the old man had wished. It came a year and a half later, in the spring of 1861. It was civil, not servile, and abolitionist peace principles, already thoroughly weakened, nearly vanished with the firing upon Fort Sumter. A small number of abolitionists stuck stubbornly to nonviolence, a handful of men and women from all factions, including anti-Garrisonians like Beriah Green. Garrison and the nonresistants were of divided mind, appalled at the carnage but increasingly drawn to the Union cause, especially after the Emancipation Proclamation turned the war (however begrudgingly) into a struggle against slavery. Many of the nonresistants were genuinely sorry that slavery would not die peacefully, and a few had the courage to ask whether the clash of arms might not bring worse sins in its trail. More common was the response of other abolitionists, less extreme peace men, who found evasions to allow them to support the war. Finally there were abolitionists, many of them never peace men at heart, who marched off to battle with little hesitation. One of Garrison's sons became an officer commanding black troops.[27]

It neither glorifies Brown nor justifies his violence to say that he was the most consistent of abolitionists; sometimes inconsistency is more humane and effective than consistency, and a greater person than Brown might have weighed the value of life differently than he did. There were, nonetheless, few places for abolitionist zeal to go once it became central to a person's sense of self. Institutions could not contain it, compromise could not satisfy it, and the American political system could not comprehend it.

When Wendell Phillips pronounced the platitudes about agitation that endeared him to historians he did not foresee the progression that brought him on a dreary December day to a rough farmhouse near North Elba, New York, where he delivered a eulogy over the body of John Brown. Yet there was a thread of consistency running from Phillips' ideas about agitation through the common rituals and artifacts of antislavery and ending at Harper's Ferry. The thread was identification of self with the cause. For its staunchest disciples, post-1830 abolitionism was a style of life. It defined their role in society, whom they associated with, what they surrounded themselves with, and—for a few—how they died.

II
CONTENT

Reform activities are external matters,
ways of communicating and living a
commitment. The commitment itself is
the vital center of reform. To understand
it, we must go to the categories of
thought and feeling that both express
and shape the reformer's vision of the
world.

3
RELIGION
Evangelical Protestantism
and the Reform Impulse

MEANS can reveal ends. Although abolitionists used secular tactics—reform organizations and political parties—their zeal and their rhetoric resembled nothing so much as a religious crusade. Antislavery could not, in fact, have been what it was after 1830 if there had not been an evangelical Protestant tradition behind it and if there had not been evangelical Protestants in it from beginning to end.

The relationship between antislavery and conventional Christianity, however, was neither simple nor peaceful. Abolitionists were the children of American Protestantism, but they were also among its severest critics. Some of them ultimately left its churches in order to remain true to Christian principles. They and abolitionists generally were part of a broad antebellum process through which moral authority in America ceased to be a monopoly of ministers and gentlemen. Indebted though abolitionism was to American Protestantism, the effect of a reform commitment was to bring the institutional power of church and clergy into question and to subvert much of the religious base from which antislavery originally drew inspiration. As significant as what evangelicalism did for antislavery are the reasons why formal Protestantism failed reformers and the manner in which they modified or replaced it.

One of the foremost evangelists of his time, Lyman Beecher, looked back on a long life and recalled how, as a young clergyman, he had been in despair at disestablishment of the Congregational churches in Connecticut in 1818. "For several days I suffered what no tongue can tell," he wrote. But it was, Beecher came to realize, *"the best thing that had ever happened to the State of Connecticut."* Denied governmental support, churches had to rely "on their own resources and on God. . . . They say ministers have lost their influence," Beecher noted; "the fact is, they have gained. By voluntary efforts, societies, missions, and revivals, they exert a deeper influence than they ever could by queues, and shoe buckles, and cocked hats, and gold-headed canes."[1] These were brave words from a preacher who once had William Lloyd Garrison for a parishioner, who as head of Lane Seminary saw his brightest group of students desert him for abolitionism, and whose daughter, by writing an antislavery novel, achieved greater moral influence than the vast majority of clergymen.

From the mid-1820s onward a wave of religious revivals swept from west to east, roaring and crashing about the heads of sinners, driving them to seize upon good works as signs of "disinterested benevolence" marking the saved from the damned. A most remarkable evangelist, Charles G. Finney, seemed to be master of it all—his followers were a host in themselves. Behind the efforts of Finney, his assistants, and his competitors were left men and women eager to demonstrate their virtue through social action.[2] Surely antislavery, the greatest of the moral crusades, must have been produced by this revival, the greatest of stimulants to reform activity. Or was that the connection? Relations between complex social phenomena are not so simple and uninteresting as mere cause and effect.

That is not, of course, to deny the very real debt antislavery owed American Protestantism. Abolitionist propaganda abounded with biblical and evangelical imagery and gained power from ancient Christian associations linking the concepts of slavery, bondage, and sin (antislavery turned them around so that the sinfulness was in holding a slave, not in being one). Revivalism and antislavery, moreover, possessed a similar grammar, with "immediate repentance" becoming "immediate emancipation."[3] They also shared techniques of persuasion: the antislavery agent travelling about urging men and women to cast off their connection with slavery was just as much an itinerant exhorter as the revivalist was. Ohio abolitionists, appropriately enough, frequently held their gatherings under the familiar tent of the camp-meeting. These similarities were not purely coincidental. Areas in the North that had been swept by revivals showed a tendency to support antislavery activities as well.[4]

Abolitionism did indeed attract a large number of individuals whose lives had been profoundly moved by the revival. Theodore Dwight Weld and the young men of Lane Seminary in Ohio had seemed far more likely to become evangelistic ministers than the pioneer antislavery agents many became after their debates on slavery in 1834. As late as 1836 several of them agonized over whether to devote their primary efforts to abolitionism or to "engage in protracted meetings and promote revivals of religion," as Finney urged. Finney himself was an important influence upon abolitionists, and he presided, somewhat uneasily, over Oberlin College, a hotbed of reform as well as of pious zeal. Revivalistic antislavery clergymen like LaRoy Sunderland and Orange Scott preached freedom from earthly and from spiritual bondage with equal fervor. The Reverend Joshua Leavitt went from being editor of the *New York Evangelist* to being editor of the American Anti-Slavery Society's paper, the *Emancipator*, and ultimately into the Liberty, Free Soil, and Republican parties.[5]

Important as revivalism was for some people engaged in secular reform, it clearly was not sufficient in itself to explain the rise of antislavery. For one thing, there were a fair number of abolitionists who were not from evangelical sects. These ranged from the calvinistic Wendell Phillips to Quakers like James S. Gibbons, John Greenleaf Whittier, Abby Kelley, and James and Lucretia Mott, to Unitarians like Charles and Eliza Follen, David and Lydia Maria Child, Francis Jackson, Edmund Quincy, Theodore Parker, Samuel J. May, and Thomas Wentworth Higginson.[6] It was also true that the most revivalistic denominations were not inherently antislavery. The Methodists, with an evangelical heritage, nevertheless showed more inclination to support colonization than immediate emancipation. Revivalism may actually have hindered Methodism from taking a genuine stand against slavery by giving the sect a strong Southern contingent opposed to abolition.[7]

Even in cases where revivalism did eventually lead to antislavery there was often a long gap between the religious awakening and the reform commitment. Marius Robinson, one of the Lane students, had been converted at least a decade before the time he became an abolitionist.[8] Theodore Dwight Weld, in an autobiographical fragment, dated his becoming "a radical abolitionist" to a series of travels he made between 1822 and 1824. This was before Finney brought him into the fold, which occured in 1825. But Weld's surviving letters, and his activities in the late 1820s, indicate he did not truly advocate immediate emancipation until near the end of 1832.[9] In either case, the revival alone obviously was not what made Weld an abolitionist. James G. Birney's redemption from what he later considered to be a life of wildness and sin came around 1826. According to him, it was seven or eight years after that "before the sound of Abolition entered my ears."[10] It took an emotional debate to awaken the already evangelical Lane Seminary students to antislavery in 1834.

J. Miller McKim suggested a plausible explanation for this sort of delay between conversion and reform commitment. He noted that two or three years before he became an abolitionist, "people's attention was directed with unusual earnestness to the subject of personal religion." He too had been swept along, but he later felt that these revivals "were, for the most part, mere imitation—simulations; without depth and without earnestness." As enthusiasm waned, he had become less sure about his faith, filled with doubts and with dismay at its narrowness. After almost a year in a Pennsylvania pastorate he resigned to become an antislavery agent. "With the subsidence of . . . religious excitement in the country," he recalled, "the feelings of the sincere and enlightened who had shared in it began to take a new turn. Their attention was called away from themselves to the conditions of others."[11] The unwillingness of many evangelists to confront social problems and the self-absorption of their converts led McKim and many of his contemporaries into a period of dissatisfaction, followed by engagement in secular reform. It was less the revival than its passing that brought men and women to antislavery.

Some abolitionists took longer than McKim to become disillusioned with revivalism, but all had to confront the fact that evangelism did not necessarily threaten slavery. In 1835 the *Anti-Slavery Record* reported the existence of a slaveholding evangelist, and there were frequent embarrassing admissions that revivals failed to affect slavery. James G. Birney reported word of one in Kentucky in which those who joined the church were ordered to desist from all sins—but not from slaveholding. To make it more galling, the converts included two men who had persecuted Birney for his abolitionism when he had lived in the area. Frederick Douglass told of a revival in New Bedford, Massachusetts, in which one of the saved refused communion after a black person had taken it. Another claimed to have been in heaven while in a trance. Asked "if she saw any black folks in heaven," she replied, after some hesitation, " '*Oh! I didn't go into the kitchen.*' "[12]

From the beginning prominent evangelists had been reluctant to take a firm stand against slavery, even though many of them regarded it as an evil. They feared dividing the church and diverting attention from their primary mission, which they saw as converting the nation. Charles G. Finney, the most famous of all, believed that "if abolitionism can be made an append[a]ge of a general revival all is well." His abolitionist admirers betrayed frustration and irritation with him on this point, being less convinced than he that secular reform should wait upon general awakenings.[13] Finney continued to hold the respect of evangelical abolitionists like Theodore Dwight Weld and Lewis Tappan and he continued to believe that slavery was wrong. But his effect on the cause was not especially constructive. He dampened Oberlin's contribution to abolitionism by raising doubts in the minds of students who considered giving up the ministry for antislavery and by influencing the *Oberlin Evangelist* to criticize abolitionist lecturers for coming to the college during awakenings. Other evangelists shared

Finney's belief that revivals were primary and that antislavery agitation merely got in the way. David Nelson tried to bring the abolitionist message to an area of Illinois where there was a "protracted meeting." "Much was said," he discovered, "about the 'danger of turning off the minds of the people from the concerns of religion, excitement,' &c." With persuasion from Nelson "it was finally concluded that the claims of suffering humanity were not incompatible with a revival of true religion."[14]

The failure of evangelists and evangelism to bear unequivoval witness against slavery led once-revivalistic abolitionists into increasingly harsh criticism. In 1840 James G. Birney recorded his disappointment with a New York clergyman during a minor awakening. "For the first time, since I first heard him," Birney wrote, "he omitted to pray for the Slaves and the Indians. If this be the effect of the Revival—away with it!" Two weeks later Birney attended a Catholic church and found less prejudice against blacks there than in New York's evangelical churches. "Revivals of religion have done immense good," Elizur Wright conceded in 1837, "but they have sometimes, perhaps done some hurt, as well as left much good undone."[15] Even abolitionists with a higher regard for evangelism than Wright showed ambivalence. In a history of antislavery published in 1853, William Goodell argued that the revival of the 1820s had "more or less connected with it . . . an increasing spirit of inquiry in respect to Christian ethics, and the bearing of the religious principle upon the social relation and political duties of man." This was a cautious statement of the idea that revivalism led to social reform. Yet Goodell went on to note that because of its refusal to take a courageous stand against slavery, American religion was also one of the chief obstacles to abolition.[16]

Abolitionists from all factions proclaimed the guilt of organized religion. James G. Birney labeled the churches "the bulwarks of American slavery." Judge William Jay, as moderate an antislavery man as there was, changed the figure slightly, asserting "the American Church . . . [is] the great buttress of American slavery." Such rhetoric was not confined to laymen. An Ohio clergyman told the World Anti-Slavery Convention in London in 1840 that "if ministers of the gospel [in North America] were united in their denunciation of *slavery*, it would die a natural death in a very few years."[17] That could never have been. American Protestantism was too much a part of antebellum society, too enmeshed in local affairs, and too fragmented into warring sects to act as a concerted force on controversial issues.

Disappointment with the churches was so pervasive and so strong after 1839 that it encouraged abolitionists to experiment with new tactics that placed less faith in religious sentiment and moral suasion.

James G. Birney's commitment to independent political action came in 1840, the year he published *The American Churches, the Bulwarks of American Slavery*. Before the decade was out a portion of the Liberty Party men drifted off into the Free Soil movement, which made its primary appeal to the self-interest, rather than the spirituality, of whites. As Lysander Spooner worked on his constitutional argument against slavery in 1847, he assailed "the tame, cowardly, drivelling, truckling course pursued by the abolitionists." Spooner decided that "if they have the constitution in their hands, why, in heaven's name do they not out with it, and use it? Why spend their breath in talking to women and children about the churches and the clergy?" Spooner was extreme in his irritation but other abolitionists came to question whether religious purity was an essential precondition to reform. Asa Mahan, a clergyman, conceded that he would work with "infidels, Mahomedeans, and Hindoos even, in vindicating the rights of crushed humanity." That was not completely candid— Mahan drew the line at collaboration with those "aiming to prostrate Christianity itself" (among whom he counted Garrison)—but it indicated he recognized that a person might be an abolitionist and not a proper Christian.[18]

William Goodell, a devout and orthodox man, was a reluctant sojourner along this path. In 1845 he asked A. A. Phelps, "What could we do, as *reformers* without the Bible?" Eight years later he published *The American Slave Code in Theory and Practice*, a work designed to circumvent religious arguments by proving that slavery is a creature of law and current custom and that biblical precedents were irrelevant. In 1859 he conceded that "the humane instincts and natural sympathies of some men are better than their Theologies." Thus there could be radical reformers who did not have "any corresponding radical theology to stand upon." Others could be more blunt. "We do not believe that it will be necessary that the conversion of the world should take place in order to rid it of so gross and palpable a wickedness and folly as American slavery," the *National Anti-Slavery Standard* decided by 1858. The distance this simple comment marked can be measured by comparison with one of the earliest issues of the *Liberator*. In it Garrison, of all people, wrote that "nothing but extensive revivals of religion can save our country from great plagues and sudden destruction."[19] Somewhere along the way a number of American Protestantism's most loyal sons and daughters began to doubt whether that religion would ever be in the vanguard of social and moral reform.

Disillusion did not lead abolitionists to a total rejection of religion;

only one, possibly two, notable antislavery men and women became athiests.[20] It did, however, spur abolitionists to make sporadic attempts to explain why the clergy and churches had failed them. Occasionally such comments were perceptive but they fell into a few predictable patterns that tell as much about what mattered to abolitionists as about the state of religion in antebellum America.

It was especially vexing to abolitionists that many clergymen were apathetic or hostile to the slave's plight. Ministers, of course, were among the most active and effective abolitionists, but their good work could not undo the ill-will generated by their ministerial brethren. William Lloyd Garrison was the most passionate critic of pastoral "plots" against antislavery, but others within the movement were equally distressed. In 1837 William Goodell thought he detected "a grand Ecclesiastical Combination" designed to effect "the preparation of the public mind, (by previous sanction of the clergy) for severe legislative enactments throughout the Country against us."[21] Even devout evangelicals like Arthur and Lewis Tappan, who preferred to work through religious organizations, ran into opposition from ministers and found it necessary to create their own Protestant associations after existing ones proved unconcerned about social reform.

Abolitionists usually argued that the problem lay in a desire among clergy to assert their authority. Theodore Dwight Weld wrote Birney in 1842 that "the ministry as a body have grasped and are clinging to power and to prerogative that they have no right to—sheer usurpation, is just as plain." Evidence that Weld was right abounded. "Deference and subordination are essential to the happiness of society, and particularly so in the relation of a people to their pastor," the Massachusetts Congregational Association grandly concluded in 1837, when attacking the Grimké sisters and other antislavery itinerants.[22] There was a subtle point here: the clergy were not seeking to maintain something they held securely; they were trying to hang on to (or increase) an influence they were in danger of losing. "The Shepherds were driven by the sheep," noted Samuel J. May, himself a Unitarian minister. Prominent laymen, "too important to be alienated, were permitted to direct the action of the churches, and the preaching of their pastors on this 'delicate question,' 'this exciting topic.'" Theodore and Angelina Grimké Weld were more trenchant. They found American preachers culpable for "connivance at cherished sins, . . . truckling subserviency to power, . . . clinging with mendicant sycophancy to the skirts of wealth and influence, . . . humoring of pampered lusts, . . . cowering before bold transgression when it stalks among the high places of power with fashion in its train."

The truth was slightly more complex. As the Welds realized, clergymen (like Jacksonian politicians) did bow before public opinion and before the selfish wishes of influential men. But ministerial authority was also compromised by the existence of secular reformers like the abolitionists. The Executive Committee of the American Anti-Slavery Society accurately described the situation when, in 1840, it remarked that "the clergy have been in the habit of taking possession of every benevolent and moral cause which stirred deeply and strongly the hearts of their societies and the community, and they disdained to play a second part in the Abolition movement."[23] Nondenominational and led by laymen, antislavery was yet another threat to clerical authority, already forced into a defensive posture by religious pluralism, separation of church and state, and the assertiveness of parishioners.

Having once regarded revivals as a force to convert and change the world, abolitionists by the 1840s began to view them as simply another mechanism clergy used to preserve their place in society. In 1841 Beriah Green, an antislavery minister, noted the "special effects" to promote revivals. "Theatrical expedients are employed, and a theatrical effect is produced." Evangelists do their work, Green told his hearers, "without touching the strong holds in which Satan is entrenched." Some years later C. K. Whipple cynically dissected Charles G. Finney's efforts, which he described as "scientifically conducted." "In Boston," Whipple wrote, "this apparatus of systematic labor, and this concert of action between the various departments engaged, have been as obvious as the ploughing, mowing, harrowing and weeding that preceed the gathering of the farmer's harvest."[24] Ministers judge the success of a revival, Whipple observed, by the convert's "incorporation of himself with the ecclesiastical system." Evangelism had become a device to perpetuate the churches and to draw in members rather than to regenerate the world.

The decline of revivalism into a hollow ritual mirrored what abolitionists saw as a more general American obsession with the superficial forms of religious life rather than with its inner meaning. Intense rivalry between Protestant denominations was the worst example of this. Garrisonians led the way in detecting "sectarianism" (sometimes finding more of it than there actually was) but non-Garrisonians also believed that denominational peculiarities stood in the way of reform and kept truly Christian men and women separated by empty creeds. Gerrit Smith, among others, drew analogy to the Jacksonian political system, which likewise demanded intense partisan loyalty from the men caught up in it. "Political and ecclesiastical sectarianism is the giant foe of our cause," he informed Theodore Dwight Weld in 1840. A year earlier William Goodell had declared that the "present denominational arrangements *cannot* continue, and *ought* not." They did, of course, but two decades later Goodell was still attempting to break them down: he began the *National Principia* as a nonsectarian paper open to investigate impartially religious, moral, and political questions.[25]

There were, to be sure, sectarians in the movement, particularly among those who could not stomach Garrison's theological peculiarities. Many of these people, however, were exceptions who illustrate the rule; they were men who detested Garrison but who agreed that no single denomination had a monopoly on truth. Joshua Leavitt, himself a clergyman, urged his brother to receive the Word from whomever might preach it—even from a Baptist, if necessary. Two other opponents of Garrison, James G. Birney and A. A. Phelps, similarly were more catholic than the Boston editor imagined. In the 1840s and 1850s Birney evolved into an antisectarian in one of the most interesting religious transformations undergone by an abolitionist. Phelps had been so set in his ways that he, a Congregationalist, refused a call from a Presbyterian church. Yet in his most famous antislavery tract he "solicited the names of persons of various denominations . . . to make the impression at the outset that this, like the cause of Temperance, is a common cause—a common work." LaRoy Sunderland, whom Garrison once considered a hopeless Methodist, left his church in the 1840s over its commitment to slavery. By 1853 he had attacked "sectarianism" strongly enough to draw applause from the *Liberator*.[26]

Garrisonian and non-Garrisonian alike never renounced their Christian moral sensibility, but by the 1840s many of them clearly had renounced the outer trappings and the institutional structure of American Protestantism. The abolitionist critique of clerical hostility, revivalism, and sectarianism converged upon a point: the Protestant sects had drifted into a sterile formalism. The mechanics of maintaining ministerial authority and church membership, abolitionists believed, had overwhelmed the Christian message, blocked the progress of social reform, and divided godly men and women into denominations that existed for their own sake, not for Christ's.

William Lloyd Garrison was the movement's most famous religious pilgrim, beginning as a fairly orthodox Baptist, dallying in the congregation of Lyman Beecher for a while, and finally turning to perfectionism, non-resistance, anti-sabbatarianism, and questioning the divine authority of the Bible. Yet Garrison was by no means the only abolitionist who fell into heterodoxy. For a surprising number of men and women, commitment to antislavery was part of an on-going spiritual quest. Such people eventually found it less easy to reconcile with the Protestant denominations than to re-enter the political system; in the

1850s fewer retreated back to theological orthodoxy than marched into the Republican Party.

Some abolitionists came to the movement with a history of spiritual restlessness. Besides J. Miller McKim there were the Grimké sisters, who had been through several changes of heart, Elizur Wright, and Lydia Maria Child. Despite pressure from his father, Wright had not joined a church until well into adolescence. Finally yielding to a revival, he presented himself to a local church but failed to answer questions satisfactorily and was admitted only as a favor to his father, a deacon. He later made an abortive attempt to enter the ministry, out of a sense of obligation rather than from conviction. Lydia Maria Child informed her brother in 1820 that she was more "in danger of wrecking on the rocks of skepticism than of stranding on the shores of fanaticism." She wished to "find some religion in which my heart and understanding could unite." She lost herself in literature and painting until she met Garrison in an experience she described as changing "the whole pattern of my life-web"—the language of a religious conversion.[27] The quest did not necessarily end with antislavery. Angelina Grimké turned to the Millerites and shared in her husband's theological changes from the 1840s onward. Elizur Wright became a free-thinker and at the end of his life referred to himself as an atheist. Lydia Maria Child was still "passing through strange spiritual experiences" in the 1850s.[28]

Other abolitionists—including Garrison—were orthodox when they arrived at the antislavery movement but in following decades drifted far from the conventional churches. This was true of Parker Pillsbury, Stephen S. Foster, and Henry C. Wright, all former preachers or students for the ministry (Foster quit a prosperous business to spend seven years in preparation to become a clergyman). All became non-resistants and withdrew from their old denominations. J. V. Himes, a former evangelist, and Reverend Charles Fitch, a signer of the Clerical Appeal against Garrison, became Millerites. Methodists disaffected with their sect's stand on slavery likewise slipped off to other pastures. George Storrs left in 1840 and thereafter professed no creed but the Bible until he became a Millerite. Shipley Wilson converted to Unitarianism. LaRoy Sunderland was among those who founded the antislavery Wesleyan Methodist Church in 1843, but by late 1849 he was giving lectures on Pantheism and was on the road to becoming a spiritualist.[29]

The prides of the evangelical wing of the antislavery movement, Theodore Dwight Weld and James G. Birney, showed a similar wanderlust. In 1842 Weld pitied an acquaintance who was pouring over "*mere intellectual theories* of religion." He knew the path well. "I have threaded the same labyrinths and stumbled upon the same dark mountains, and shivered and frozen amid the same congealings," Weld wrote. That approach, he decided, had been mistaken. "The simple *practicals* of religion, *these, these* are the Alpha and Omega." The acquaintance should turn "to direct communion with God . . . by bringing his spirit simply and utterly in contact with infinite purity and love." In 1848 Weld asserted proudly, "*creeds* have lost all hold upon me." A visitor in 1852 noted that "Mr. and Mrs. Weld and Sarah [Grimké] have laid aside all forms of religion."[30]

Birney once was as properly evangelical as Weld, yet by 1840 he remarked to his diary on a decline in "religious emotions." But the coldness of the churches bothered him more than the coldness of his heart. "The church cannot disappoint me much in its anti-slavery measures," he told a Christian Anti-Slavery Convention in 1850, "because I look for so little—hardly any thing, indeed—from it." His diary entries for that year show him musing over theological issues, coming to doubt eternal punishment, divine authorship of the Bible, and predestination. Moving to live with the Welds in New Jersey speeded Birney along into heterodoxy. He also opened a correspondence with Theodore Parker, who brought him close to Unitarianism (a tendency he stifled out of deference to his trinitarian wife). Birney, the man Garrisonians accused of surrendering antislavery to the claims of orthodoxy, made—belatedly—a journey nearly as long as Garrison's.[31]

Few abolitionists speculated as daringly as Garrison or Birney. Simple withdrawal from existing churches was the more typical response when a serious antislavery commitment met denominational resistance. Here again Garrisonians, and the controversies swirling about them, clouded things by associating "come-outerism" with men like Parker Pillsbury and Stephen S. Foster, flamboyant characters who went beyond quiet secession and actually interrupted services, demanding the startled congregation hear their denunciations. That behavior was so well-publicized it made Garrisonians appear to have a monopoly on attacking pro-slavery churches. Garrisonians, naturally, encouraged the view. They taunted Liberty Party men for supposed hypocrisy in withdrawing from corrupt political parties but (allegedly) not from corrupt churches. Like most of the bickering following the division of 1840 that exaggerated differences between factions and obscured a common pattern among abolitionists.

The heart of "come-outerism" was renunciation of fellowship with those who tolerated slavery. A related position was refusal to hold communion with slaveholders, a practice that most definitely was not a Garrisonian monopoly. One of the earliest issues of the *Emancipator* contained a letter from a Presbyterian abolitionist declaring noncommunion an antislavery obligation. Oberlin, in 1835, declined to invite slaveholders to preach or participate in communion.[32] From there it was not far to withdraw from sects that held slaveholders to be members in good standing.

Some, of course, could not take the step, but even among evangelical abolitionists there was a stronger streak of "come-outerism" than Garrisonians acknowledged. The *Emancipator* in 1838, under the editorship of Joshua Leavitt (a former revivalist), argued it was inconsistent for abolitionists to rebuke men for supporting "dumb representatives at the polls" while "themselves supporting dumb pastors in the pulpit." It concluded that " 'Come out of her, my people, that ye be not partaker of her sins and her plagues,' is already written on the great proslavery church North and South."[33] James G. Birney and Lewis Tappan dealt with the problem as early as 1836. "I concur with you entirely on the subject of forming churches anew," Birney wrote Tappan. "We can no more reform the present church, than Luther could, the Roman, or merely the Episcopalian." This was the beginning of Birney's travel away from revivalistic orthodoxy and the process continued steadily until by 1846 he assumed "come-outerism" as a matter of fact. "How to reconcile an intelligent love of freedom and a desire to remain in a proslavery church, under the preaching of a pro-slavery minister, I do not know," he told Gerrit Smith. "The duty of leaving them appears so plain, I have long since withdrawn from them."[34]

In one evangelical abolitionist Garrisonians did recognize a kindred spirit. William Goodell was an unlikely ally for them on theological issues—he had an affection for Calvinism and an antipathy to perfectionism. But in 1843 Goodell produced an essay on the "Duty of Secession from a Corrupt Church," which the *Liberator* reprinted with praise. Samuel May sent a copy to a friend, noting that Goodell ("an orthodox man") "strongly dissented from Mr. Garrison, when he, some time earlier, took essentially the same ground."[35] In 1845 the American Anti-Slavery Society published a version of the essay, prefixing its old title with "Come-Outerism." Goodell and Gerrit Smith, in fact, enjoyed a privilege open only to the very pious or the very wealthy: they founded their own churches. Goodell's began in 1843 in Honeoye, New York, erected on a foundation of temperance and antislavery. Smith, appalled at sectarianism in the local Presbyterian church in Peterboro, New York, withdrew to form his personal—presumably more comprehensive—sect, "The Church of Peterboro."[36]

In quieter fashion other non-Garrisonians were urging or doing similar things. The New York State Anti-Slavery Society refused to countenance nonabolitionist ministers and accused churches that were not antislavery of bearing the "stain of hypocrisy." The Ohio Anti-Slavery Society, after a secession of Garrisonians, resolved that churches having any connection with slavery, or refusing to denounce it, "must work the speedy forfeiture of the favor of God, the confidence of man." "Every true convert to abolitionism," its executive committee believed, "must first be emancipated from thraldom to sect and party." Abolitionists like John Rankin, Orange Scott, and LaRoy Sunderland, advocated or led separations from slaveholding brethren. Lucius Matlack, an abolitionist historian of Methodism, found examples of local schisms throughout the North. An elderly retired minister and twenty-two others in Troy, Ohio, were "come-outers" as much as Stephen Foster or Parker Pillsbury, even though they were far from being Garrisonians. In January 1843, according to Matlack, they presented their preacher with a document of withdrawal. "The Methodist E. Church has ceased to be an antislavery Church, and has become, emphatically, a slaveholding and slavery-defending Church," they charged. After detailing how the denomination had stifled their abolitionism they concluded "All this, and much more, we have borne, and would continue to bear, if we could hope that the Church could ever be reformed; but we cannot longer dream of such a state of things." The following Sunday they organized their own congregation.[37]

Such secessions were inevitable and involved abolitionists from all factions and all denominations. The reform conscience granted itself the right to judge everything by reform standards. By those standards institutional Protestantism failed.

Dangerous implications lay ahead. After years of religious speculation, uncertainty, and dissatisfaction with Protestant denominations, Lydia Maria Child decided "the church of the future is to be a church of deeds, not of doctrines of any kind." Asa Mahan concluded that no man could be a Christian who was not also a reformer; another antislavery clergyman, Beriah Green, declared that Christianity derived "all its significance and worth . . . from its relation as a Means to the prevalence of Justice and Mercy."[38] That logic came from the evangelical belief that spirituality could be measured by what people did, but it also could push men and women to the brink of scepticism.

To make reform the test of faith might well be to call the fundamentals of Christianity into doubt. "If it can be shown to me that religion is calculated to harm the human race," Charles Stearns wrote in 1865, "it matters not that a stack of Bibles mountain high teach its necessity." Asked if he would believe slavery to be right if God declared it so, Henry C. Wright answered "no." "I would fasten the chain upon the heel of God, and let the man go free," he declared.

"*For such a God is a phantom.* I would discard the phantom and liberate the slave." Wright was ready to reject the Bible as "a lie and a curse to mankind" if there was conflict between it and mankind's right to liberty. "Man is an appendage to nothing," Wright asserted in 1850, "not even to his creator." A correspondent to the *Liberator* two years later made much the same point. "Man's highest authority is himself. . . . In obeying himself, he obeys God."[39]

Wright had a gift for tracking arguments on into absurdity, and as usual he was more extreme than most of his colleagues. Yet even earlier, and in the hands of more orthodox men, the biblical argument against slavery betrayed signs that the Bible was assessed not by what it said but by what a nineteenth-century reformer's moral code held it *should* say. In his *Strictures on African Slavery* Samuel Crothers rehearsed what became the standard rebuttals to the biblical defense of slavery. Yet in proving that servants in biblical days were not slaves, he digressed from the text, insisting that Abraham could not really have condoned certain kinds of behavior since he was a good man. That gave greater weight to what Crothers intuitively felt to be moral than to what was actually in the Bible. James G. Birney, in probably the last letter of his life, tried to have it both ways. "Whether we believe in the inspiration of the Bible—in the personality of the Holy Ghost appears to me a small and deceptive business," he told Gerrit Smith. "The question truly is do we do what good things the Scriptures and Christ and the Holy Ghost tell us to do?"[40] Birney wanted to be done with looking for simple and already-known truths in the Bible—but he wanted them to be there anyway.

The logic of reform was driving antebellum Americans like Birney toward secularism and scepticism, but they were too fundamentally Christian to go beyond the point where piety and religious formalism parted company. Faced with the choice, they selected practical piety and abandoned formalism. They left it to later generations to abandon piety in favor of practicality.

In withdrawing allegiance from old denominations, abolitionists risked falling into a kind of sectarianism similar to that they criticized in others. In this instance it was a retreat into self-contained communities of reformers. Garrison himself fretted about that, arguing in 1842 against creation of separate churches because of their reliance upon principles of "exclusiveness, partiality, and selfishness."[41]

More than balancing that tendency was a genuine, thoroughly evangelical desire to unite true Christians. Even Gerrit Smith's pathetic Church of Peterboro was created to bring together men and women formerly kept apart by denominational rivalries. There is irony, not necessarily contradiction, when people separate themselves from corruption in the name of unity and comprehensiveness.

"To me Quaker and Catholic are alike," John Greenleaf Whittier wrote in 1842, ". . . separated only by a *creed,* to some, indeed, a barrier like a Chinese wall, but to me frail and slight as a spider's web." Lucretia Mott expressed similar sentiments to friends in England. "The distinctions among Christian professors are found, on an analysis, to be but hairbreadth," she thought, "and it is puzzling to bear in mind the distinctive points in their creeds."[42] Mott had reason to dislike creeds: she and her husband had seen bonds of love and respect snap during the Hicksite schism in the Society of Friends. Quakers like Whittier and Mott came from a tradition that placed less emphasis on formal doctrine (although no less on orthodoxy) than did most Protestant sects; but abolitionists from other backgrounds reached the same position. Beriah Green, once an evangelically-minded professor of Sacred Literature, committed treason to his old craft in 1847 when he announced, "the distinctions gotten up and magnified and insisted on by the Ecclesiastics around us of one and another denomination, with me have no good significance. They seem to me to be no better than the gambling tools of Godforsaken sharpers; generally employed for no better—often for ineffably worse, purposes."[43]

Such feelings led many reformers to seek a highly generalized, all-encompassing religion of humanity. That is where James G. Birney eventually arrived, and Gerrit Smith, Elizur Wright, Lydia Maria Child, and Garrison as well. After the Civil War, Smith, Lucretia Mott, and other old abolitionists found an institutional expression of their yearning for a nondoctrinal union of moral men and women. It

was the Free Religious Association, formed in 1867. But the religion
of humanity could not quite be captured in an institution (Mott felt
even the Free Religious Association placed more emphasis on theology than suited her).[44] Nor did it need to be.

There was another religion available, promising unity although
fragmented with its own schisms and sects: that was the reform commitment itself. From the beginning abolitionists conceived of their
crusade fulfilling a religious function. William Goodell described reform organizations as gatherings of men from all denominations
"united together to do what *the Church OUGHT* to do." Samuel May
believed the "anti-slavery movement . . . has applied Christianity, in
its whole spirit and purpose, to the state of society existing around
us." When the churches failed to lead, as they did in the 1830s, it
was easy to transpose terms and make antislavery, not formal religion,
the spiritual force and redeemer of American society. A correspondent
to the *Liberator* in 1846 described abolitionism as the salvation of
church and state alike, "the very nucleus of the civilization and Christianity of our time." A Virginia-born convert to the movement, Moncure Conway, recalled the Fourth of July celebration at Framingham,
Massachusetts, during which Garrison burned a copy of the Constitution of the United States. "That day I distinctly recognized that the
antislavery cause was a religion;" Conway wrote, "that Garrison was
a successor of the inspired axe-bearers,—John the Baptizer, Luther,
Wesley, George Fox."[45] As Conway perceived, abolitionism led its believers into a secular priesthood. Abolitionists who abandoned settled
ministries merely sacrificed the comfort of a preacher for the wander-
ing of a prophet of reform; in antebellum America either role was
available and the latter was less morally confining than the former.
There was truth, as well as an edge of irony, when the Reverend
Henry Ward Beecher, evangelist son of Lyman Beecher, informed
members of the American Anti-Slavery Society that "An uncanonical
Church you are, a Church without ordination, but in my judgment a
Church of the very best and most apostolic kind, held together by
the cohesion of a rule of faith, and an interior principle."[46]

Itself an heir of the revival, antislavery *was* a church, an appropriate one for men and women who had both a fiercely Protestant
morality and a disdain for metaphysics. It expressed perfectly their
abhorrence of the spiritual emptiness, moral cowardice, and denominational rivalries they found in their traditional churches. It gave
them a means to withdraw from clerical domination and sectarian
narrowness while permitting them to maintain a vision of Protestant
unity—the solidarity of moral men and women brought together in

godly works. Much of the appeal of antislavery lay in this ability to merge essentially religious impulses and spiritual discontent into a constructive, acceptable social role.

There was more to abolitionism. It did, after all, deal with real issues—with race, exploitation, and power—and it interwove them with concerns generated by the transformation of antebellum America into a new kind of society. It was this broad reform theology, of which Protestant morality was only a part, that gave coherence to the dissatisfactions of antislavery men and women. Its reward was a sense of personal meaning and moral direction reformers no longer found within the formal structure of American religion.

4
MORALITY
Racialist Thought,
the Moral Sense, and
Environmentalism

RELIGION shaped it and a religion it became—but antislavery mingled Protestant imagery and impulses with a vocabulary influenced by philosophy and natural sciences. Like all patterns of rhetoric this was partly a function of class, partly of culture, and partly a response to events. Its importance is that it expressed and limited the manner in which abolitionists dealt with the problems that preoccupied them.

Antislavery had more trouble with man than with God. Abolitionists felt mankind had urges that needed to be controlled and yet that human beings also had to be set free, liberated from evil institutions and stifling environments. This tension between desires for control and for liberation was not peculiar to abolitionism: it was part of a general struggle in antebellum America to reconcile the flux of democracy and economic expansion with orderliness and moral security. Within the terms of antebellum culture people could engage in that struggle in a variety of ways—antislavery was simply one response out of many. But the particular strength of abolitionism was that it permitted men and women to see the problem of control and liberation in a manner that was both emotionally compelling and focused upon a specific institution. Slavery served as an archetype of complicated and threatening forces abolitionists saw at work within mankind and within American society, North and South.

The prevalence of abolitionist ideas about human nature makes it easy to dismiss them: they, after all, could not have caused an antislavery commitment if abolitionist and nonabolitionist alike found nothing exceptional in them. But they are a part of the cultural anthropology of antebellum reform, the intellectual and perceptual framework within which it took place. Certainly assumptions about mankind cannot much explain why William Lloyd Garrison or anyone else became an abolitionist; but they can help explain why, when men and women became abolitionists, their response fastened upon the things it did and followed particular courses rather than others.

Abolitionists acquired a rich reputation as extreme individualists. Antislavery attracted people like N. P. Rogers and Stephen Pearl Andrews. Rogers eventually found all associations overly repressive, even reform societies, and Andrews fastened himself to the aptly named theory of the Sovereignty of the Individual.[1] Abolitionists more temperate than Rogers or Andrews likewise believed society and its institutions were at war with human nature.[2] Theodore Dwight Weld lamented that the "tendencies of the times to sink the individual and exalt the social are so strong as to have become utterly morbid." Gamaliel Bailey, a future Republican, shared the feeling. "The power of party (we speak both of churches and political organizations) over the individual, is most lamentable," he wrote in 1842. "We are sometimes tempted to abjure every species of organization, as hostile to personal independence."[3]

Abolitionists often made their case against slavery by appealing to the absolute necessity of freeing individuals from external restraints. "SELF-RIGHT is the foundation right—the post in the middle, to which all other rights are fastened," Theodore Dwight Weld insisted. "Does not [slavery's] essence lie in the counteraction of the human will?" James G. Birney asked. "Can any man be happy when his will is liable at any moment to be crossed?"[4] Without the right to protect and govern themselves humans were degraded and brutalized.

There were, nonetheless, anti-individualistic and restrictive elements to the abolitionist conception of freedom. Antislavery men and women never argued that true liberty involved allowing anyone to do anything. That was license, not liberty. The freedom abolitionists envisioned was for people to exercise the virtuous part of their nature: it allowed no latitude for evil conduct—it was not freedom to sin. Liberty, abolitionists thought, rested on suppression of ungodly passions and it was a precondition to genuine social order, to a state in which humans could come together out of love and sympathy rather than out of force and base motives.[5]

Nonresistance was the exception confirming the abolitionist rule of equating freedom with social and moral orderliness. Although they were indeed anarchists, nonresistants (in common with other abolitionists) aimed to make relations between humans more rational, predictable, and virtuous, not more fluid and chaotic. Henry C. Wright claimed "non-resistants hold as a fundamental principle THAT MAN WAS MADE TO BE GOVERNED." They wished to dispense with human governments, which are based on force and are morally undependable, and in their place "establish God's authority and dominion over the world." With governments gone humans would obey divine justice, the highest and most exacting law of all. So committed were nonresistants to moral order that there was no irony intended when one of their number bemoaned the "present anarchical state of society" in 1845.[6]

Abolitionists felt strongly enough about some questions to mute their emphasis on personal freedom and advocate outright compulsion. "The era of discussion and opinion is over;" Wendell Phillips said of debate over sale of alcoholic beverages, "the era of legislation has come—the time when the minority sits down and obeys." Lewis Tappan was charmingly candid in describing his brother on a similar occasion. "He was now," Lewis reported, "as he had ever been, a zealous advocate of moral suasion; but when the community was ripe for it, he was for using prohibition with incorrigible transgressors."[7]

Rather than being extreme libertarians, abolitionists were in the difficult position of wanting people to be free to act as their own moral agents, and yet also wanting to be sure that once set free they made the right choices. Abolitionists, of course, had no doubt what those right choices were—Protestantism and their reformist consciences told them that. What they lacked was a coherent set of assumptions about mankind's potential for moral behavior—in other words, a consistent view of human nature.

Some abolitionist writings implied that there were a variety of human natures, each with its own capabilities. As we shall see, abolitionists spoke of innate differences of character between men and women. More vexing for abolitionists, however, was the issue of whether races also differed in mental and moral strength.

There are problems determining exactly what abolitionists meant when they spoke of race. They were not necessarily well versed in scientific thought, nor did scientific thought in their day possess a great deal of precision on the question of human differences. "Race" was an amorphous concept, and antislavery men and women spoke of the "Anglo-Saxon" or the "British" race and contrasted it with the "Irish" or "Celtic" races, and then contrasted them all with the "Negro" race—with no sense of confusion, even though genetic and cultural factors were hopelessly muddled. Making the subject more confusing, abolitionists did not want to pander to the prejudices of other whites and consequently were less open in proclaiming their true feelings on race than they were on other matters.[8]

Although critical of racist defences of slavery, abolitionists themselves often adopted a patronizing tone toward blacks. By the 1850s even devout racial egalitarians like Wendell Phillips and Theodore Parker were not above picking up the "white man's burden." Parker believed that "civilization hitherto has belonged only to the Caucasian race." After the failure of John Brown's raid to incite a black insurrection, Phillips argued that the slave's redemption will come from the interference of a wiser, higher, more advanced civilization."[9] In Parker and Phillips this did not pass beyond paternalism on into segregation and imperialism. Weighed by our standards, they, and abolitionists generally, rank as racists and yet as considerably less malignantly racist than their white contemporaries.

Racism, of course, stood as a considerable barrier to antislavery propaganda. Abolitionists had to convince whites that black people were indeed men and women just like themselves. Sentimental appeals asking readers to imagine themselves in the place of slaves depended for their effectiveness on whites believing that they and blacks had common emotions and common reactions. There was also the matter of persuading whites that blacks were not content with their status. Abolitionists could best do that by asserting a love of liberty innate to all humans—"that spirit of freedom, which knows no distinction of cast [caste] or color; which has been kindled in the heart of the black man as well as white."[10]

Still, abolitionists had nagging suspicions that all humans might not be the same; these suspicions were even occasionally turned to advantage in antislavery propaganda. Like literature glorifying the old South, abolitionist rhetoric sometimes rejoiced in the "mildness, fidelity, and generosity" of the Negro. A black abolitionist made explicit what a number of his white colleagues only hinted—that the racist image of the docile black man was correct and not at all insulting. "The heart is the king of the head," he asserted. "In that better day when mere calculating intellect (for this is the only kind of intellect in which the Caucasian excels the African) shall have only its place —and no more, the African will unquestionably stand at the head of a true civilization." The argument that whites were superior mentally and inferior emotionally "exalts the African race above *all* the races."[11] In an age that admired sentimentality and gentle emotionality, those once offensive stereotypes rebounded to the credit of black people.

Racial differences even helped explain such embarrassing things as why, if blacks truly desired freedom, so few of them rebelled. "The negro's heart, spite of all the maddening influence of oppression, is too kind, too full of tenderness and love," was A. A. Phelp's answer. "The white man might [seek vengeance], but not he."[12]

There was a real ambivalence here since many abolitionists firmly expected a race war in the South—foresaw one with dreadful fascination—and yet, at the same time, pictured the black man as forgiving, gentle, and unvindictive. Lydia Maria Child illustrated the difficulty (without meaning to) in a story appropriately entitled

"Black Anglo Saxons." Set in Virginia at the time of the American Revolution, it centered on a group of slaves who gathered secretly to plot to gain their freedom. There were two choices. They might flee their colonial masters and seek refuge with the British. Or they might exact revenge by murdering slaveholders and ravishing "wives and daughters before their eyes, as they have done to *us*." Although the debate took place among slaves, it assumed a racial character. The most blood-thirsty spokesmen for retribution were mulattoes whose white paternity was much emphasized. The chief speaker for mercy was a pure-blooded black man. He repeated the Christian message of returning forgiveness for evil and "the docility of African temperament responded to his gentle words."[13] The same dichotomy appeared in *Uncle Tom's Cabin,* in which Harriet Beecher Stowe also made a nearly white slave vengeful and potentially violent while the purely African Uncle Tom bore the message and martyrdom of Christ.

Criticized by a black abolitionist for stressing the gentleness of the Negro, Theodore Parker responded with an evasion. He had only been speaking of the past, Parker claimed; he longed for the time in the future when American blacks would imitate their Haitian brothers and sisters and prove their courage "by rising and achieving their freedom by the only method which the world thoroughly and heartily accepts, and that is, by drawing the sword and cleaving the oppressor from his crown to his groin, until one half falls to the right, and the other half falls to the left." This lurid image in mind, Parker concluded in a tone which was both defensive and wistful. "I have said many times, I thought the African would not be content to be a slave always; I wish he would not a single day more."[14] The best argument Parker, and abolitionists like him, could manage was that even natural forgiveness had its limits and that these were rapidly approaching.

It was hard for abolitionists to turn the black man into a vengeful but liberty-loving Anglo-Saxon, but it was possible to convert his patience into a sign of deep spirituality. "It is the glory of Christianity that it teaches its disciples to return good for evil," wrote a contributor to the *Anti-Slavery Record* in 1836. "But what Christian nation can show more or nobler instances of this virtue than the poor, despised, enslaved Africo-Americans?"[15] This was in line with a tendency among abolitionists to associate blacks with a special religiosity. "The Christ of the present Age approaches us, in this land, in the mutilated form of the American Slave," Edmund Quincy thought, anticipating Uncle Tom by over a decade. "Scourged, mocked, [word illegible], crucified every day afresh, He presents Himself, daily, to a world full of His nominal disciples & titular ministers, & implores their aid."[16] Quincy easily shifted from believing in the gentleness of blacks to

identifying blacks with the Redeemer, and finally to depicting blacks
as agents of redemption.[17] Harriet Beecher Stowe was to do much
the same when at the end of *Uncle Tom's Cabin*, she hinted to whites
that the torch of Christian mission might be passing from their un-
worthy hands to Africa.

With its promise that the meek shall inherit the earth and that the
last shall be first, Christianity made it possible for abolitionists to find
solace and salvation in the lowly condition of black people. For this
to have occurred required a geographical distance that allowed abolitionist imaginations to see slavery abstractly, as a moral drama rather
than as interaction among real human beings. Also required was a
shift in antebellum values from belief in the church militant (and
masculine) to the church sentimental (and feminine)—an identification of godliness with those mild, emotional, and forgiving qualities
of Jesus that neatly corresponded to the stereotype of the docile Negro. In the past Anglo-Americans, ambivalently satisfied with their
culture and themselves, found comfort in measuring their civilization
against what they thought was the barbarity of blackness.[18] Abolitionists, ambivalently discontented with Jacksonian America, measured the depravity of their society by contrasting it with the spirituality of its oppressed.

Although abolitionists believed in the importance of some kinds of
racial differences, they had to persuade whites that other supposed
racial differences did not exist or did not matter. Many lines of racialist thought abolitionists simply dismissed as ultimately irrelevant.
"Whether the different varieties of human species are equal in mental
endowments, and whether they had a unity or diversity of origin are
questions rather curious than useful," argued David Lee Child. In
1834 William Goodell conceded to scientists their measurements of
brain weights and facial angles, which were supposed to reveal mental
characteristics of blacks and whites. "The question is," Goodell said,
"whether the two races partake of the same [moral] nature." For
Goodell they did.[19]

Abolitionists had a number of ways of disposing of racial differences
when it was necessary to do so. They could be dismissed by "the
declaration of God himself, that he hath made of one blood all the
nations of men to dwell upon the face of the earth." Or they could
be obscured in the doctrine that "the black man has rights which are
as sacred as the rights of a white man," which maintained political
equality but left other kinds of equality open to debate. Or differences
might be resolved by reference to a higher unity, by presenting them
as complimentary, with each group contributing something lacking in
the other. Theodore Parker, awkwardly positioned between antislav-

ery and a strong belief in the fixity of racial and cultural characteristics, sought to extricate himself by that route. "God makes us one
human nature, but diverse in nationality, that we may help each
other. So the hand is one," said Parker, "but it is separated into five
fingers, to make it pliant and manifold useful."[20]

Somehow Parker and his fellow abolitionists wanted to believe both
in human unity and in racial diversity. Their culture insisted upon the
latter and their reform commitment depended upon the former. Abolitionists did speak of black and white "characters" (and of male and
female ones, for that matter); but when they did so, it was with little
analytical rigor and often as a way of marking the moral distance
between oppressor and oppressed. As much difficulty as abolitionists
had with racial differences, their hopes, fears, and reform strategies
really rested on an abstract and generalized creature called "man."

The *Emancipator* in 1836 took satisfaction in noting that "the mind,
limited though it be, . . . is fitted in its nature, on all questions of
moral right, to see the right and do it." The intellectual foundations
of that faith were laid over a half-century before by the popularization in America of Scottish Common Sense philosophy. The key was
belief in an innate moral sense—something like a conscience, an inner
voice within each and every person able to tell right from wrong.[21]
The abolitionists were not the first to apply that doctrine to racial
issues: a feeling that blacks possessed the same moral apparatus as
whites bothered Thomas Jefferson when he tried to reconcile a mind
divided over slavery and race. Yet thanks to circumstances in antebellum America the doctrine of a moral sense assumed special importance in post-1830 antislavery.[22]

"Slavery is a self-evident wrong," Garrison declared. Nothing more
had to be said, and the reformer only pointed out to men and women
what should have been apparent to them. Higher law and knowledge
of natural rights were brought to earth, given to everyone, not just
to priests and statesmen. "In all cases involving the *inculcation of
correct moral principles, and the condemnation of sinful practices,*"
wrote William Goodell, "the moral sense itself, sustained by direct
scripture precept, gives imperative direction." The conscience, an
antislavery clergyman agreed, "is still employed by our Creator as
His representative in the soul." Garrison, quite early in his career,
drew the obvious conclusion. "Let every one settle it as a principle,"
he urged, "that his conscience, and not his lay or spiritual leaders,
must be his commander."[23]

Such an application of the moral sense doctrine allowed reformers
like Garrison to maintain a dogged faith in human beings while de-

spising the way they behaved. Mobs and hostility against abolitionism were creations of sects, parties, selfish aristocrats, and demagogues, not signs that the people themselves were beyond redemption. This was a whiggish resignation to Jacksonian democracy, not a concession that the people were always right, but an admission that they would eventually be right—if they could be removed from sectarian darkness and their moral sense could be properly unfettered.

The doctrine of a moral sense also shaped part of the abolitionist critique of slavery. Depriving people of their will, reducing them to items of property, meant they had no chance to exercise and develop their better nature. "Man is justly subjected to moral law," George Bourne wrote; "but property, a slave who has no will, cannot be the proper object of rewards and punishments."[24] If the moral sense marked mankind from the beasts, then inability to exercise it reduced a human being to brutishness. Slaves became symbols of godly individuals rendered unable to exert moral strength because of oppressive institutions and willful men (human beings in much the same situation as antebellum reformers felt themselves to be in, harnessed as they were by unresponsive churches and politicians).

A slight but significant transformation of values in the antebellum period fused still other new and immediate meanings onto the moral sense doctrine. The idea of a moral sense had always been allied with a traditional dichotomy between intellect and emotion, between head and heart. Eighteenth-century figures like Jefferson, who strongly endorsed the intellect, could concede emotional or moral equality to black people and still consider them inferior because they presumably did not measure up to white standards of rationality. By the 1830s there existed in America and in Europe a greater suspicion of intellect and a higher faith in emotions; the moral sense, as a result, gained stature from being identified with sentiment and feeling. The inevitable conclusion was that the moral sense—or humankind's best, most intuitive emotions—should be supreme over the intellect, which always needed moral guidance. That made reform a matter of sensibility, not a problem for the head to ponder. "Nothing can be done to abolish slavery, unless we are waked up to feel," Henry B. Stanton believed. "Publicola" informed Garrison that "abolitionists need more heart than mental preparation to carry forward their holy enterprise."[25] Such statements, of course, only reflected the spirit of the day—the heart was a staple of Victorian literature, and it even reached the apex of academic prestige in 1856 when a Miss Plummer, of Salem, Massachusetts, endowed a chair at Harvard to be a "professorship of the heart, not the head."[26]

When pressed far enough by abolitionists, emphasis on the heart made the question of the relative intellectual capacity of the races largely irrelevant, even though this had been a serious issue for Jefferson and for antislavery writers in the 1790s.[27] "Human beings have *rights*, because they are *moral* beings," wrote Angelina Grimké; "the rights of *all* men grow out of their moral nature; and as all men have the same moral nature, they have essentially the same rights."[28] Belief in a common moral sense, an annoyance to Jefferson, a half century later became the anchor of man's right to control his own life, an assurance that he had the potential to do so morally, no matter what his intellect was. The moral sense, thanks to a sentimental age's revaluation upward of emotionality, finally became an egalitarian doctrine. It contained the revolutionary implication that if education and intellect corrupted human beings, and if women and blacks were mentally inferior but emotionally equal (perhaps superior) to white males, then indeed the last might well be first. That dangerous possibility aside, the moral sense doctrine promised to tie freedom for all kinds of people to the rock of moral certainty. It provided assurance that "God, in making human beings, has given to each a power of self-government, which needs, which admits of, no other rule—a conscience, to govern the movements of soul and body."[29]

The doctrine of moral sense could not fulfill this and its other hopeful promises. Belief in intellectual differences between the races never quite died, even among abolitionists. Moral certainty, in addition, was not easily clung to in antebellum America. Adin Ballou, an early abolitionist, remembered how he had begun a utopian community with the conviction that it was possible for "man's being and doing right from the law of God written on his heart, without the aid of external bonds." Yet the community collapsed and Ballou learned, to his sorrow, that the consciences of men were too variable and too contentious to sustain harmony, even within a utopian venture.[30]

The moral sense doctrine was a convenience, a part of the intellectual baggage of the time, an assumption to carry into reform activity. In itself it was not an answer to the question of human nature, especially since the moral sense of antebellum Americans was so reluctant to assert itself by taking a stand against slavery.

Abolitionists made other assumptions about human beings. These were important in shaping abolitionist perception of reality and they, like racialist and moral sense doctrines, were unconsciously and unsystematically articulated. Modes of thought which disciplined minds distinguished from one another, and which posterity can separate clearly, all tumble happily together in the mentality of people like the abolitionists, bound by the terms of their culture even in their discontent with the way things were. In antislavery propaganda the rhetoric of the moral sense (and, for that matter, the rhetoric of inherent racial characteristics) coexisted with that of another intellectual tradition, which held man to be a product of his environment.

Some environmentalism in abolitionist writings may have gotten there by direct transmission. James G. Birney studied at Princeton in Samuel Stanhope Smith's day—Smith having been an advocate of the idea that skin color was a product of climate and social conditions. Birney's son later claimed that his father had been deeply influenced by Smith (very little else about Princeton affected Birney).[31] For most other abolitionists, however, environmental explanations of skin color and racial differences simply were available for the taking, with little thought required. "M.," writing in the *Quarterly Anti-Slavery Magazine,* seemed almost annoyed to have to bring the matter up. He asked, "*Can* anyone doubt that custom and climate fully account for the diversities of the human form?" As late as 1849 the *National Anti-Slavery Standard,* ignoring a growing body of contrary material, asserted that "the most important general conclusion to be drawn from the study of ethnology is that the differences in type exhibited by different races of men is not greater than may be found existing in individuals of the same race subjected for a long period of time to the action of climatic or other physical causes." For good measure it went on to add that white skin, not black, was the divergent type.[32]

Despite such statements, environmentalism was neither clearly articulated nor consistently upheld. For instance, it is difficult at times to discover what theory of racial characteristics lay behind statements by antislavery authors. "That the races of mankind are different, spiritually as well as physically, there is, of course, no doubt," Lydia Maria Child conceded;

> but it is the differences between the trees of the same forest, not as between trees and minerals. The facial angle and shape of the head is various in races and nations; but these are the *effects* of spiritual influences, long operating on character, and in their turn becoming *causes:* thus intertwining, as Past and Future ever do.

Consequently, "Similar influences [to those enjoyed by caucasians] brought to bear on the Indians or the Africans, as a race, would gradually change the structure of their skulls, and enlarge their perceptions of moral and intellectual truth." Having gone that far toward environmentalism and human commonality, Mrs. Child was prepared to retreat again toward diversity. "The same influences cannot be brought to bear upon them;" she added, "for their Past is not *our* Past; and of course never can be." Undaunted, she foresaw the result

as "variety, without inferiority."[33] In addition to being vague on just
what produced racial dissimilarities, Mrs. Child obviously did not
make a sharp distinction between such physical differences as the
shape of skulls and what we would consider to be largely cultural
matters—"perceptions of moral and intellectual truth."

This confusion was perhaps fortunate, for there was the awkward
problem of explaining why slaves, who were supposed to be innately
spiritual, did not always display the moral refinement a New England
lady might desire. Environmental assumptions were as available here
—and as haphazardly utilized—as they were for dealing with varieties
of skin color. Mrs. Child herself, putting the best face on things, insisted that moral turpitude among slaves was part of "a merciful
arrangement of Divine Providence, by which the acuteness of sensibility is lessened when it becomes merely a source of suffering." It was
the brutality of slavery, not any kind of innate brutishness in black
people, that accounted for whatever lack of higher feelings might be
apparent in slaves. Abolitionists similarly—and very correctly—cred-
ited slavery with encouraging idleness, theft, and promiscuity. Quite
typical was the simple assertion by a correspondent to the *National
Era*, who wrote of blacks that "their apparent inferiority is owing to
circumstances, and not to the endowments of nature."[34] When blacks
displayed higher qualities, these were presented as emblematic of a
deeply spiritual nature; when they fell from grace it was attributed
to a crushing and destructive environment.

Environmentalist assumptions, nevertheless, were too deeply ingrained simply to be crude propaganda weapons, picked up and dis-
carded cynically and self-consciously. They served the important but
largely unrecognized function of allowing abolitionists to hold fast to
their belief in human unity while explaining why groups of people
looked and acted so different from one another. The most obvious
such application of environmentalist thought was to race, but abolitionists brought the same assumptions to bear upon the slaveholder.
Environmentalism permitted abolitionists to denounce the master class
in the bitterest terms and yet to feel empathy and to see the white
Southerner's sin as one any person might be in danger of commiting.

George Bourne, a blunt and angry man who had seen slavery at
first hand, was sure he knew what slavery did to the master. It produces "Haughty self-conceit," "marble-hearted insensibility," and it
"destroys every correct view of equity." Masters "become sensual,"
"irrascible and turbulent"; and slavery "renders men violent in cruelty." As if that were not enough, the institution was a "prolific source
of all infidelity and irreligion." Another abolitionist, his view confirmed by a stay in a Southern prison, determined that slavery "causes

and nourishes pride, laziness, haughtiness, cruelty, oppression, deceit, fraud, theft, lying, Sabbath-breaking, drunkenness, adultery, fornication, and all uncleanness, murder, and everything that is hateful and abominable in the sight of God!" The environment of slavery, abolitionists further believed, also accounted for the master's hatred of his human chattel. The Ninth Annual Meeting of the Massachusetts Anti-Slavery Society put it succinctly when it resolved that "the prejudice which exists in this country against our colored population is not the creature of physical organization or complexion, but of slavery." Prejudice, abolitionists generally maintained, was not "natural" but was itself the result of arbitrary power given whites by slavery and of the subsequent degradation of blacks.[35]

Hidden behind glare of rhetoric was an implication abolitionists were prepared to acknowledge and to accept. A correspondent to the *American Anti-Slavery Reporter* in 1834 believed that "had the labor always been performed by slaves in N. England, the people would have been very similar to the inhabitants of the southern states." The real difference between Northerners and Southerners was not anything deep or permanent but rather in circumstance, in the blighting institution peculiar to the South. Harriet Beecher Stowe gave popular form to the idea in the character of Simon Legree, a transplanted Northerner who became the epitome of an evil master. Richard Hildreth,

an independent figure in antislavery and in New England letters, faced bravely the logic of such a position. "So we are slave-holders or abolitionists, not because we differ much either in moral character or intellectual capacity, either in sentiment or opinion," he wrote, "but mainly from differences of social and topographical position."[36] Remove slavery and you would remove the cause of differences between Northerners and Southerners. On that blessed day Southerners would act virtuously and work industriously—they would become, in other words, much as Northerners imagined themselves to be.

Up to this point environmental explanations fulfilled admirable functions. They explained human diversity while allowing for human commonality. They made slavery stand both as an evil in itself and as the cause of the evil of prejudice. Yet environmentalism led to horrifying conclusions if pushed too far. Richard Hildreth pressed on toward them when he assessed sexual immorality among slaves, which, of course, he attributed to the conditions of slavery. "Chastity like courage is, to a great extent, an artificial virtue," he decided, "the existence of which principally depends upon education and public opinion." This made morality not an absolute thing, but variable from situation to situation. Hildreth appeared to recognize as much for he added that "To persons so situated [as slaves], we cannot justly apply ideas founded upon totally different circumstances."[37] A doctrine excusing the misconduct of slaves, however, could easily excuse misconduct of all sorts by making morality strictly a condition of time and place.

Confronted with this kind of environmentalist implication, abolitionists hastily withdrew. In 1836 Elizur Wright mounted an attack on the philosopher William Paley, because of whose influence (he believed) "the educated class are more averse than others to any attempt at a general reformation of morals. They have been taught to regard man as a mere creature of circumstances." Garrison grappled with the problem in 1843 and 1844. John A. Collins, a trusted antislavery agent, defected to "Robert Owen's absurd and dangerous dogma, that men are 'the creatures of circumstances'—not sinful, but unfortunate—not inwardly corrupt, but outwardly trammelled." Garrison was appalled, feeling this meant man was "not accountable—not worthy of any praise or blame for any of his actions." Publicly joining the issue, Garrison swung away from environmentalism. "The root of evil," he argued, "was in the heart of man, and not in external circumstances, though these often operated disasterously on the manners and morals of the truly unfortunate." And so back once more to the individual: "Of one thing we feel certain: an internal regeneration must precede the external salvation of mankind from sin and misery."[38]

There was a dilemma here. If abolitionists saw sin as an individual matter, they nevertheless focused attention upon an institution—slavery. Although the slaveholder's sins were both environmental and personal (and amenable to repentance), the sins of the slave were social: the slave was locked in a perverse system which put a premium upon theft, laziness, and sexual immorality. The master sinned by choice; the slave sinned because of circumstances. Did responsibility for evil rest with the hardened heart of the individual or with society? Abolitionists answered one way one time, the other way another time.

The only escape for someone who took the problem seriously was to find refuge in generalities about reciprocal relationships between circumstances and conscience, or else to fall all the way back from environmentalism to the moral sense. Lydia Maria Child took the former course, telling her readers in 1860 that "human nature is essentially the same in all nations and ages; being modified only by the laws that control and regulate it, and the social conditions under which it is developed. Hence, laws and social institutions are of immense importance." George Bourne took the other recourse. Although he portrayed the effects of slavery upon the master, he dismissed the argument that Southerners ought to be excused for their transgressions because, having grown up under the system, they knew no better. Bourne at this point ceased to be an environmentalist. Excuses, he felt, were nonsense—all Americans were brought up with the Declaration of Independence, and all persons possessed enough moral sense to realize the sinfulness of an evil so hideous as slavery.[39]

Environmentalist assumptions, like those of innate racial differences and of a moral sense, if pursued too far, led to a god-forsaken thicket in which either human unity or human responsibility, or both, got lost.[40] And that, to an antislavery sensibility, was unacceptable.

Quite clearly, if logical and systematic thought about race, environmentalism, or common sense philosophy were all-important, abolitionists would have to be marked as utter failures. And if we operated on the assumption that ideas by themselves brought men and women to antislavery, then we, no less than they, would be left in confusion. Abolitionists conceived of human beings in terms of the moral sense and environmentalism because they had to, just as they had to deal with racial differences and could only do so in certain ways. But environmentalism and the moral sense did not necessarily lead to anti-slavery; neither doctrine stopped at the Mason-Dixon line, and both found their way into the minds of people who were either hostile to abolitionism or apathetic. The important thing is not that abolitionists used the assumptions of their times, but how they used them and how they refused to use them.

Both environmentalism and the moral sense, in antislavery writings, served to assert that at heart all of mankind were the same. Even in their acceptance of some fixed racial differences abolitionists often tended to resolve diversity into a grander unity, finding comple-mentary functions for the bold and vigorous Anglo-Saxon and the spiritual and forgiving Negro. On the other hand, most abolitionists refused to go any farther when the moral sense brought them to moral relativism. They could not accept an individualism that defended the absolute sanctity of every person's conscience. They likewise re-fused to follow environmentalism into a moral relativism that would excuse human beings for their actions by placing responsibility on to social conditions. The consistency in abolitionist thought about man-kind was not in doctrine but rather in yearning: in longings to be-lieve in human unity and to find moral security—longings appropriate to a society rapidly becoming more diverse and in which the old moral loci, the state and the church, no longer commanded the respect they once had.

Abolitionist belief in inherent racial characteristics, in the moral sense, and in environmentalism, all contained relatively optimistic assumptions about human nature. Abolitionists emphasized the spirit-uality of blacks (rather than consigning them to permanent infer-iority), placed a guide to right and wrong in all men, and prepared to forgive a limited number of the slaveholder's sins. Antislavery rhetoric, moreover, effectively located the source of evil outside of human nature, usually in institutions that stifled men and women and thwarted their better instincts. Here abolitionists were not far from the older and less strident antislavery of earlier generations, which likewise drew upon common sense philosophy and environmentalism; nor were they distant from contemporary transcendentalism, which similarly sought to extricate mankind from repressive institutions. But the post-1830 abolitionist was driven by still another, grimmer, set of attitudes constantly in tension with moral sense and environmentalist doctrines, yet more distinctive and probably stronger. If the solution to social sins was individual repentance, as abolitionists commonly argued, then there had to be something wrong with mankind after all.

5

CONTROL
Sexual Attitudes, Self-Mastery, and Civilization

MORALITY was self-evident to the abolitionist. Other people found it much less obvious and evaded its demands with little difficulty. Although reformers sought human liberation they, as citizens of a sinful society, could not believe that mankind should be left to the claims of the flesh. Just as the potential for moral behavior seemed to lie in human nature, so did some of the forces preventing that potential from being realized.

Charles K. Whipple described slavery as "absolute, irresponsible power on one side, and entire subjection on the other." Like virtually all abolitionists he grounded his objections to bondage on this relationship of utter submission and total dominance between slave and master. There were, of course, other kinds of emphases possible. Earlier humanitarian reform had stressed the suffering of slaves, but, no matter how useful examples of inhuman treatment might be in stirring sentiment against slavery, most post-1830 abolitionists denied that cruelty was what made the institution so terrible. After combing Southern newspapers and exhausting eye-witnesses for horror stories about slavery, Theodore Dwight Weld declared that these were not the basic fact of the institution. The "combined experience of the human race," he thought, proved that such "cruelty is the spontaneous and uniform product of arbitrary power." Abuse was only an effect of submission and dominance. Even those who began by looking at slavery in still another way, in terms of "the chattel principle," came around (like Weld) to a definition which was neither economic, nor institutional, nor based on specific kinds of treatment. "Slavery is the

This essay originally appeared, in a slightly different form, as "The Erotic South: Civilization and Sexuality in American Abolitionism," *American Quarterly* 25 (1973): 177-201, copyright, 1973, Trustees of the University of Pennsylvania, and is reprinted with permission.

act of one holding another as property," a correspondent to the *Philanthropist* declared, adding "or one man being wholly subject to the will of others." In his mind slavery (as a property relationship) resolved itself into a matter of power just as surely as it did for Whipple or Weld.[1]

A. A. Phelps constructed an imaginary state of nature to show how it came to be acceptable to hold some humans as property. Phelps' original man "loves, and is grasping after power," and the white Southerner was his direct descendant. So driving was this urge to dominate, abolitionists believed, that it outdistanced all other possible motives, including greed. When Garrison assessed "the master-passion in the bosom of the slaveholder" he found it to be "not the love of gain, but the possession of absolute power, unlimited sovereignty." His words echoed those of Angelina Grimké shortly after her arrival in the North. "There are hundreds of thousands at the South, who do *not* hold their slaves, by any means, as much 'for purposes of gain,' as they do from the *lust of power*," Miss Grimké exclaimed. "This is the passion that reigns triumphant there."[2]

Achievement of authority brought destructive results for its possessor as well as for his victim. Having helped her husband compile the material for *American Slavery as It Is*, Angelina Grimké (by this time Mrs. Weld), told a sister that these stories were designed "to show the awful havock which arbitrary power makes in human hearts, and to excite a holy indignation against an *institution* which degrades the oppressor as well as the oppressed." William Goodell gave it as "an old maxim that the exercise of unlimited power will make any man a tyrant." "It is," he noted "no slander to say that the slaveholder is a man!"[3] Goodell's phraseology was not just an accident. Abolitionists did not maintain that slaveholders were somehow peculiar in their failings but rather that they demonstrated what all people should beware of.[4] After having detailed in their different ways the devastating effects of slavery, C. K. Whipple and Theodore Dwight Weld each reminded his readers that the danger was a general one, not confined to white Southerners. "No human being is fit to be trusted with absolute irresponsible power," Whipple claimed. "If the best portion of our own community were selected to hold and use such authority [as masters possess], they would very soon be corrupted." Weld believed "arbitrary power is to the mind what alcohol is to the body; it intoxicates."[5] Man might have an innate moral sense, he might at times be moulded by his race or environment; but abolitionists, not obligated to cling to any theory to the end, were at the bottom certain that mankind also had a deeply implanted drive to dominate others —a drive that required constant vigilance and suppression.

Enslavement of blacks was not the only kind of coercion and "arbitrary power" disturbing to abolitionists. Slavery was a special case because of its magnitude, but the principle behind it appeared in countless places, many of them closer to home. Few abolitionists were so extreme as Abby Kelley who—lest she be a tyrant—was "very conscientious not to use the least worldly authority over her child."[6] But even abolitionists less dogmatic (or fool-hardy) than she were outraged by the tyranny of preachers, politicians, public opinion, and institutions.[7] Quite early William Goodell perceived that slavery served a symbolic function as the extreme example of what happened when man's drive for power ran rampant. "We acknowledge that there is a propriety in holding up 'NEGRO SLAVERY' from age to age, as the perfect image of oppression personified," he wrote, "so that everything insufferably dreadful, and superlatively hateful in despotism, to the end of time, may be branded with infamy simply by showing its affinity with SLAVEHOLDING."[8]

Americans of an earlier generation had been just as suspicious as Goodell was of man's ability to wield authority. Such wariness was epidemic at the time of the American Revolution, and it had affected the way individuals saw slavery, just as it would again after 1830. Almost a life-time before Garrison's career began, John Woolman argued against the institution because "so long as men are biassed by narrow self-love, so long an absolute power over other men is unfit for them." In 1765 John Adams wrote of "the love of power, which has been so often the cause of slavery."[9] Fear of power has always been an appealing perception of reality in times when the political system seems unrepresentative and unresponsive. It took on new vitality in the antebellum period as moralistic whites saw political and economic affairs increasingly dominated by ambitious, uncouth men.

There was, in addition, a subtle cultural shift between the Revolutionary and antebellum periods. The concept of "power" was coming by the 1830s to fit into a web of associations that ensnared some of the deepest and most mysterious forces that abolitionists believed to be in all men. This included the deepest, most mysterious, most fearful force of all: human sexuality. By 1831 there was not a great distance from the concept of lust for power to that of mere lust.

Abolitionists did not dwell "excessively" on sexual misconduct in the South—their writings have little merit as pornography. From the beginning whites perceived (and cultivated) an erotic potential in interracial contact. Nevertheless, this potential could be organized into more than one pattern of perception and post-1830 antislavery propaganda directly reversed a prevalent assumption by presenting

white men, not black men, as the sexual aggressors. Early in his career Garrison set the tone. He was accosted by a slaveholder who
posed the classic question of American racism: "How should you like
to have a black man marry your daughter?" Garrison replied that
"slaveholders generally should be the last persons to affect fastidious-
ness on that point; for they seem to be enamoured with amalgama-
tion."[10] The retort was unanswerable, and it survived down to the
Civil War. It was, in part, simply fine strategy, pointing both to an
obvious hypocrisy and a very real condition of slavery.

But abolitionists did not stop with this simple and expedient formula. They did not argue that erotic activity always was at the instiga-
tion of white males. Gerrit Smith believed planters would not fight
an insurrection effectively because they would be too "busy in trans-
porting their wives and daughters to places where they would be
safe from that worst fate which husbands and fathers can imagine
for their wives and daughters." George Bourne pondered, "What may
be the awful consequences, if ever the colored men by physical force
should attain the mastery?" "If," he decided, "no other argument
could be adduced in favor of immediate and universal emancipation,
that single fact is sufficient. Delay only increases the danger of the
white women and augments the spirit of determined malignity and
revenge in the colored men." Abolition would lead to forgiveness and
to sexual security for the white woman as well as for the female
slave.[11]

Rape was only one form of sexual retribution abolitionists foresaw
slaves exacting upon the master class. Louisa Barker believed black
women lured young slaveholders into illicit attachments with female
slaves as a way of lessening the chance that the slave might be sold—
and to destroy the constitution of the master through physical over-
indulgence. Still another writer argued that "women who have been
drawn into licentiousness by wicked men, if they retain their vicious
habits, almost invariably display their revenge for their debasement,
by ensnaring others into the same corruption and moral ruin." This
placed on female slaves much of the responsibility for stirring the
sensuality of their masters, thus degrading the slaveholder as they
had been degraded. But there were even more horrifying prospects—
lasciviousness did not stop with white men and black women enticing
each other. "Were it necessary," John Rankin stated primly, "I could
refer you to several instances of slaves actually seducing the daughters
of their masters! Such seductions sometimes happen even in the most
respectable slaveholding families." It was impossible for daughters of
slaveholders always to "escape this impetuous fountain of pollution."[12]
Comments like these touched the white South at a sensitive point—

its image of itself and of its women.[13] Futhermore, they moved the
argument from the idea that whites were sexual aggressors over to the
more comfortable position (for whites) that blacks represented sensuality after all.

Emotional associations concerning miscegenation undoubtedly
played their part, but the horror of Southern sexuality for abolitionists
was not in its interracial nature. At work was a more generalized
sense that the South represented a society in which eroticism had no
checks put upon it. "Illicit intercourse" was embedded in the very
conditions of Southern life, abolitionists believed. For the master "the
temptation is always at hand—the legal authority absolute—the actual
power complete—the vice a profitable one" if it produced slaves for
market, "and the custom so universal as to bring no disgrace." One
author, using the apt pseudonym, "Puritan," was appalled that

> not only in taverns, but in boarding houses, and the dwellings of in-
> dividuals, boys and girls verging on maturity altogether unclothed, wait
> upon ladies and gentlemen, without exciting even the suffusion of a
> blush on the face of young females, who thus gradually become habit-
> uated to scenes of which delicate and refined Northern women cannot
> adequately conceive.

To make matters worse, the free and easy association between slave
children and white children spread the depravity of the back cabins
to the big house. "Between the female slaves and the misses there is an
unrestrained communication," Southern-born James A. Thome explained to the American Anti-Slavery Society. "As they come in contact through the day, the courtesan feats of the over night are whis-
pered into the ear of the unsuspecting [white] girl and poison her
youthful mind."[14]

In its libidinousness the South could only be compared to other
examples of utter depravity and dissolution. Thome informed an audience of attentive young ladies that "THE SOUTHERN STATES ARE
ONE GREAT SODOM," and his account was seconded by another
abolitionist, who had lived in Virginia and Maryland. In 1834 the
Pennsylvania Freeman spoke of the "great moral lazarhouse of Southern slavery." Thomas Wentworth Higginson decided that, compared
to the South, "a Turkish harem is a cradle of virgin purity." Henry
C. Wright preferred a comparison with the notorious Five Points
district in New York—much to the latter's advantage, of course.[15]
Like Sodom, brothels, or a harem, the South appeared to be a place
in which men could indulge their erotic impulses with impunity.

Yet, in the nature of things, there must be retribution. It could be
physiological since—nineteenth-century moralists assumed—sexual ex-

cesses ultimately destroyed body and mind. Planters, according to Mrs. Louisa Barker, exemplified the "wreck of early manhood always resulting from self-indulgence." They were "born with feeble minds and bodies, with just force enough to transmit the family name, and produce in feebler characters a second edition of the father's life." Mrs. Barker's comments were consistent with the way other abolitionists viewed the South and with the way her times viewed sexuality, but they were almost unique in antislavery literature—although the character of the languid but erratic planter was not.[16] The more usual form of retribution predicted from Southern licentiousness was social and demographic.

At the beginning of the antislavery crusade there was a sense among some abolitionists, that (in the words of James G. Birney) "from causes now operating, the South must be filled in a few years with blacks and, it may be, that in our lives it will be given up to them." Birney, in the letter that marked his public renunciation of colonization, detailed the "alarming rapidity" with which the process was operating in his native Kentucky. In a similar vein, John Rankin warned that slavery will "increase their [blacks'] numbers, and enable them to overpower the nation. Their enormous increase beyond that of the white population is truly alarming." Liberation, however, would disperse them and make their population growth "proportionate to the rest of the nation." LaRoy Sunderland quantified the increase, using censuses through 1830, and explained why he thought it was occurring. "That the blacks should increase faster than the whites, is easily accounted for," he remarked dryly, "from the fact, that the former class are increased by the latter, but the blacks cannot increase the whites."[17] Such statements seem to have decreased in time and with additional censuses (although complaints about licentiousness persisted), but they and fears of imminent insurrections glare luridly from early abolitionist propaganda—they were twin expressions of a belief that the South faced an overwhelming chastizing event and that white dominance might soon become submission. In both cases —insurrection and the fruits of unchecked sexuality—the only security rested with abolition.

There were wonderful propaganda advantages here. The issue of miscegenation forever dogged the antislavery movement and by stressing Southern licentiousness abolitionists turned the tables. They could both speak of the "dreadful amalgamating abominations" of the slave system and argue that they would "experience, in all probability, a ten fold diminution" with emancipation. Elijah Lovejoy went so far as to state the "one reason why abolitionists urge the abolition of slavery is, that they fully believe it will put a stop, in a great and almost entire measure to that wretched, and shameful, and polluted intercourse between the whites and blacks, now so common, it may be said so universal, in the slave states."[18] Yet the propaganda advantages—if they were only consideration—would have been greater had abolitionists not also insisted, as they did at times, that "the right to choose a partner for life is so exclusive and sacred, that it is never interfered with, except by the worst of tyrants." Garrison, with his usual boldness and lack of tact, asserted the perfect equality of the races and drew the conclusion that "intermarriage is neither unnatural nor repugnant to nature, but designed to unite people of different tribes and nations."[19] Such assaults on antimiscegenation sentiment, if nothing else, show that abolitionists were not just saying what they thought their audience wanted to hear when they spoke out on sexual matters. Instead, what abolitionists wrote about Southern sexuality must be put in relation to nineteenth-century assumptions, to conditions in the North that gave urgency to concern for licentiousness, and to the other reform interests of antislavery men and women.

Abolitionists did not perceive the South as lustful simply because unhallowed sex occurred under slavery. Erotic activity between master class and bondsmen, after all, did not originate in 1831 (nor did disgust with Southern morals; New England Federalists had that in abundance a generation earlier). Miscegenation itself may well have been decreasing at the very time it became a staple of antislavery propaganda.[20]

Abolitionists were especially sensitive to Southern eroticism because, like most middle-class moralists of the day, they saw a certain interchangeability between power and sexuality. Sexuality, as far as they were concerned, was not a peculiarly Southern problem: it was intrinsic to any situation in which one person's arbitrary will could rule over others. Abolitionist revulsion at Southern sensuality was, to be sure, very much in line with Victorian morality; but it was also in large measure part of a more general abolitionist revulsion against domination and possession. The abolitionists' association of sexuality with power and dominance had some validity, and it was unique neither to them nor to the antebellum period. But such an association did have much wider currency and more fearsome connotations in nineteenth-century America than in previous centuries or in our own day. To take an extreme but revealing example, Victorian pornography exploited situations of power and powerlessness more than the contemporary variety does (despite some noteworthy exceptions) and probably more than ancient bawdy literature did. In one nineteenth-century classic the action took place in a harem where "The Lustful Turk," a darkly sensual being, reduced women (even good English women!) to sexual slaves. His power was both political and erotic, and his desires were as unchecked as they were varied. This was strikingly similar to antislavery images of the South and the slave-holder—a similarity increased when one of the lustful Turk's victims made a speech in which she attacked slavery as "the most powerful agent in the degradation of mankind," a charming bit of abolitionism amidst depravity. In more respectable Victorian circles it was thought that servants, another class of underling, were both sexually corrupted and agents of corruption, a matter which later attracted the attention of Sigmund Freud.[21] Anti-Catholic diatribes likewise played to a sense that subordination led to debauchery. George Bourne, an early and important abolitionist, doubled as a professional Catholic baiter, and he found the two careers quite easily reconciled. He pictured the South as an erotic society where whites "have been indulged in all the vicious gratifications which lawless power and unrestrained lust, can amalgamate." Much the same, he believed, prevailed in the convent, another kind of closed society. There the absolute power and unchecked erotic energy of the priest replaced that of the planter (in Bourne's imagination) and the seduction and seductiveness of nuns replaced female slaves.[22]

Enough licentiousness existed under slavery to fuel the minds of men like Bourne; but as much as anything, Southern sensuality illustrated a general principle which abolitionists held to be true about man and what possession of power did to him. "We know what human nature is; what are its weaknesses, what its passions," the *Philanthropist* asserted confidently, as it remarked upon the potential for depravity on the plantation.[23] Certainly abolitionists saw what was actually there—erotic encounters did occur—but they were able to do so because culturally determined associations of power with sexual domination prepared them to see and to react strongly to it.

Southern licentiousness took on further meaning for abolitionists because it intersected some typically nineteenth-century judgments about what mankind and society ought to be. In 1939, unconsciously forecasting a later and more famous Victorian moralist, Theodore Dwight Weld wrote that "restraints are the web of civilized society, warp and woof." James G. Birney, musing to his diary in 1850, decided

> the reason that savage & barbarous nations remain so—& unrighteous men, too—is that they manage their affairs by passion—not by reason. Just in proportion as reason prevails, it will control & restrain passion, & just in proportion as it prevails, & passion diminishes nations emerge from ignorance & darkness and become civilized.

Here was a feeling that civilization, if not its discontents, depended on curbing what another abolitionist called "the fatal anarchy of the lowest passions."[24]

Of course, these passions were not exclusively sexual. Birney would not have argued that "savage & barbarous nations" governed themselves by erotic means. But in the minds of abolitionists sex was clearly among the most formidable components of the "animal nature" that had to be subdued before humans or society could be counted as civilized. Henry C. Wright gave as a general principle that "it is for man to keep himself in the image in which he was made, with a power to grasp and control, for the welfare of the race, every element of his own nature and the external world." Yet the specific element that concerned Wright was the reproductive, the husband's "natural propensities" to indulge himself sexually. Theodore Parker decided when a man "is cultivated and refined, the sentiment [of love] is more than the appetite [of sex]; the animal appetite remains but it does not bear so large a ratio to the whole consciousness of the man as before." Sarah Grimké agreed with Parker's estimate. It was impossible for men and women to enjoy the relationship God intended until "our intercourse is purified by the forgetfulness of sex."[25] This resonated almost as a linguistic pun with a biblical tradition, restated by Beriah Green, holding that "all visable slavery is merely a picture of the invisable sway of the passions."[26] Slavery had long borne with it imputations of sin and human willfulness, but nineteenth-century American culture transferred the sin from the slave to the master and combined its suppression with a drive for civilization and self-control. In antislavery propaganda the plantation was less a real place than an imaginary one where the repressed came out of hiding.

Slavery was a guidepost, marking the outer limits of disorder and debauchery; but abolitionists consistently defined their own moral responsibilities and those of fellow Northerners in the same terms they applied to Southerners. "And how is slavery to be abolished by those who are slaves themselves to their own appetites and passions?" Beriah Green asked. William Goodell informed the American Health Convention that "no efforts of yours, nor mine, nor of those who labor with us for the enfranchisement of the enslaved, will ever raise human beings, of any complexion to the true dignity of freemen, so long as they permit themselves to be the slaves of their own appetites, the panders of their own lusts, the forgers of their own fetters." Some years before, the *Emancipator* had noted "the common acceptance of things" in which "men deem themselves the most happy when they can the most easily set aside known prohibitions and indulge in certain propensities." It contrasted this with the "early propagators of the religion of the cross" who had "no animal passions to gratify" as they were led to martyrdom. The lesson was unmistakable: the person who would do good must first conquer himself.[27]

The courtship of Theodore Dwight Weld and Angelina Grimké, a veritable orgy of restraint, revealed that reformers were willing to practice what they preached. Weld regarded the intensity of his emotions for Miss Grimké as a challenge to be overcome, and it was with triumph that he wrote her in March 1838. "It will be a relief to you," he assured Angelina, "to know that I have acquired *perfect self control,* so far as any *expression* or *appearance* of deep feeling is visable to others." Angelina earlier chided him for carrying things too far. "Why this waste of moral strength?" she asked. But she too thought of civilization as a repression of the deeper and more mysterious forces in mankind. She responded ecstatically upon finding how elevated Weld's views of courtship were—how similar to her own, how unsensual. "I have been tempted to think marriage was *sinful,* because of what appeared to me almost invariably to prompt and lead to it," she wrote.

> Instead of the higher, nobler sentiments being first aroused, and leading on the lower passions *captive* to their will, the *latter* seemed to be *lords* over the *former.* Well I am convinced that men in general, the vast majority believe most seriously that women were made to gratify their appetites, *expressly* to minister to *their* pleasure.

The couple's control extended beyond the awkwardness of courtship. A few years after their marriage James G. Birney visited them, remarking to his diary, with a touch of envy, "their self-denial—their firmness in principles puts me to shame."[28] For abolitionists like the Welds the goal was self-mastery and the reward was an orderly life in which affection, even spontaneous joy, had a place—but only after the animal passions were subdued.

Abolitionists saw restraint as a problem for all Americans, not just for themselves and for Southerners. The mass of humanity, Thomas Wentworth Higginson proclaimed, was mired "deep in sensual vileness." William Lloyd Garrison attacked an opponent for refusing to believe that "licentiousness pervades the whole land." Somewhat later Garrison bemoaned the large number of human beings "caring for nothing but the gratification of their lusts and appetites, and dead in trespasses and sins!" William Goodell felt that licentiousness "pollutes the atmosphere of our splendid cities, and infects the whole land with the leprosy of Sodom." Less metaphorical, Stephen Pearl Andrews flatly stated that "prostitution, in Marriage and out of it, and solitary vice characterize Society as it is."[29]

A great many factors lay behind the sexual jeremiads of people like Higginson, Garrison, Goodell, and Andrews. Their warnings echoed the rumblings of nineteenth-century spiritual and medical authorities, who counseled erotic restraint and spoke gloomily of the dangers of erotic excess for body and soul. For some reformers complex psychological impulses also figured in—Henry C. Wright and Stephen Pearl Andrews mingled the rhetoric of control with fantasies of transcendental sexual rapture. Yet the significant thing for antislavery men and women was that antebellum culture defined loss of moral control and a consequent growth of licentiousness as major threats to civilization. At that point perception and real conditions converged. Southern sensuality forecast growing Northern sensuality and Southern "barbarism" confirmed abolitionists in their fears about unbridled human nature. The South led the way in debauchery, but prostitution in America's growing cities and a seeming nation-wide moral breakdown demonstrated to abolitionists that the sin of licentiousness jeopardized the North as well. It jeopardized the North, that is, unless ways could be found to curb it.

Abolitionists seem crankish for all the various other reforms they drifted into, but many of these auxiliary causes fit the same mold as antislavery. They demonstrate that abolitionists were driven as much by a generalized desire to control the "animal nature" standing between man and civilization as they were by a specific quarrel with the South, which was only the worst of offenders, the logical extension of human depravity. Time after time abolitionists turned their guns toward the same kinds of lack of restraint in the North as they imagined in the South. In these numerous and occasionally subtle ways they betrayed how much of their concern stemmed from a fear that man was giving in too easily to his passionate self. The most frequent attacks of this sort probably were reserved for the tyranny of the bottle; but despite the near universality of temperance sentiment among abolitionists, they found their most spectacular examples of sin in presumably prevalent sexual immorality, a more literal surrender of mankind's "higher" qualities (its civilization) to the claims of the body than was alcoholism.

Numerous abolitionists devoted themselves to sweeping back "the wild sea of prostitution which swells and breaks and dashes against the bulwarks of society." Almost coincident with the rise of antislavery was a moral reform movement designed to eradicate prostitution and promote purity. It had appeal at antislavery centers such as Oberlin and Western Reserve, and many abolitionists became involved in the efforts of one of moral reform's chief promoters, Reverend John McDowall. McDowall's spicy account of sexual depravity in New York City in 1831 brought tremendous criticism on his sponsor, the local Magdalen Society, and on Arthur Tappan, a prominent member of that society and a future president of the American Anti-Slavery Society. A successor to the Magdalen Society, called the American Society for Promoting the Observance of the Seventh Commandment, drew upon abolitionists for its officers. Beriah Green was president; three abolitionists, including Weld, were vice-presidents; others, Joshua Leavitt and William Goodell among them, were on the executive committee. Lucretia Mott's support of an organization to redeem fallen women was dampened only by her discovery that it did not offer its services to black women.[30] William Lloyd Garrison's interest in moral reform continued unabated to the end of his life. Among the last items in his personal papers is a newspaper clipping recording a speech he made at a reception given him by "The New York Committee for Prevention of Licensed Prostitution."

Some abolitionists were convinced that things were drastically wrong with the very institution designed to contain erotic impulses. "The right idea of marriage is at the foundation of all reforms," Elizabeth Cady Stanton decided in 1853. She complained that "man in his lust has regulated long enough this whole question of sexual intercourse."[31] Henry C. Wright produced a work on *Marriage and Parentage* which not only attacked promiscuity outside of marriage but also "THE UN-NATURAL AND MONSTROUS EXPENDITURE OF THE SEXUAL ELEMENT, FOR MERE SENSUAL

GRATIFICATION" within marriage. He presented as ideal two husbands able to "control all their passional expressions." Stephen Pearl Andrews preached an individualism that bordered on free love—except he argued that a liberalization of marriage and divorce practices would actually "moderate the passions instead of inflaming them, and so . . . contribute, in the highest degree, to a general Purity of life."[32]

So sinister was man's erotic nature that it was not satisfied with brothel and marriage-bed, and abolitionists found it necessary to warn against the "secret vice" of auto-eroticism. Their admonitions were likely to crop up anywhere. Lewis Tappan interrupted the biography of his brother to urge readers to warn their children that "youthful lusts" could lead to "idiocy, insanity, disfigurement of body, and imbecility of mind." Garrison used the columns of the *Liberator* to review a book entitled *Debilitated Young Men*, taking occasion to rail against "the dreadful vice of Masturbation."[33]

All of this put a terrible burden on the erotic offender. The prostitute spread disease and misery; the lustful husband destroyed his wife and transmitted his sins to his unborn child; and the masturbator faced self-destruction. In fact, one did not even have to be consciously lustful to be harmed by his sexuality. Theodore Dwight Weld badgered his son, suffering both from a mysterious lethargy and an apparently unstimulated loss of semen, by warning that "all authorities agree that this drain upon the seminal fluid will . . . lead ultimately to insanity or idiocy."[34]

Such beliefs were conventional wisdom, and abolitionists were not the only people in their day to think that sexual excess caused insanity and other frightening ills. But abolitionists fit such diffuse and prevalent attitudes into a special pattern of concern, a large part of which resulted from an antebellum turn to find the key to reform within man—not just within man (for others had done that too) but in man's physical nature. A feeling in the Jacksonian era that man's animal self had to be conquered in favor of his immaterial being came around, in reform thought, to emphasize the body once more. Control and liberation were to be found there.

Also coincident with the rise of the antislavery and moral reform movements was health reform, exemplified by Sylvester Graham, whose memory lives decadently in the Graham cracker. Graham, and others like him, sought to purify the body and heal it of infirmities through a proper diet. Graham's regimen, which seemed laughable to many Americans at the time, found adherents among abolitionists and not just among the Garrisonians (who have a reputation for susceptibility to fads). Henry B. Stanton and Lewis Tappan attended the American Health Convention, a Grahamite gathering, in 1839. Stanton, while a student at Lane Seminary, suggested Graham as a candidate for a professorship in the natural sciences. Oberlin greeted Graham, and a fellow dietary reformer, William A. Alcott, enthusiastically and made physiology a required course of study in the early years. The Graham system declined there in the 1840s after David Cambell, who began as an abolitionist before becoming a health reform publicist, set up a campus boarding house on "correct principles." Cambell's rigorous stewardship evoked a student protest, and by 1845 Oberlin's president, Charles G. Finney, repented his support for the Graham system. But in its heyday the regimen secured the fierce loyalty of such staunch immediate emancipationists as the Welds, Sarah Grimké, and William Goodell. LaRoy Sunderland went so far as to claim that he owed his life to Graham's diet; Amasa Walker merely attributed regularity to it.[35]

There was also a considerable interest among abolitionists in exercise and gymnastic programs which, like proper diet, were presumed to help in bringing the body under control and in preventing it from interfering with man's spiritual nature. Theodore Dwight Weld had been a missionary for the manual labor school idea before he turned to antislavery. This was a plan designed to mix education and work, both for financial reasons and to put body and spirit into right relation. After his career as an abolitionist had virtually ended, Weld taught in Dio Lewis's gymnastic institute—where William Lloyd Garrison sent at least some of his children and where the Welds themselves sent the son who exhibited signs of excessive loss of seminal fluid.[36] Charles Follen, an early and beloved abolitionist, had been one of the first to bring German ideas of physical culture to the United States. Although Follen died tragically before Thomas Wentworth Higginson entered the movement, Higginson proved to be his spiritual heir, managing to serve as a bridge from antebellum reform to the "vigorous life" of the late nineteenth century. So persuasive was Higginson's campaigning for exercise that his efforts, according to one abolitionist, produced an outburst of ice-skating in Worcester, Massachusetts, which earned the title of "Higginson's Revival."[37]

Such activities seem innocent—and innocuous—enough; and, like dietary reform, they sought a genuine and necessary improvement in the quality of life. All that they were. But connected with dietary reform and the cult of exercise was, once again, the familiar drive to subdue the physical, particularly the sexual, aspects of man. Prophets of health reform like Sylvester Graham and William A. Alcott wrote extensively on the terrible effects of sexual excess and presented proper diet as a means of suppressing erotic impulses. Propagandists for physical culture such as Dio Lewis and Russell Trall likewise counseled sexual control and likewise saw health reform as a way of achieveing it. "A vigorous life of the senses not only does not tend to sensuality in the objectionable sense," Higginson claimed in an essay on gymnastics, "but it helps to avert it."[38] Dietary reform and even exercise programs, like antislavery, fastened upon man's erotic nature in order to overcome it.

The other side of a fear of man's physical being was a belief that properly understanding it could lead to salvation. Certainly Grahamites and gymnastics enthusiasts aimed at a kind of redemption, a freedom from the infirmities and corrupt desires of the body. Given the right sort of social engineering, it might be possible to turn those same desires to the task of regeneration—regeneration of the race, if not the individual. Garrison's tutor in perfectionism, John Humphrey Noyes, produced the clearest example of this in his Oneida Community, where a form of contraception was practiced, as well as plural marriage, in hope that "scientific combination" might be "applied to human generation." The result, Noyes believed, would be increasingly perfect children.[39]

Few, if any, in the antislavery movement were willing to take their ideas to the scandalous extreme of Oneida. Yet abolitionists of various sorts did accept Noyes' assumption that regulation of sexuality might become a means of human betterment. Henry C. Wright, as usual, wandered as far along the way as any abolitionist. Wright believed that all sorts of antenatal influences shaped the development of human beings. Diseases, alcoholism, and the parent's attitude at the time of conception passed on to the child. Wright acknowledged that this put a weighty responsibility for sexual restraint on a couple, particularly on the father, and it was with such matters that Wright expended most of his polemical energy. Yet he realized the possibilities, as well as the dangers, of sexuality. If ungoverned it could blight humanity; but proper regulation of it meant the power to produce better men and women. People simply had to use sex wisely, for progress rather than gratification. Wright, ever the visionary, believed, "to the LAW OF REPRODUCTION will human beings, in the future of this world, look as the one great means to expel disease from the body and soul."[40]

Elizabeth Cady Stanton, like Wright, believed such traits as drunkenness descended to children, and she was impressed by an essay entitled "Cerebral Dynamics" because it "shows so clearly that children are the victims of the vices and excesses of their ancestors." Mrs. Stanton, again like Henry C. Wright, had been affected not only by contemporary writings on hygiene but also by phrenology, which similarly directed attention to inherited physical characteristics, particularly to configurations of the head. Mrs. Stanton, much later in life, recalled that influential writers, "proving by their Phrenological discoveries that the feelings, sentiments, and affections of the soul mould and shape the skull, gave new importance to woman's thought as mother of the race."[41] In Mrs. Stanton's interpretation there was room for manipulation and improvement; the race was not absolutely at the mercy of heredity but could guide it. Stephen Pearl Andrews envisioned the time when the marriage-relation might be changed so that the woman could "accept only the noblest and most highly endowed of the opposite sex to be the recipients of her choicest favors, and the sires of her offspring, rejecting the males of a lower degree." He suggested that "by this means, Nature has provided for an infinitely higher development of the race."[42]

This was eugenics—and hereditarian thought—only in embryonic form. There was, as yet, no real sense that biological laws might have man in an iron grip from which there was no escape. Even phrenology, which asserted that character was irrevocably revealed in the shape of the skull, allied itself with hygiene, exercise, and an interest in the environment. In his philosophical meditations, James G. Birney, claimed that "a large, or well developed brain & head" might be partly the product of "early training & sufficiently & good nourishing food." Birney's speculations were consistent with those of professional phren-

ologists, who often tried to improve skulls already in existence rather than just condemn inferior ones to genetic hell.[43] The mechanisms, and perhaps the social pressures, for eugenies were not available in the antebellum period. The whole issue of birth control (another attempt originating in the 1830s to regulate sexuality) was still bound up with fears of promiscuity;[44] racialist thought was crudely developed and attacked the human unity abolitionists wanted to believe in; and Darwinism lay in the future when Henry C. Wright and Stephen Pearl Andrews and Elizabeth Cady Stanton formulated their attitudes into opinions. But in their drive to control mankind's animal nature, particularly its sexuality, abolitionists were part of a continuum from romantic reform, with its emphasis on the individual, to those middle-class moralists at the end of the century who ultimately cast their faith and anxieties onto race.

This was a continuum from religiously based perfectionism to a sort of physical perfection, from enthusiasm to eugenics. Standing mid-way along it, abolitionists sought to reconcile both ends with each other as well as with human equality. Physical salvation, in these pre-Darwinian days, could not be just a matter of biological necessity. It was God's mandate, not evolution's, which, according to Theodore Parker, made it man's task on earth "to unfold and perfect himself, as far as possible, in body and spirit." There was a transition, nonetheless, when Harriet Beecher Stowe, who bore with her the seed of the great revival, exclaimed, *"Perfect* spiritual religion cannot exist without perfect physical religion."[45]

Abolitionism began, and ended, with mankind: it began with a call for individual outrage and repentance and ended with the Yankee schoolmarm in the South. It sought to liberate slaves and, at the same time, to control all human beings, to make them moral, to direct their most fearful energies toward their salvation. When it drew upon the moral sense and upon environmentalism, it casually used the assumptions of its time, and it echoed the language of an earlier reform tradition. When it drew upon its sense of mankind's physical nature (and, unfortunately, when it drew upon belief in innate racial differences), it looked toward the future. To its credit, antebellum reform was too optimistic—and perhaps too naïve—to see mankind, even at its most beastly, imprisoned by biology. There was hope among abolitionists that human nature could be overcome, that civilization depended on a struggle within human beings, not on struggle among men.

And yet there was that transition. Younger abolitionists drifted elsewhere. The Garrison children absorbed Darwinism. Moncure Conway went to England, to a friendship with Herbert Spencer and to another kind of revelation: "Darwin's discovery made a new departure in my pilgrimage necessary," he exclaimed. Shortly after the Civil War, Elizabeth Cady Stanton declared that Spencer's popularization (and socialization) of Darwin had achieved the grand objective of "teaching us to lose sight of ourselves and our burdens in the onward march of the race." As he neared the end of his days, Parker Pillsbury took satisfaction in the career of Loring Moody. Moody had been general agent for the pioneer organization, the Massachusetts Anti-Slavery Society. He went from there to the Society for the Prevention of Cruelty to Animals, and then to "a similar association in behalf of poor children." According to Pillsbury, Moody's "last labor was doubtless most important of all in his life of nearly seventy years. He originated and organized *The Institute of Heredity,* perhaps viewed in all its aspects and relations, the most important enterprise to universal human well-being of the nineteenth century."[46]

The distance from the moral sense to evolution was small enough to be crossed in a lifetime. Among antebellum reformers it was virtually the distance between man's moral nature—the universal human being who could be trusted to behave correctly, who would not abuse freedom—and man's animal nature, the passionate creature needing to be kept tightly under control, the physical being over whom civilization was to triumph.

III
CONTEXT

Religion, philosophy, science, and culturally determined concerns about mankind created the hidden grammar of antislavery, the categories of thought and language abolitionists brought to bear on the world around them. But the world itself also shapes reform. It supplies the sins reformers attempt to suppress and it provides the conditions, material and cultural, that make it possible for reformers to see those sins as sins and to organize for their elimination.

6

FAMILIES

The "Centre of Earthly
Bliss" and Its Discontents

CONTROL, as abolitionists conceived of it, was largely an individual matter. Although willing at times to use compulsion to achieve victory, they never could quite accept it as an adequate substitute for the regenerated conscience of the believer. But clearly there were unregenerate individuals in American society, and no moralist could rest easily until dependable mechanisms existed to promote virtue in a dangerous and promising world. Religion had proven too diffuse and too untrustworthy for the task. Voluntary associations like antislavery societies served the purpose, yet they were only temporary and organized to meet specific problems. Society needed a permanent rudder, agencies to steer it through troubled times and to keep it on a morally true course. Abolitionists often looked to family-life and to women to fulfill such a role. In so doing, antislavery brought together conventions of middle-class culture, the particular situation of antebellum reform, and changes in the nature of American society.

With the confidence of an earnest young man, James A. Thome assured the "Females of Ohio" that "the *centre* of earthly bliss lies within the family circle." There, he thought, was the heart of "social happiness." The women Thome addressed may or may not have found his description accurate, but his enthusiasm for the family was fully shared by other abolitionists. Theodore Parker, likewise taking the masculine view of things, was rhapsodic. "A man's home—it is to him the most chosen spot of the earth," he believed. "It affords him a rest from the toils of life."[1] But the importance of family went far beyond simply providing the weary husband with a refuge from the work-day world. The anonymous author of a tract entitled *The Family and Slavery* felt that since human beings "are born despots" the family was "intended to be a little model Church and State," commissioned to do the "all-important work" of teaching men "the great truths of equality and disinterested love." Everything hinged on family, for good or for ill. When it "falls into decay," William Goodell warned, "no other true institution can be preserved in a healthful state." On the more optimistic side, the author of *The Family and Slavery* reminded the public that "The predicted renovation of the world will be largely secured by it." The family, it seems, was not just a man's castle; it was also the Kingdom to come.[2]

So sacred was the home to staid abolitionists like John Greenleaf Whittier that they dreaded Henry C. Wright's version of Christian anarchism for fear it might lead to "no family government." Theodore Dwight Weld, himself very close to nonresistance, took seriously the task of distinguishing between "legitimate" power like that exercised in the family and "arbitrary" power like that exhibited under slavery. Whittier and Weld need not have worried about the nonresistants; even they, who were scornful of most institutions and who sought liberation from all kinds of human authority, valued the home highly. Henry C. Wright did argue that man had no right to dominion over woman (and thus both partners to a marriage should be truly equal), and he did believe that parents should govern their children by moral means, not force. As for the family itself, he was no less optimistic than anyone else. If anything, his disdain for other institutions made him put still more weight upon it. "In their power over organization, character and destiny of human beings," he wrote, "the Church is nothing, the State is nothing; religion, government, priests and politicians, are nothing, compared to marriage and parentage, to the husband and wife, the father and mother." No one "who is engaged in a work of moral reform, and is seeking instrumentalities to regenerate and save the world, will overlook the family institution," he argued.[3]

It would be a greater surprise had abolitionists attacked the home and motherhood. Their rhetoric was fully in tune with more prevalent antebellum attitudes. This was an era, after all, that produced sugary hymns of praise to the family and made an industry out of books and magazines giving advice to homemakers.[4] As yet it is unclear exactly what was happening with (or to) the family in the antebellum period —or even whether there was such a thing as *the* family, since we do not know how significant differences were between regions, classes, and generations. Articulated opinion about the family, nevertheless, was changing by the 1830s and it was verging on worship.

On the eve of antislavery there were quantifiable changes in family structure, particularly in New England, where immediate emancipation found its most zealous advocates. The American birth rate tended downward in spite of an increasing percentage of women in the child-bearing years, suggesting a self-conscious limitation of conception much like that apparently practiced by the English middle-class.[5] Families were also losing some economic functions they once had. By 1830 household manufactures had declined considerably. Not only were fewer goods produced in the home—at least in urban and middle-class homes—but the household was also serving less and less as a place of business. Even in Western cities such signs of a diversified and specialized economy as suburbs began appearing in the decades preceding 1830: men no longer worked where they lived.[6] The family, upon which so much seemed to rest, was declining as an economic unit at the very moment it was assuming more ethical authority. Just as some of the most obvious traditional functions of the family disappeared, it took on the burden of assuring society's moral stability; it came to serve as the moral locus that the church, fragmented into sects and no longer coincident with the community, could not be.

Believing in the divine nature of the family is not the same thing as believing that the contemporary family is perfect. Among abolitionists there was a strong undercurrent of criticism of family life, particularly of marriage. The great antislavery wedding, the union of Theodore Dwight Weld and Angelina Grimké in 1838, served to draw forth bitter lamentations about the usual state of things, the most articulate ones coming from the bride and groom themselves. Angelina bemoaned the motives impelling men to matrimony, and Theodore added "the fact that among the dislocations of the age marriage and the relations of husband and wife are perhaps as they now are the most horrible perversions." Thirteen years later Sallie Holley expressed, in less urgent tones, the same ambivalence the Welds brought to matrimony. "A true marriage is beautiful and desirable," Miss Holley felt. "I believe, in the millenium, every body will be married." Yet in the present, Miss Holley thought, "alas! all outward marriages are not real ones."[7] Stephen Pearl Andrews felt the situation to be so bad that "*There are to-day in our midst ten times as many fugitives from Matrimony as there are fugitives from Slavery; and it may well be doubted if the aggregate, or the average of their sufferings has been less.*"[8]

Some of this discontent was part and parcel with abolitionist dread that sexuality was running rampant and that, even within conventional marriages, there was too much license, particularly for the husband's erotic nature. But there was a wider, less overtly sexual, sense that conventional marriage was an exploitive relationship, especially for the wife. James G. Birney, as conservative an abolitionist as there was on woman's rights, regarded the "patriarchal family" idealized by proslavery writers as "one of the lowest forms of civilization, just emerging from savageism."[9]

The critique of family life was no indication that abolitionists themselves endured especially unhappy marriages. The Welds, the Garrisons, the Motts, the Childs, and so many others, seem to have formed
warmly loving families by nineteenth-century standards. For all his
rhapsodic prose about the home, Henry C. Wright stands as one of
the few exceptions. The desire to establish a better national home life
was, moreover, far too prevalent in antebellum America to be dismissed as a mere fantasy of a handful of maladjusted individuals
(even if it could be shown that abolitionists were "maladjusted").
The numerous antebellum communal societies generally took it upon
themselves to rearrange society's usual sexual and child-rearing practices. One of the bolder innovators, John Humphrey Noyes, noted that
outbursts of spiritual enthusiasm in his time "all recognize the right
of religious inspiration to shape society and dictate the form of family
life." Very different men and women (including Reverend Nehmiah
Adams, a proslavery Bostonian) engaged in a loose domestic reform
movement designed to perfect the conventional family. And, of course,
Southern defenders of slavery frequently justified the institution by
comparing it to a well-ordered, benevolently patriarchal family that
the North lacked and should have.[10] To most articulate antebellum
Americans the family was the one morally reliable institution in a
fluid and diffuse society.

Abolitionists found slavery's effect on domestic life to be both an explanation and a symbol of the disorder they saw in the South. The slave family was the immediate victim. "The voluntariness and independence necessary to take the conjugal vow can not belong to slaves," one writer asserted. Without it there was no such thing as marriage and thus no legitimate family (a belief abolitionists amply documented from Southern practice and law). The slaveholder, wrote Stephen S. Foster, was under no obligation to uphold "this sacred relation." The master's "very position makes him the minister of unbridled lust. By converting woman into a commodity to be bought and sold, and used by her claimant as his avarice or lust may dictate, he totally annihilates the marriage institution."[11] Slave parents, powerless to protect each other or themselves, had no call on their children, no real control over them. Ties between slave father and mother, made tenuous by the master's sensuality or his willingness to sell one or the other of the partners, all too often became merely sexual.

The slaveholder's family also suffered. He violated his own marriage vows as he wished, inflicting upon his legal wife the mental and physical effects of his philandery. The master callously sold those who, in biological fact, were his own progeny or his brothers and sisters. No less hateful was the effect of his behavior upon his legitimate offspring. "The children of slave-holders observe all these proceedings from their youth; and having no other examples before their eyes, and no counteracting instructions either from the literary preceptor, or from the professed minister of Jesus Christ, . . . they grow up in a reckless unconcern to all the miseries which they behold."[12] And so the sins of the fathers passed on to the children, to be endured or imitated.

Families of both races felt the evil effects of slavery; but, more important, so did society. "The Family is the head, the heart, the fountain of society," proclaimed one abolitionist, "and it has not a privilege that slavery does not nullify, a right that it does not counteract, nor a hope that it does not put out in darkness." There is little wonder that Harriet Beecher Stowe believed the "worst abuse of the system of slavery is its outrage upon the family." In an apocalyptic mood the *Anti-Slavery Record* warned in 1836 that "the attempt to build the wealth of a nation on the ruin of *domestic ties*, will fare worse than that which was confounded on the plain of Shinar. God's foundation stands sure, and the nation that despises it shall feel his wrath in all her institutions."[13]

Destruction of the home fit with slavery's symbolic function as the exemplar of what could go wrong with society. Abolitionists after 1831 took slavery's impact on family more seriously than their ancestors had, because social, economic, and demographic alterations made family life generally an issue of concern in the three decades before the Civil War. Southern family life, furthermore, helped explain Southern depravity. Religious and political institutions might be expected to fail to keep the proper balance between liberty and control, but when the family fell the last bastion was gone.

Revaluation of the family partially explains the broadening nature of much antebellum reform activity—its appeal to women and children as well as to the white adult males who formed the most politically significant segment of the nation. The household was not a political unit, and once attention shifted to it, the father, despite his special privilege as a voter, was not the only person for reformers to consider.

In the early nineteenth century there was increasing emphasis placed on the child. The notion that children have a different world from adults, so natural to us, was then first gaining prominence.[14] This new image of childhood coincided with some intriguing demographic changes, particularly in New England and in urbanizing areas, which (thanks to declining fertility) showed a lower proportion of children in the population than there had been before. Even at that, a low infant mortality rate meant America's population was youthful: up to 1860 every census showed half the whites to be under twenty years of age; 70 percent in 1850 were under thirty, as compared with 63 percent in England and 52 percent in France.[15] The child was coming into its own in literature in the United States just as proportionally fewer were born and as people were publicly advocating birth control to continue the trend. At the same time, the world itself and America in particular was populated with younger human beings.

Under the circumstances early nineteenth-century moralists could hardly avoid a reassessment of youth. An aspect of this was a widespread attempt to bring the energies and sensibilities of children to the task of social regeneration. Even abolitionism's predecessor and great rival, the staid and distinguished American Colonization Society, relied upon juvenile assistance. There was also an antebellum debate over the correct kind of education to give children in schools and at home in order to guarantee they would become a force for good. Horace Bushnell, in 1847, reduced the traditional Protestant stress upon conversion in favor of *Christian Nurture*, through which a person would be brought up to religion rather than smitten by it. Grasping something of the same principle two decades earlier, laymen organized the American Sunday School Union to provide children with the religious training forbidden them in public schools. By 1855 a properly proper newspaper like the *Boston Evening Transcript* could assert that "mental impressions, and in particular those of early childhood . . . are for the most part indelible." Children were not only "the greatest of his [God's] earthly blessings," they were also potential footsoldiers in the vanguard of righteousness.[16]

In common with other antebellum moralists, abolitionists both utilized and informed youth. They encouraged antislavery organizations of young people and, in the first decade, the American Anti-Slavery Society appointed an agent, Henry C. Wright, especially for them ("he never fails to produce a deep impression upon their minds," Garrison said in what was undoubtedly an understatement). Wright took it as a "settled truth . . . that if we would regenerate and save this world, we must direct our efforts to children."[17] His belief was shared by more temperate abolitionists, who eventually fretted over *what* he was teaching youngsters.

The child of antebellum America was not the child of recent times, to be exempted from adult cares, and abolitionist propaganda directed at youth made little pretense to being anything other than didactic. An issue of the *Slave's Friend* warned its small readers not to throw it down as they did other new books, and candidly informed them that it was not written "merely to amuse you." The *Child's Newspaper* promised to tell "of things that are taking place in the world—of the little children that are drowned, or killed by accident, or murdered by their wicked parents. Above all it will tell you that you were born sinners against God." Dead and dying slaves abounded and so did tearful separations of parent and child. Morbid as this appears to modern sensibilities, it carried into action the assumption that reform had to begin in the home and with the rising generation, not with those who presently held power but rather with those who might hold it in the future. "It is in the house that we must rear up those tender plants which are one day to be a hedge to keep the world of wickedness out of the garden of our civilization," gushed Theodore Parker. It was appropriate for the *Anti-Slavery Alphabet* to bear as its motto "In the morning sow thy seed."[18]

Of course other reformers besides abolitionists might have taken the same motto, so pervasive was the concern for youth in antebellum America. Yet in its efforts toward reaching children, antislavery played out themes that resonated with its own peculiar interests. Some of these had to do with the abolitionist conception of reform as being above and beyond politics and as involving total commitment. Since abolitionists accepted the idea that character was formed early and in the home, they were bound to look optimistically toward childhood as a time before human beings became ensnared in corrupting institutions or perverted by unholy desires. There was another important implication to the prevalent high regard for childhood. Abolitionist writers assumed that defenders of slavery reversed the correct scheme of things when they declared that the "child-like nature" of black people suited them for slavery. Childlike natures, abolitionists believed, had a great deal to offer by way of example to adult society.

There were occasional assertions that children might be innately depraved, but Protestantism had wandered so far from Calvinism and infant damnation that these sounded anachronistic and churlish. More common was the assumption articulated by Henry C. Wright: "Children are all born abolitionists. All we have to do is keep them abolitionists." Antislavery literature contained numerous characters like Phil, "about three years old, and a noble boy he was. He had a great head and a great heart, and his beautiful blue eyes beamed with intense interest at the simple story of the wrongs and sufferings of the slaves." As an older brother unfolded the evils inflicted upon slaves, Phil interrupted to explain "if I were there, wouldn't I set Tig [his dog] on the naughty men that do such naughty things?" Phil's abolitionism was present in his youthful character and only needed direction, or perhaps restraint.[19]

Moral prodigies like Phil could well uplift adults. A mother in an antislavery story made an analogy to temperance, in which "many a poor drunkard has been raised from the gutter, and baptized into newness of life, through the saving power of his little child!" One brave lad, having attended an antislavery picnic, supposedly wrote in a letter to his nonabolitionist family that "if the men don't all do something about slavery soon, we boys had better see what we can do, for it is too wicked." The *Philanthropist,* under the editorship of James G. Birney, took pride in recounting how a girl, given a copy of the *Slave's Friend* by a visiting physician, burst into tears because "she could not help crying, when she thought of the poor little negro boy about whom she had been reading in her little book." Shortly the whole family, initially not abolitionists, was reading it.[20]

For Theodore Parker children were "those heralds of holiness, prophets of new things . . . sent to preach the gospel of innocence again, and baptize mankind anew to single-heartedness and love." This view marked one of the many differences between Parker and his spiritual ancestors, the colonial New England clergy who had proclaimed infant damnation. Henry C. Wright, a sometime Congregational minister, also identified the child as a redeemer. "A perfectly healthy LOVE-CHILD, is a joy unspeakable and full of glory to the parents," he enthused. "What a Saviour is such a child to the parents! What a God manifest in the flesh to their hearts!" Sarah Grimké, explaining to Gerrit Smith the way to salvation, could best describe the process by analogy to the child's nature. Miss Grimké believed "so far as we trust in God we are his children." But "the moment we lose the character of children and set up for ourselves a separate interest from Gods," all is lost.[21]

There was something of a paradox here. Abolitionists conceived of civilization as a matter of overcoming man's animal nature, putting it under the dominion of his "higher" self. Yet they saw the most unformed state of human development as the most perfect. This was true not just spiritually but even physically, where children in reality are less developed than adults. Thomas Wentworth Higginson described the goal of gymnastics as "perpetual youth,—that is, a state of positive health." Health, he felt, was to "feel the body a luxury, as every vigorous child does." In a long, remarkable rhetorical question Harriet Beecher Stowe captured it all:

> Shall there not come a day when the little child . . . shall be the type no less of our physical than our spiritual advancement,—when men and women shall arise, keeping through long and happy lives the unperverted appetites, the joyous freshness of spirit, the keen delight in mere existence, the dreamless sleep and happy waking of early childhood?[22]

Mrs. Stowe's choice of "unperverted" to describe childhood unlocks the mystery. The Stowes and Parkers existed in a breathing space between the older theological concept of inner depravity and a newer secular one which would take shape toward the end of the nineteenth-century, when mankind explored its nature by the light of Freudian psychology and Darwinian biology. Although profoundly mistrustful of uncontrolled humanity, abolitionists preserved enough faith in human beings to think that they might basically be good, at least before circumstances drew out the beastliness that also was there. The child, naturally emotional and not yet tainted by sexuality (so it was thought), was the heart, the counterweight to the shrewdly calculating, corrupted, mature person.

Once more, the tension: abstractly it was between the innately moral self and the self needing to be controlled, between the human nature to be liberated and that to be repressed. But the drama could also be cast with real actors—the spirituality of the slave matched against the lustful tyranny of the master, the innocent good will of the child played off against the brutal insensitivity of the adult. There was, as we shall shortly see, still another combination possible. The pattern, however, is apparent, and in all its repetitions it was clearly set by both culture and society. Ideas and attitudes about the family and the child intersected demographic and economic conditions which made children and families subjects of particular interest. Social developments threw upon youth and the household a burden of hope abolitionists could no longer place upon politics or formal religion. Imposed on actual changes in institutions and in social configurations was a drive to reconcile freedom and order in a bustling nation that offered both and jeopardized both.

Woman was caught in the middle of the family and of change. Increasing numbers of young females were actually leaving the home to take factory work, especially in the mills of New England. But few if any of the mill-girls gained a prominent voice in the antislavery crusade, and the abolitionists, their nerves most sensitive to the role of the middle-class, thought of women in a different plight. The females of whom abolitionists were most aware were losing their obvious economic functions (as the family itself was) and were trapped within the household.

In 1838, Sarah M. Grimké lamented that too often "the wife and daughters and sisters take no part in the support of the family." Theodore Parker, from the perspective of fifteen years later, was able to grasp industrial heart of the matter. "When all manufactures were domestic," he said,

> then the domestic function might well consume all the time of a very able-headed woman. But nowadays, when so much work is done abroad; when the flour-mills of Rochester and Boston take the place of the pestle and mortar and the hand-mill . . . ; when Lowell and Lawrence are two enormous Old Testament women, spinning and weaving year out and year in, day and night both; when so much of woman's work is done by the butcher and the baker, by the tailor, and the cook and the gas-maker . . . you see how much of woman's time is left for other functions.

The lower-class woman might find herself in the mills of Lowell and Lawrence (a fact Parker neglected to mention), but the middle-class woman produced fewer goods for family use. Moreover, the advent of an Irish servant might even take from her much of the menial responsibility for tending her own house and for raising her own child.[23]

In many respects, the image was not fair to middle-class women. Though less visible, their economic role was not necessarily less, since they managed what could be large households with sizable budgets. When Elizabeth Cady Stanton phrased her personal discontent it was hardly in terms of irrelevance. She objected to "woman's portion as wife, mother, housekeeper, physician, and spiritual guide, the chaotic conditions into which everything fell without her constant supervision."[24] Still, the ill-defined and unrewarding economic role allotted women seemed to produce the evils that befell them in American society. Lucretia Mott hoped that in the near future "cultivated and refined woman would bring all her powers into use." When that day arrived "the energies of men need not then be wholly devoted to the counting-house and common business of life, in order that women in fashionable society may be supported in their daily promenades and nightly visits to the theatre and ball-room." Lydia Maria Child strongly deplored those for whom "usefullness is ungenteel," the women who have "moved on, in their daily automation revolutions, with a vague, half-smothered hope that life has something in store for them, more interesting than the past has been."[25]

Discontent with woman's role inevitably led abolitionists to describe the "true" female character—and it led them into some of the same pitfalls they encountered when they assessed the black man's character. In both cases there was a strong compulsion to assert sameness—to deny sexual as well as racial distinctions—since a sense of difference formed the keystone of oppression.[26] There was, nevertheless, ambiguity in the orthodox doctrine, which described antislavery as "the cause of philanthropy, with regard to which all *human beings* . . . have the same duties and same rights."[27] Moral obligation is not identical with character, and there was room here for a belief in differences of emotional and intellectual capacity between men and women (or between blacks and whites).

Some abolitionists managed to hold sameness and dissimilarity in a wonderful jumble of confusion. Theodore Parker, preaching on "The Public Function of Woman" asserted that "she and man have the same human nature, and, of course, the same natural rights." Among these, he went on, was for each man "a natural and inalienable right to the normal development of his peculiar nature as a man, where he differs from woman." Women had equal rights—they could develop their "peculiar nature as woman, and not man."[28]

Other abolitionists, and Parker himself at times, found a more graceful way out. This was to acknowledge that the sexes had different characters, but to make them complementary, just as the supposedly emotional and religiously inclined African could provide the "heart" presumably lacking in Anglo-Saxons. When humans finally approach "the truest life," Lydia Maria Child thought, they "will be one; but it will be as affection and thought are one; the treble and bass of the same harmonious tune." Samuel J. May took advantage of the sentimental image of Christ to make the point. "Jesus of Nazareth, the perfect man, exhibited as much of the feminine, as he did of the masculine character," May said. "And doubtless every individual, of either sex, will approach the perfection to which all are called, just so far as he or she combined in one, the virtues and graces of both."[29] This had the neat effect of accepting differences and denying their relevance.

It did not work. As social conditions removed woman from some traditional economic functions, she was being cast into a new kind of role, although too decorative a one to satisfy intelligent and determined females. Woman (or at least the lady) was being placed on a pedestal. Keeping her there was the task of a set of assumptions—part of a "cult of domesticity"—that stressed feminine gentleness, purity, virtue, and passivity. But like stereotypes of black spirituality, such doctrines could be twisted to radically different purposes. The frustration of the middle-class woman, economic and social in origin, was heightened at times by the fact that she was excluded from the world of public events while being told she had spiritual qualities it desperately needed. Anxious to assert his mental and physical superiority, man had conceded too much. The first Woman's Rights Convention, held in 1848 and drawing many abolitionists, caught the difficulty perfectly when it resolved that "inasmuch as man, while claiming for himself intellectual superiority, does accord to woman moral superiority, it is preeminently his duty to encourage her to speak and teach, as she has an opportunity, in all religious assemblies."[30] There was no reason to restrict that logic to religious assemblies. Leading the thrust of women into reform were presumptions of innate mental and moral differences between the sexes, including some of the very assumptions first used to keep middle-class ladies at home.

Abolitionists attributed an impressive amount of power to women, who were most notable for their lack of power in American society. Angelina Grimké thought it was through woman's "instrumentality that the great and glorious work of reforming the world is to be done." That faith was not confined to such future advocates of woman's rights as Miss Grimké. Under the evangelical editorship of Joshua Leavitt, the *Emancipator* proclaimed, "the influence of woman, under God, is omnipotent." Slightly more guarded, James A. Thome thought "it would appear to be a *prominent feature* in the divine plan for the recovery of our race, to secure the *agency of woman.*" Leavitt, Thome, and many others drew back from the conclusion that females ought to participate equally with men in reform societies; yet even abolitionists who balked at a full commitment to woman's rights nevertheless believed in the redemptive capacity of women. They simply felt women ought to redeem the world by means of separate organizations. Faith in woman's ability to regenerate society persisted among abolitionists after the Civil War, impelling efforts by some of them to secure the franchise for her in order that her votes might "save the State from debauchery and utter demoralization." Thomas Wentworth Higginson spoke for the antislavery tradition when, in 1888, he wished for "the Woman of Influence," hoping she would "modify and control all the habits of society."[31]

Of course, powerlessness has its advantages, especially in the eyes of people who fear power. Abolitionists thought woman's very deprivation freed her from the worldly entanglements that kept men from following the voice of morality. "Men are afraid, or perplexed with their social interests," a "Puritan" explained, "and therefore they are vacillating and uncertain. With all these contradictory motives, female Christians have no connections." Theodore Parker noted "the great moral enterprises of this day so often find favor with women, when they are mocked at by men whom business trains to look only at the profitable side of abuses." One lady turned this into both a justification for action and a damning indictment of the opposite sex. "As *women*, it is incumbent upon us," she commanded, "instantly and always to labor to increase the knowledge and the love of God, that such concentrated hatred of His character and laws may no longer be so intrenched in men's business and bosoms, that they dare not condemn and renounce it."[32]

It was not simply freedom from the corrupting worlds of trade and politics that made women morally pure. They were assumed to be innately purer than men by those who wanted to liberate them as well as by those who wished to keep them at home. "However ambition and the love of political power may blind the stronger sex," Harriet Beecher Stowe remarked, "God has given to women a deeper and more immovable knowledge in those holier feelings which are peculiar to womanhood, and which guard the sacredness of the family state." Reverend Ludlow, addressing the New York State Anti-Slavery Society in 1836, could not believe there might be a woman who was not an abolitionist. "A woman not an abolitionist! No. This truth hath a lodgement in the heart of every female that understands it, and deserves the name of a mother and wife."[33] Supporting him—of all things—was the cult of domesticity itself, with its assertion that women were more religiously inclined and less sensual than men, and that females possessed greater emotionality, sensitivity, and intuitive goodness. Angelina Grimké liked the antifeminist argument that "all the power and all the conquests that are lawful to woman are those only which appeal to the kindly, generous, peaceful and benevolent principles." From that, she retorted, ". . . I would suppose that *woman was the superior,* and that *man the subordinate being,* inasmuch as moral power is immeasurably superior to 'physical force.' "[34]

One need not even make it a question of superiority and inferiority to see that idealization of woman could lead her away from home, rather than confining her to it as her peculiar domain. Elizur Wright acknowledged a belief that "woman's gentleness and love are gifts of God to make men better, to make society better, to refine the coarseness, melt away the surly hate, and mitigate the fighting, tyrannizing, brute force propensities by which man has always more or less degraded himself." Wright held that "all the moral qualities peculiar to her sex, were meant to have a controlling influence in human affairs." He would have hated to see women in politics, because contemporary politics were too corrupt, but he had to admit that "society would be the gainer if the men would give up the whole business of legislation, politics and diplomacy into the hands of woman."[35] Woman's controlling hands—that was a dangerous concept for a man like Wright to endorse. Yet, it reflected the common belief that woman stood on the side of civilization and progress since she represented refinement of humanity's higher, or spiritual and emotional, faculties.[36]

Drawing upon such attitudes, reform activity in general provided a way outward for woman's inborn goodness and a way upward for individual women. In 1836 Angelina Grimké rejoiced at the growth of benevolent societies, for in them she saw "*woman* rising to that influence and elevation in the world for which she was destined under the Gospel Dispensation." Even moderate abolitionists could not deny woman a place, having conceded her redemptive qualities. "She, equally with her rugged partner, was destined to exert a healthful influence on others," Gamaliel Bailey wrote in 1842; "and this is to be done, as in his case, not by restricting herself exclusively to household affairs, but by the proper attention to the affairs of the great house-hold of the earth." Twelve years later he attacked the idea that women should "turn to their firesides, and effect reforms there" and pointed out that "slavery is a fireside evil of the most heinous stamp."[37] Bailey, a political abolitionist, was a strange ally; but even stranger was the fact that when ambitious and articulate middle-class women broke out of the family circle, they found support from some of the chains that had originally bound them to it. The "cult of domesticity," a rationale for female economic and political irrelevance, carried implications that justified public activity by women, particularly in reforms to suppress mankind's animal nature and to liberate the downtrodden.

The abolitionist image of Southern sexuality focused a generalized Northern discontent with power and loss of moral control. In the same fashion abolitionists joined together the plight of slaves and of middle-class women in a network of emotionally charged associations—a web spun partly out of culture, partly out of objective conditions.

There were enough coincidences in commonly held views of women and of blacks that Theodore Tilton, as a matter of course, was able to assert that the "negro race is the feminine race of the world." Lydia Maria Child thought

> the comparison between women and the colored race is striking. Both are characterized by affection more than by intellect; both have a strong development of the religious sentiment; both are exceedingly adhesive in their attachments; both, comparatively speaking, have a tendency to submission; and hence, both have been kept in subjection by physical force, and considered rather in the light of property, than as individuals.

Gilbert Haven likewise saw the similarity in an "excess of a submissive, peaceful, religious spirit" which allowed blacks and women to be easily dominated.[38]

William Goodell went from editor of the *Female Advocate* to editor of the *Emancipator* after it had become the organ of the American Anti-Slavery Society. He saw no particular change. Both papers spoke for "the helpless and uncomplaining," and a nation practicing slavery could "hardly be expected . . . to be very solicitous to assign the female sex in general the elevated stand the God of nature designed them to occupy." Deprived by law of control over their own property after marriage, generally denied custody of their children in divorce, not given much real chance to escape intolerable husbands, and always forbidden the vote, women no less than slaves were not allowed to be morally responsible human beings. "[T]he very being of a woman, like that of a slave, is absorbed in her master," observed Sarah Grimké.[39]

It was the same master—slaves and white women shared oppressors as well as kinds of oppression. Nathaniel P. Rogers thought "Anti-slavery is peculiarly woman's work—slavery man's. Man is a tyrant. He has enslaved woman among his other slaves." Sarah Grimké traced man's urge to dominate and possess back to the Garden of Eden. "The lust of dominion was probably the first effect of the fall," she speculated; "and as there was no other intelligent being over whom to exercise it, woman was the first victim of this unhallowed passion."[40] Power, the old abolitionist enemy, sought its usual sort of expression—licentiousness. If one were to believe Elizabeth Cady Stanton, Henry C. Wright, Stephen Pearl Andrews, Sarah Grimké, and other abolitionists who commented on the sexuality of the times, then northern white women no less than black females suffered from the unrestrained erotic nature of white males.[41]

Antislavery both overtly and covertly challenged man's lustful dominion over his own women. The crusade threw down the gauntlet by renouncing the process through which political decisions were made (by men) and by denying the stereotype of the obedient, cloistered female. There was also the antislavery woman's personal identification with the slave, a double-edged reproach to the cruelty and insensitivity of the white man, to the hardness of his character. The most psychologically revealing of these reproaches to men came in antislavery fiction, especially in efforts directed at children.[42] It was inevitable and proper that some such works would fasten on the sufferings of slave mothers; but suffering women occurred in them with a frequency and a touch that indicate a coded message of personal unhappiness beneath the antislavery moral, a message reverberating to abolitionism's stress on feminine virtues and to the role of middle-class women in the North.

The emotional focus of literature for "young abolitionists" alighted upon an adult woman almost as commonly as it did upon a child. The *Slave's Friend* printed the familiar picture of a kneeling, manacled female slave and coupled it with a story, aptly entitled "The Afflicted Mother." For two pages the tale portrayed the anguish of slave mothers. Only at the end, virtually as an afterthought, was the youthful reader beseeched to "remember their poor children too, who are driven like beasts by the slave-driver, with his cruel whip." The *Anti-Slavery Almanac* for 1837 regaled juveniles with a dialogue in which Mrs. S. explained to tiny Caroline the meaning of a picture of a slave woman about to kill her peacefully sleeping child with an ax. The emphasis again was on the mother's turmoil, upon her sensibilities. Such an approach was common in stories for children and stands as something of an exception in the general run of antislavery propaganda, which often urged the reader to identify with his slave counterpart. White children were frequently asked to imagine themselves as slave children; yet, significantly, they were also asked to empathize with the plight of another kind of person, with an adult woman.[43]

The white mother as well as the slave mother fairly consistently played a sympathetic role in these stories, generally as a benevolent instructress in morality to her children, awakening them to the evils of slavery. In one such instance she succeeded so well that a member of her flock exclaimed that he wanted to become an abolitionist so "mothers could take care of their children" (he said this as his Irish nursemaid listened on!). Matilda G. Thompson pulled out all the stops in a contribution to *The Child's Anti-Slavery Book*. In the story a slave woman in Missouri explained her unhappiness to a slave owner's wife, Mrs. Jennings. Mrs. Jennings had not thought much about slavery before, but her good nature quickly manifested itself. She intervened to try to purchase the slave woman's husband and in the process met Mrs. Nelson, wife of the man who sold him. Mrs. Nelson, a careworn woman, had been beaten down by having tried, along with her children, to convert her insensitive husband. Mrs. Jennings became so revolted by slavery that she convinced her own husband to move to Chicago, where she became an antislavery worker and the narrative ended. The story underwent a decided shift between beginning and conclusion. It started with the desire of a slave woman to be united with her husband but the bulk of the story dealt with Mrs. Jennings' good moral urges seeking to assert themselves. Entitled "Mark and Hasty: Or, Slave-life in Missouri," it was not about Mark and Hasty, the slave couple, at all. Hasty died before it was over and all sight of Mark was lost after his sale southward.[44] It was, again, a middle-class female sensibility that counted most.

Some of this was recruitment for the battle of the sexes, a war-cry

THE VALENTINE.

to rally sympathy for the female as she resisted the male, whose moral obtuseness in these stories was more striking than his benevolence.[45] But in more subtle and disembodied fashion the same assumptions permeated general antislavery literature, including that by males. Beneath the specific resentment of man's dominion and immorality there was a sense that the "feminine" virtues of spirituality and intuitive goodness ought to regulate, actually to predominate over, masculine calculation and aggressiveness in American life.

For women these themes were both too broadly social and intensely personal to remain abstractions. "The investigation of the rights of the slaves has led me to a better understanding of my own," Angelina Grimké wrote in 1838. Abolitionism first drew women and then, from 1837 onward, helped push a number of them on into the crusade for woman's rights.[46] That journey could not have been made had the "investigation" Miss Grimké spoke of not taken place and had events not amply demonstrated how restricted women were when they actually tried to move the nation. Woman's influence might have been confined to the home had her peculiar virtues not seemed so necessary to refine contemporary society and had it not become so apparent that outside the home, and even within it, she was something of a victim, more idolized than socially influential, more thwarted than listened to.

Even though woman's rights advocates succeeded in converting the pedestal into a base for liberation, they did so at a cost. It was acceptance by women of an unfair measure of culpability—those who are better sin more when they fall. Bad women, Lydia Maria Child thought, went farther into evil than bad men. "Corrupted *sentiments* are more depraving in their influence, than perverted intellect," she asserted. "Hence, of all the vices and crimes which disease human souls, none is more completely hardening, so thoroughly debasing to the whole character, as that which changes the sacred sentiment of love into mere sensual passion." Woman's superior purity, Sarah Grimké likewise acknowledged, made her "more guilty" than man in vice and immorality, since man "only accepts what she prepared for the gratification of his lust."[47]

The power to effect redemption means the possessor of that power bears fearful responsibility for *not* using it, for sustaining sin. "The *women of the South* can overthrow this horrible system of oppression and cruelty, licentiousness and wrong," Angelina Grimké believed in the 1830s. "If only fifty women in Virginia or South Carolina would make such an appeal as they could offer to the women of New-England, unfolding the condition of all their sex among slaveholders, slavery would be abolished in one year," George Bourne argued at virtually the same time. An upsetting implication followed. "Had American females come forward in all the mightiness of their legitimate and resistless influence, and imperatively demanded extirpation of that complicated iniquity," one pamphleteer thought, "long ere now the term 'American Slavery' would have been used only to express a dead monster, loathed amid universal execration." Mrs. Eliza Lee Follen, two decades later, was blunter. "The mothers in the Free States could abolish slavery; American mothers are responsible for American slavery." Jonathan Walker broadened the indictment. "Why have the past and present generations proved to be so unkind, oppressive, war-like and revengeful toward each other?" he asked. "The fact stares us in the face at every turn, that in nearly every department of society and of life, our mothers diffused and cultivated physical and moral disease in their offspring and neglected to plant and mature that which is kind, beneficial, pacific, and noble."[48] The irony here is that a set of beliefs giving woman a special role in imposing moral order rebounded to make her responsible for social sins.

Few went so far as expressly to blame women for the evil world they were supposed to be able to regenerate. Abolitionists, in their own crusade and through the campaign for woman's rights, pointed up how badly confined women were, how little real influence they had. But abolitionists clearly put too much weight upon women and upon the family when they looked to them to redeem society and to provide its moral balance in the future. Women and family-life were themselves caught up in change—that was part of the problem.

In a similar fashion abolitionists had once expected too much of religious institutions, more than fragmented Protestantism, trapped by worldly matters, could fulfill: then the disillusion had set in. There was no comparable loss of faith in the family, only an undercurrent of feeling that it needed purification. Belief in the redemptive power of women likewise survived, continuing on into the drive for woman suffrage after the Civil War. That was possible because women seemed innately to embody principles that were bound to prevail in the onward course of civilization and because the family seemed to be the one potentially stable institution in a society cursed with a morally suspect political and religious system.

So many things came together here: the search for a moral community in an apparently a-moral society; fear of power and an identification of goodness with those who lack power; belief that civilization is the suppression of animal nature, yet also that emotion is the surest guide to right and wrong; and a stereotyped set of attitudes about women and black people. Beneath it all was the social and economic flux that battered about the role of the family and of women, making each an issue for concern and freeing each to take on new significance.

7
ECONOMY
Toward a Yankee
South

FAMILIES destroyed, femininity corrupted, virtue's guardians in ruins: the South, to abolitionists, was a morally devastated land. What they saw was there (although not to the degree they imagined) but it was also the reversed image of their own design for society. In attacking the South, abolitionists defined what they felt the nation should become.

Defenders of slavery responded in kind, glorifying the plantation as a utopian alternative to the evils commerce and industry brought the North. With a slight bit more intellectual effort, proslavery propagandists might have gone still farther and caught abolitionists in their ambivalence toward industrialization. Like their Southern critics, abolitionists were fearful of what commerce and industry did to human relationships. Unlike their Southern critics, abolitionists were reasonably certain that economic growth, despite dangers, represented progress. The structure rising in the North was destined to be sound (so abolitionists thought); it was even going to be the epitome of civilization—if its spiritual foundation could be strengthened.

Yet there was uneasiness. Abolitionists measured the North's superiority by contrast with the South's blighted moral and economic condition; but the South, a model of decay and stagnation, was also a terrible reminder that progress in America, whether calculated morally or economically, might not be inevitable.

"Is it right to be rich?" Lewis Tappan wondered.[1] For Tappan, a moralist as well as a businessman, the answer was "no" if success came at the expense of fairness, decency, and charity for fellow man. In antebellum America, however, there were tempting ways of acquiring wealth that did not rise to Tappan's standard, and slavery was chief among them. Abolitionists only seldom portrayed greed as the master's chief motive for keeping slaves and they admitted that man's urge to possess and dominate might even lead to unprofitable behavior, as when a cruel slaveowner maltreated his human property to the point it could not work.[2] Still, slavery was an economic institution—that could not be ignored—and abolitionists had the nineteenth-century habit of mingling moral and economic judgments so thoroughly that the line between them nearly vanished. For antislavery men and women avarice was not the modern economist's bland "maximization of profit." It was a sin.

It was a sin that permeated the whole nation. Although slavery was the most lurid case of unrestrained greed, Northerners as well as Southerners had an excessive love of money and a tendency to warp human relationships into business transactions. "I sometimes think I see, with the clearness of a death-bed vision," the Reverend George B. Cheever prophesied, "that the spirit of gain, and of a commercial expediency, and of an indolent love of ease and prosperity, even in spiritual things, has taken hold of the people." Cheever expressed his forebodings in 1857, but other abolitionists had had them long before. The *Philanthropist,* commenting on "Hard Times" in 1842, presented a trinity of national evils: "Speculation, Extravagance, and Slavery." Only the last was peculiarly Southern. Reverend John Pierpont wondered, "Was there ever a country so blessed, and at the same time, so cursed, as is ours:—so blessed of God—so cursed by the avarice and servility of man?"[3] In actuality the country was blessed, and cursed, by the mentality of a boom-or-bust economy, and by a number of energetic, unscrupulous men with few moral restraints upon their drive to seize material advantage. Pierpont's own grandson, J. P. Morgan, would be a latter-day, more genteel version; but when the antislavery crusade began two generations earlier, the economic expansion of America was already in its vigorous and troubling infancy.[4]

Antebellum prosperity, although it was uneven, played to a long American tradition of concern for the ill-effects of "luxury" upon the morality of a people.[5] This set of attitudes, a hardy perennial, blossomed at the time of the American Revolution, but expansion and growth in antebellum America made wonderfully fresh soil for it to flourish once again. Flourish it did, throughout the antislavery crusade. In 1833 William Goodell wrote that "luxurious living, is the principal instrument and precursor of national guilt and ruin. It springs from pride, and leads to licentiousness, intemperance and oppression." Twenty-one years later Theodore Parker, preaching on the "Moral Dangers of Prosperity," noted that "for forty years the nation has had no outward peril, no war, no famine, nothing to fear from abroad. We have increased amazingly in numbers and riches." Instead of delighting in this situation Parker bemoaned it. "Now the nation is drunk with power and nauseous with wealth," he concluded.[6]

In that line of argument there was both a critique of America and an excuse for the failure of abolitionism to win over the mass of men and women. "We gain very slowly on a prosperous, industrious, money-loving country, intensely devoted to the love of material gain," Wendell Phillips complained. "It is hard to plant the self-sacrifice of a rigid Anti-Slavery, or any other principle, in the heart of such a people." Marius Robinson repeated what was almost an abolitionist cliché. "The Wealth of the South and the Wealth of the North are combined to crush the liberal, free, progressive spirit of the age," he wrote. "Gentlemen of property and standing" set their weight against the movement; the Money Power of the North joined hands with the Slave Power of the South to protect each other's avarice. Much like slaveholders, "our great capitalists are speculating, not merely in lands and banks, but in the liberties of the people."[7]

Had abolitionists pressed onward with such remarks, they might have built a bridge from traditional Christian hostility to amoral acquisitiveness over to an analysis of capitalism, an assessment of its spirit, its political power, and its interest in oppression. Two very different groups of contemporaries, radical socialists and Southern defenders of slavery, were doing precisely that.[8] For their part, abolitionists drew back. Slavery merely served to focus their discontent with the corrosive effect of greed upon antebellum morality. That discontent was severe enough to stand them firmly against slavery,

but it owed too much to the values of an industrializing society to take them any farther.

Abolitionists were capable of specific criticisms of capitalism and of industrialization, but if they had a fundamental hostility to commercial society it was remarkably well concealed and they were spectacularly unsuccessful in communicating it even to their own kin. Perhaps J. P. Morgan is not a representative example of what antislavery stock became, but a striking number of children and grandchildren of abolitionists adjusted quite well to the industrial order of post Civil War America—and yet had no visible sense of alienation from their ancestors. James G. Birney's son, William, became a prominent Washington lawyer, a United States attorney for a time, the author of an admiring biography of his father and a genteel reformer himself as president of the Anti-Imperialist League of Washington in 1899. William Lloyd Garrison's beloved daughter, Fanny, married Henry Villard, soon to become a wealthy railroad organizer. Fanny kept the heritage alive (as did her son, Oswald Garrison Villard) through concern for civil rights and opposition to war. Harold Garrison Villard, another son, became an authority on accident insurance and financial matters, while still another grandson of William Lloyd Garrison, not a Villard, became an investment banker. J. Miller McKim's son combined his career with pious remembrance of his tradition. One of the nation's prominent (and expensive) architects, he designed the Boston Public Library, in which many of the sacred relics of New England antislavery were enshrined.[9]

The fact that their descendants succeeded in late nineteenth-century America does not prove that antislavery advocates were themselves committed to commerce and industry. Yet a number of the original abolitionists did display a fine entrepreneurial spirit of their own. Early in his life John Greenleaf Whittier edited the *American Manufacturer*, a paper designed to promote industry and internal improvements. Arthur and Lewis Tappan were wealthy merchants when they came to antislavery; Amasa Walker was on the brink of retirement from profitable manufacturing and railroad interests when he entered the abolition and peace crusades. When their antislavery days were over, Elizur Wright and Marius Robinson found careers in insurance, Robinson as president of his own company and Wright as a significant figure in the development of actuarial tables.[10] After the Civil War, even Samuel May, Jr., saw no incongruity in discussing purchases of railroad stock with a long-time Irish antislavery correspondent.[11]

More impressive than direct abolitionist participation in commercial transactions was the enthusiasm with which antislavery men and

w   d technological advances. Nowhere was
th   an in rhetoric about the railroad, that
he   Rather than being an unwelcome intruder
in   alden, the railroad evoked much ecstatic
p   led analogy. A member of the Hutchinson
f   antislavery gatherings, penned a number
e   k." According to N. P. Rogers, it "repre-
             d [of abolitionism] in characters of living
             terrible enginery and speed and danger."
             ine "Liberator" with its clanging "Liberty
             Higginson likewise hitched his muse to
             etic tribute to the railroad. In a later essay
             rguing that its speed called forth images of
             ne charge at Balaklava." The railroad, he
             virtue of courage in modern life because it
             d danger.[12]

             ss aesthetically inclined and less committed
             Higginson, similarly found good things to say
             slavery prophets as diverse as Elizur Wright,
             maliel Bailey, and the *National Anti-Slavery*
             me or another sang their hymns of praise.[13]
             nsportation revolution, William Lloyd Garrison
             e day when a "voyage around the world will
             rare event, but it will be undertaken with as
much .... one goes from Boston to Liverpool." But he
too reserved special gratitude for the railroad (a form of enterprise
his future son-in-law would later organize brilliantly). Garrison felt
obligated to "bow down with veneration to the heads that conceived
and the hands that have made so admirable a mode for transportation,
and offer praise and thanksgiving for so sublime an achievement."
Instead of imagining that it would compromise America's moral fibre
and further the heartless exploitation of the country, Garrison believed
it would foster human unity by bringing men closer to each other in
time.[14]

The railroad, smoke-belching symbol of mechanical power, was
not the only aspect of antebellum economic growth congenial to
abolitionists. Garrison had once been a promoter of Henry Clay's
"American System." In 1828, three years before beginning the *Liberator,* he glorified its vision of national commercial and industrial
development. "We wish to see a manufactory by the side of every
suitable stream," he wrote,

> and, if possible, the entire amount of cotton that may be grown in the
> country made into good, substantial fabrics for home consumption and

exportation. Every day's experience teaches this whole people that their interests are best promoted by the erection of *national houses of industry;* that Providence has made them necessarily dependent on no other country for the comforts of life; and that the great secret of national aggrandizement consists in improving their own resources.

Deeper awareness of the sin of slavery brought Garrison to reconsider cotton production and made him despair for his country, but he never ceased to cast his faith for America at least partly in terms of economic expansion. Shortly after the Civil War he took a tour of the West. Much impressed with what he saw, he told his wife the region "is a mighty theatre for enterprise, labor, business of every kind. It is a vast empire in process of rapid development, and its capacity for growth and prosperity seems boundless."[15]

Other abolitionists likewise found hopeful signs in the approaching industrial age. Theodore Parker, in 1841, believed machines "will at last set free a large portion of leisure time from slavery to the elements. The brute forces of nature lie waiting man's command, and ready to serve him." Elizur Wright's enthusiasm at American prospects knew no bound. He expected man to turn coal-power into "the efficient sub-gardener of the world's Paradise Regained." The steam engine was destined to be "our artificial slave" or "the illustrious Man Friday of our modern civilization." Noting that God is "an infinite mechanic," Wright added a sublime flourish: "Are we ourselves less godlike building mills than sitting in pews?—less in the image of our Maker, endeavoring to subdue matter than endeavoring to ignore its existence?" he asked. As the Civil War approached, Wendell Phillips rested his confidence on the ability of Northern "mechanical progress" to bring freedom to the South. He was sure "you cannot make a nation with one half steamboats, sewing-machines, and Bibles, and the other half slaves."[16]

Abolitionists were not motivated by greed or by a self-serving desire to justify the new economic order. Far from it. The rewards of antislavery were never financial. Some abolitionists, like N. P. Rogers and C. C. Burleigh, gave up promising careers to take the movement's vows of poverty. Others, like James G. Birney, Elizur Wright, and Henry B. Stanton, were virtually driven from the field in the 1840s because of their need to secure a dependable income. Men of wealth who supported antislavery—Gerrit Smith, the Tappan brothers, Henry Chapman, and others—jeopardized what they had and almost certainly suffered losses for their commitment.

The fact that abolitionists seldom turned a profit from antislavery does not preclude the possibility that they may have been defending a class interest, one which was as much psychological as directly economic. Certainly historians have devoted great effort to determining whether abolitionism was particularly attractive to people from groups of declining status.[17] That enterprise, however, is most likely eventually to show that, in terms of class, status, and occupation, abolitionists did not look dramatically different from their more articulate Northern enemies. Economic conditions and social dislocation in Jacksonian America were not the beginning of a tight causal chain, the final link of which was abolitionism. Instead, economic and social changes led elements of the Northeastern and Midwestern middle classes to be especially sensitive to issues they found reflected in the institution of slavery. Objective conditions and culture framed the question—they did not determine which individual would ask it and which would ignore it.

Abolitionists obviously were not reactionaries yearning to revoke the machine age. Even Christian anarchists like Garrison and Edmund Quincy did not want to smash the steam engine in order to bring about the Christian utopia—they hoped to have both. But neither were abolitionists embryonic Rockefellers, Vanderbilts, and Carnegies. Much of their energy was expended in opposing the "aristocratic spirit," manifested most notably by slaveholders but also by Northern capitalists, by anyone who felt himself better than those whose labor supported him. "Gentlemen of property and standing," abolitionists believed, were responsible for the Boston mob of 1835, which nearly took Garrison's life.[18]

Bitterly aware of aristocratic hostility, abolitionists sometimes presented themselves as quite the opposite of the wealthy and well-born. Garrison informed a Scottish audience in 1840 that the "anti-slavery principle has been left to the care of the humble and the poor . . . to those without influence in society." But he quickly added what was more than a qualification. "He had said that the abolitionists were not the high and mighty of the land," a reporter recalled; however, "neither were they the degraded nor the rabble. They were the moral worth of the country." This was similar to the assumption behind James G. Birney's prediction of an onslaught upon "our free institutions, by the aristocracy and the thoughtless rabble of the cities and the large towns."[19] Birney phrased his ideal in terms of America's "honest yeomanry," almost an antique expression. His identification, like Garrison's and that of nearly every other abolitionist, was with an industrious, virtuous, and comfortable style of life located midway between wealth and poverty. This ideal was not necessarily agrarian, nor did it allow any great sympathy for the poor.

Abolitionists never made the middle-class nature of their economic assumptions clearer than when they failed to deal incisively with the exploitation of Northern workers by the "Money Power"—a form of oppression much closer to home than was the South's peculiar institution. On a superficial level abolitionists were able to sympathize with the problems of white workers. Elizur Wright, in 1848, admitted that "slavery is only a species under a genus of wrong and oppression." The solution, he believed was "the union of all that work, whether bond or free, to throw off the yoke together."[20] Other abolitionists brooded sentimentally about the sufferings of workers or made occasional appeals to the "WORKING-MEN of our country" to realize "that the present is a struggle between them and a fat, heartless and most insolent aristocracy." Stephen S. Foster began in the 1840s to fret that antislavery had not sought "the elevation of the laboring classes to an equality with the capitalist, and the professions, in the enjoyment of social, civil, and religious rights and privileges."[21]

Such attempts of abolitionists to join their cause to that of the worker were not successful, in large part because immediate emancipationists were neither extreme nor perceptive in their critique of the exploitation of whites.[22] A few were appalled enough by conditions in the North to drift into socialism or into the primitive communism of utopian societies. Those who did soon became painfully aware of how restricted most other abolitionists were in their economic thought. William H. Channing, something of a Christian Socialist, felt that Garrisonians went too far in attacking religion but not far enough in their assaults upon "the whole domain of OWNERSHIP and WORK."[23] Yet even abolitionists like Channing who came close to class analysis did so out of impulses which were diffusely moral and Christian, not as the result of any systematic examination of material conditions. Theodore Parker saw the basic conflict in America to be "between money on the one hand, and men on the other; between capital and labor; between usurped privilege and natural right." This led Parker to an indictment of greed, not to rejection of capitalism and not to great empathy with the worker.

Abolitionists like Parker, furthermore, combined their economic pronouncements with sniping at the vices of the poor. They had the American faith that honest toil always brought rewards, and it made them hold unsuccessful free men responsible for their own failure. In a debate with English Chartists in 1840 Garrison conceded the crushing effect of environment on workers but still advocated self-reform as the first step to liberation—he never was willing to believe that white workers might not be personally to blame for their poverty. Although Lydia Maria Child was able in the abstract to condemn the extravagances of all classes, when it came to specifics she found the luxuries of the poor more detestable than those of the rich.[24]

Even the abolitionists most concerned about economic matters thought more in terms of an organic society than a noncapitalist one. Elizur Wright wanted to see "capitalists and laborers . . . integrally associated, made partners, each sharing in the just profits in fixed proportions, and thus each interested in the other's welfare as well as his own." Wright's system would have achieved a middle-class ideal, "making every workman in fact his own employer." Garrison, granting that capital received more than its proper share, wished to see different interests "blend harmoniously together with those of the common weal." He did not want an "abolition of all individual interests." Speaking of Reconstruction in the South after the Civil War, Marius Robinson pronounced the radical formula: "he who would degrade and rob labor anywhere would degrade all labor; he is the enemy of mankind." His solution was to leave the land open to "fair competition in occupancy by those who have the muscle to till it" and to pay "fair wages" in the South and the North.[25] Opportunity and the ballot, he thought, were all that was required to secure the rights of social classes and peace between them. Redistribution of wealth was not the answer.

Friction between capital and labor was only one aspect of industrializing America; equally apparent was the rise of the city. Here too the abolitionist response was less an attack on the new economic order than a patchwork of old attitudes, moralistic pronouncements, and ultimate acceptance—although, once again, bits and snippets of it might have led to a more fundamental critique.

Lydia Maria Child at first was jaundiced about New York. "In Wall-street, and elsewhere, Mammon, as usual, cooly calculates his chance of extracting a penny from war, pestilence, and famine," she noted; "and Commerce, with her loaded drays, and jaded skeletons of horses, is busy as ever 'fulfilling the World's contract with the Devil.'" Garrison agreed that in New York "Mammon reigns in filthy splendor, and humanity finds none to sympathize with it."[26]

Abolitionist perception of the city drew on an American tradition of believing rural life to be the most moral kind of existence. Still, what abolitionists objected to was urban immorality, not to the city itself.[27] In 1846 Garrison described the horrors of solicitation by London's prostitutes rather than the misery of its poor. Paris, he thought in 1867, "must be Elysium to those who live in their animal nature, and only eat and drink and dissipate *ad lib.*, but the reverse to the spiritually minded." Abolitionists like William Goodell and the Tappan brothers became interested in efforts to suppress vice, in part to cope with evils endemic to life in New York City.[28] With covetousness and libidinousness reigning, the city was hostile territory for the moralist.

But it was not beyond redemption—voluntary associations such as moral reform societies promised to check dissipation—and there were good aspects as well as bad to urban life. Against her will Lydia Maria Child found in time that "though New York remains the same, I like it better." "If you wish to see a commercial age in its ultimate results, come and observe life in New York," she urged. She began to think, nonetheless, that it was "a beautiful city, every year increasing in beauty." She eventually committed the heresy of preferring the Battery to the Boston Common. Henry C. Wright, maddened to ecstasy by Progress, claimed in 1856 he had not "seen the city that presents to my mind such a picture of human skill, energy and power, as Chicago." Garrison may not have liked New York—"the great American Babylon"—but he found the sudden growth of Manchester, New Hampshire, into a manufacturing town to be a blessing. Temporarily exiled to Northampton, Massachusetts, for reasons of health, he discovered he missed Boston: "I have been so long accustomed to the bustle and excitement of a city life, that it is quite essential to the activity of my brain," he complained.[29] There was no yearning for an agrarian past here—a mistrust of unbridled greed and of licentiousness, certainly, but such a mistrust was no more a rejection of capitalism and industrialization by abolitionists than was their tepid middle-class sympathy for exploited laborers.

Abolitionists tended, in fact, less toward radical economic analysis than they did toward values associated with post-Civil War capitalism, particularly toward the twin assumptions that order would emerge out of competition and that government should let well enough alone in economic matters.

Some had not started out with those values. Amasa Walker and William Lloyd Garrison, like many other abolitionists, had been Whigs and supporters of governmental intervention in economic life. They had endorsed the "American System" of tariffs, internal improvements, and federal assistance in promotion of manufacturers. Walker later became a theoretician for free trade. Three years before becoming a Christian anarchist, Garrison backed the Bank of the United States (the "monster bank") in its war with Andrew Jackson.[30]

Other abolitionists had been Democrats before they were actively antislavery and they merely persisted in advocating an open society, with little government activtiy on economic issues except to promote competition. One of them, Gamaliel Bailey, while editor of the *Philanthropist* from 1836 to 1847, often presented slavery as part of a larger question of monopolies, a Jacksonian concern of the sort expressed in the struggle against the Bank of the United States. Bailey had not altered his views in 1847 when he opposed "all schemes to stifle labor's mobility and to prevent free circulation of land or to exclude competition, and preclude or lessen the rewards of individual merit."

In the 1840s others began to move in the same direction, as one of James G. Birney's supporters lamented when he detected Birney bending toward William Goodell's position that "the business of Government, . . . [is] *chiefly*, or *only*, to protect each individual in doing whatever he pleased, so that he did not injure others." Wendell Phillips, summing up the opinion of a convention on woman's rights, believed the sense of the delegates (and himself) was that "in government, every individual should be endowed, as far as possible, with the means of protecting himself." Eight years later he praised Robert Peel for weakening government in England. In 1859, he asserted "the idea of our civilization, underlying all American life, is that men do not need any guardian."[31]

That was hyperbole. Yet after the enchantment of the American System wore off in the 1840s political intervention did not appear necessary for economic growth.[32] Prosperity was virtue's reward just as prosperity unregulated by morality was virtue's enemy.

Abolitionists applied their economic assumptions to the South in a way that allowed them the best of two worlds. On the one hand, the South epitomized the sins of commercial society—greed and reduction of human relationships to financial transactions chief among them. On the other hand, the triumphs of the bourgeoning Northern commercial order were a measure of the South's failure.

There could be no doubt in the minds of abolitionists that slavery violated fundamental tenets of economic morality. For one thing, it encouraged idleness, among slaves because they had no incentive and among masters because they had someone else to work for them. The *Emancipator* reversed the old argument that black people had to be "prepared" for freedom. The real preparation must be of the masters since they would have to be taught to live morally and honestly on their own toil. "Our Southern brethren do not believe in compelling anything to work except the negro," Gilbert Haven wrote. Beriah Green sniffed that "no place can be found for slavery among a people generally inured to useful industry."[33] The South challenged the abolitionists' bourgeois compulsion to find occupation for idle hands, and Southern immorality proved, to the satisfaction of emancipationists, the wisdom of that compulsion.

Worse than engendering sloth, slavery deprived human beings of their "grand central right—the right of a man to himself." There was an old Anglo-American tradition holding (in the words of a prospectus written by Garrison in 1830) "that by the name of a slave, we understand a man who can neither dispose of his person or goods, but enjoys all at the will of the master." Garrison cited Algernon Sidney's *Discourses on Government* and various documents of the American Revolution to buttress the point.[34] As Garrison recognized, Englishmen and Americans long before him had associated freedom with the right to govern one's own labor, to enjoy its fruits or voluntarily to dispose of them in the market-place.[35] Such a tradition helped make sober and practical men in the era of the American Revolution think of taxation without representation as a form of slavery since it deprived them of control of their property without their consent. And it helped abolitionists organize their objections to real slavery after 1830. "God has committed to every moral agent the privilege, the right and the responsibility of personal ownership . . . Slavery annihilates it," Theodore Dwight Weld proclaimed.[36]

From the right of humans to self-ownership there flowed still more bills of indictment against the South. "The proposition that one man can hold another as his property, fundamentally subverts the right of property," the *American Anti-Slavery Reporter* asserted. "Admit it, and you cannot prove that any product of human industry is the property of the producer, for it does not appear that the powers and instruments by which he produced it were his own." William Goodell thought by "the very act of claiming a slave, a man denies all rights of property, by denying the inherent right of self-ownership in all men, upon which all other rights are based." From this followed inevitably the conclusion of Edmund Quincy that "it is the slaveholder, and not the abolitionist, that strikes at the very root of all property."[37] There clearly was a propaganda advantage here. Accused of undermining the slaveholder's right to property, abolitionists reversed things and cast the slaveholder in the role of menace to property rights. Specious though that reasoning seemed to Southerners, it permitted abolitionists to mount an assault upon the institution of slavery while remaining within ancient, ultimately conservative, assumptions about the rights of individuals to possess the goods accumulated by their own labor.

Respect for work, disdain for southern laziness, equation of freedom with self-ownership, belief in the sanctity of property—these were attitudes too deeply American to be mere rhetorical weapons. Still, immediate emancipation was not just a matter of applying old traditions to an old institution. In this case tradition fit tightly with a newly awakened concern for property, seemingly made insecure by the speculative fever of the Jacksonian era, with its rhythms of inflation, deflation, and dishonored debts. In the 1830s slavery became a metaphor for the perilousness of economic freedom just as it had been in the 1760s and 1770s. Behind abolitionist fears of bondage stood an abhorrence of an irresponsible commercial mentality and a hatred of the act of degrading human relations into matters of power and possession. What upset abolitionists were vices prevalent in an expanding society like that of the North as well as in a slaveholding one like that of the South.

Old attitudes toward property and freedom gained renewed vitality from the successes of the antebellum economy as well as from its excesses. Although appalled by greed and speculation, abolitionists were enough a part of the nineteenth-century middle classes to believe in progress and to imagine that it appeared in the smoke of Northern industrialization and in the material blessings of economic expansion. By that standard the South seemed positively un-American. Its relatively undeveloped condition confirmed the abolitionist conviction that greed and licentiousness brought failure, evidence of which appeared in the South's "sterile land, and bankrupt estates," its "once fruitful fields, now slavery-cursed with bareness." Pondering the physical desolation of Virginia, Lydia Maria Child marveled that "statesmen, for temporary purposes, are willing to spread over the rich prairies of Texas, this devastating system [of slavery], to devour, like the locusts of Egypt, every green thing in its sight." It was a Yankee eye Gilbert Haven cast upon Annapolis. "With admirable opportunities for growth, with a harbor and shores that would be filled with enterprise and taste were it not for this crime," he felt, "the capital of this freest of the Slave States, is as shabby, mean, and crowded as the dirtiest quarters of the North End." Lacking its rightful prosperity, Annapolis was a cursed city, archtypical of the South.[38]

The contrast with the North was obvious. "No merely agricultural nation ever yet attained a high degree of prosperity, or civilization," Richard Hildreth asserted. "To attain that result it is necessary that manufacturing and commercial industry should combine with agriculture." Lest his readers miss the point, he was more blunt a few pages on. "It is a fact too obvious to be denied even by the most prejudiced observers," claimed Hildreth, "that the slave-holding states of the Union are far inferior to the free states, in every thing that constitutes civilization." B. F. Grandin noted that on

Northern farms are produced all the staple provisions needed in a flourishing community, and all the mechanical arts are cultivated in the highest degree to which they have severally attained. The wealth and population are double the wealth and population in the Southern section, although the latter contains more than double the number of acres, and mostly of better quality than the former.

(To clinch his argument Grandin remarked that the few items the South produced successfully catered mainly to vice: tobacco, rum, and whiskey.)[39]

The Census allowed abolitionists to quantify the South's failure. Just having read the report for 1840, James G. Birney told Lewis Tappan that "the South, compared with the North, is almost in a state of dilapidation." Southern population lagged far behind, as did the South in value of land and most other economic categories. "The South trembles at the publication of the Census-returns," Theodore Parker gloated in 1852. Among abolitionist editors Gamaliel Bailey was especially adept at using those returns for his purposes, but even Garrison (not an especially empirical thinker) reviewed with high praise a book entitled *The North and the South: A Statistical View of the Condition of the Free and Slave States*. Based primarily on the Census of 1850 it was, he wrote, "precisely such a compilation as we have long been wishing to see." Garrison added, however, that it only confirmed what abolitionists had known all along, which was that slavery, in addition to being a sin, did not pay.[40]

Often conceding the South advantages over the North in natural resources, abolitionists felt the root of the South's lack of prosperity was its peculiar institution. The antislavery emphasis on lust for power as the master's motive complemented the abolitionist view of the South as an unproductive and desolate land. How could men be obsessed with profit where there was none to be had?

Slavery threatened to blight the national economy as well as the South's. A depression in the late 1830s and early 1840s brought certainty that slavery was "the chief source of the commercial and financial evils under which the country is groaning." Particularly dire and widely circulated was Joshua Leavitt's address upon "The Financial Power of Slavery."[41] Leavitt's grim words became Liberty Party clichés. In accepting the party's presidential nomination, James G. Birney wondered, "What can a free, republican and commercial state look for, but confusion and ruin, when they entrust their affairs to a people without commerce, without manufactures, without arts, without industry, whose whole system of management is one of expense, waste, credit, and procrastination?" The Liberty platform for 1844 dealt with the "withering and impoverishing effect of slavery on the free States." In speeches on behalf of political antislavery Alvan Stewart hammered at the insolvency of the South, its refusal to pay debts to Northerners; he further blamed the South for manipulating federal policy toward banks and tariffs in a ruinous fashion.[42]

Abolitionists who were not Liberty Party members made much the same charges. David Child, a Whig, argued that the South was undertaxed and that it twisted tariff policy for its selfish purposes. Edmund Quincy presumed "statistics would show that the free half of the Union had gained nothing by their adulterous marriage with slavery." The South, he believed, "is one scene of public and private bankruptcy." Northerners "stagger beneath the blows which their prosperity has received from that much courted region." Although always insisting that economic considerations should not affect moral decisions, William Lloyd Garrison referred to slaveholders as "rogues, pickpockets, swindlers, and tyrants . . . who have already defrauded the North of an untold sum of money." He added that an end to slavery would make Southerners "customers worth having."[43]

In coldly economic terms abolitionists quite probably had things reversed: the South was at least as much exploited by the North as it was an exploiter of the North. But the question, for abolitionists, was one of progress and of intuitive moral economy, not of academic political economy. Few of them bothered to make any pretense of a thorough study of commercial relations between the sections, nor did they regard that as a particularly relevant task since nothing could absolve the sin of holding one man captive to the will of another. In addition, abolitionists thought affluence was as much a function of individual virtue and divine blessing as it was a result of economic laws. Garrison's sense of the business cycle went no deeper than a faith that "banishment of sin will be the restoration of prosperity" and that a depression was a judgment of God upon "that Vesuvius of crime, that maelstrom of blood, that pandemonium of oppression, the slave system."[44]

Economic comparisons between North and South, and assessments of the baneful effect of slavery upon prosperity, were merely outward confirmation for an inward certainty of the South's moral depravity. Such calculations had the added benefit of making it possible to explain the instability of the Northern commercial order—its periodic panics and depressions—by placing the blame on slavery and on economic sins exemplified by slavery. Americans could have plenty if they did not seek it at the expense of virtue and especially if they abandoned slavery. Abolitionists, then, held out to the South—really to the whole nation—the American promise of abundance and peace. The price, for the South, was to become like the North, to join it

in a rush toward true civilization. William Lloyd Garrison sketched
for a black audience in 1838 the glory Southerners would realize following abolition.

> We will remove from them all source of alarm, and the cause of all
> insurrection—increase the value of their estates tenfold—give an Eden-
> like fertility to their perishing soil—build up the old waste places, and
> repair all breeches—make their laborers contented, grateful and happy
> —wake up the entombed genius of invention, and the dormant spirit
> of enterprise—open to them new sources of affluence—multiply their
> branches of industry—erect manufactories, build railroads, dig canals
> —establish schools, academies, colleges, and all beneficient institutions.

As if that were not adequate, emancipation would "extend [Southern]
commerce to the ends of the earth . . . unite the North and the South
by indissoluble ties—change the entire moral aspect of society." Gilbert Haven's image of the South redeemed was as much an idealized
North as it was Eden. After the destruction of slavery he predicted
"Railroads shall rush through every valley. . . . Beautiful roads will
wind beside every stream, scale every mountain, pierce every forest."
He foresaw "rich embowered cottages" lining roadways and multiplied
"at brief intervals, into great communities, with the gigantic factories,
and warehouses, and spacious stores, and crowded streets of growing

cities." Prosperity, as well as the schoolhouse, free labor, and steady habits of control, were assumptions behind Wendell Phillips' Civil War assertion that "the claim of the North to govern must be founded on the ground that our civilization is better, purer, nobler, higher, than that of the South."[45] The civilization Phillips spoke of was commercial as well as Christian and middle-class as well as moral in its values.

Lewis Tappan and his brother Arthur were merchants and developers of a credit-rating system, the forerunner of Dun & Bradstreet. Credit-rating was an appropriate occupation for the businessman-moralist, fully as appropriate as insurance, which lured Elizur Wright and Marius Robinson. Credit-rating and insurance: the former (especially as the Tappans conceived of it) gives economic preference to virtue; each aims at security and predictability and also profit. And yet both tend to translate ties between human beings into matters of dollars and cents, the very sin of slavery.

But then neither the Tappans, nor Wright, nor Robinson, nor any abolitionist, would have argued that commerce and industry were unmitigated blessings. There was a danger in greed, and prosperity had its perils. Still, abolitionists found it easier to pin faith on the bourgeois economic progress of America than on its political or religious institutions. If man could control himself, if society left him freedom to be a responsible moral agent, then abundance and civilization might ride together.

Their perceptions owed much to the values and dislocations of a commercial society, but abolitionists were not simple prophets of industrialization. They would be appalled by some of its latter-day consequences and they believed harmony and brotherhood were consistent with competition. The capitalism they envisioned was not that of J. P. Morgan; it was socially responsible, almost utopian. Lewis Tappan, for instance, saw the corporation as a number of men coming together to pool labor and capital to work in unity for a useful goal.[64]

Arthur Tappan, in Lewis's retelling of his life, assumed the guise of the perfect Christian capitalist. "He loved business, he was pleased with prosperity, he delighted in handling goods and money, he was gratified with domestic comforts and surrounded his family with them," Lewis wrote,

> yet he ever felt that he was after all but a STEWARD; that what he had, or could lawfully gain, was not his, but belonged to his Master; that he had no right to expend his goods in luxurious living, in vain

show, or waste them in any way; that he had no right to lavish them upon himself or family; that he was to give an account of his deeds done in the body, at the GREAT ASSIZE.[47]

Such a man could not help being a reformer as well as an entrepreneur, a cautious and temperate conqueror of all wilderness, moral and physical. His task was to reconcile traditional moral categories to the unique circumstances of an industrializing nation. Southerners and other sinners let him explain (to himself if no one else) what might happen in those perilous times if mankind let baser impulses like greed, sensuality, and lust for power take over, as Americans seemed to be doing.

8

UNION
A Divisive
Nationalism

THE ECONOMY of abolitionist morality was partly individualistic and capitalistic: it rested upon a sense that freedom meant a person's right to control his or her own property and labor. But it was also strongly social and even nationalistic: it insisted that the North and South unite in virtue and prosperity.

That was only one of many yearnings toward unification in the antislavery movement. Abolitionists sought a human brotherhood transcending artificial barriers of political party or religious sect and the biological distinctions of sex or race. Although often divisive in effect, these were genuine impulses of reconciliation in a society increasingly torn by partisan warfare, denominational rivalry, and conflict among groups jarred loose by an expanding and diversifying economy. These were, in fact, impulses for something like a Christian community of morality, self-control, and reform amid the breakdown of older, more formal communities.

So contentious were abolitionists, so vigorous was their rhetoric against the South, and so bound up was their crusade with the coming of the Civil War, that it is difficult to realize how deeply post-1830 antislavery depended on a desire to bring Americans together. Particularly difficult to detect, but quite important to abolitionism, was a strange reformist variety of that common nineteenth-century species, nationalism.

By the 1840s Europeans had embarked on a period of romantic nationalism, and one branch of American antislavery had started on a new, more intense phase of political action. Also in the 1840s the Garrisonian faction of abolitionism began to pursue a strategy which seemed both antinationalistic and impolitic. It has earned them a reputation for irresponsibility, commendable radicalism, or treason—depending on the historian's point of view. In May 1844 the American Anti-Slavery Society, the Garrisonian organization, went on record in favor of a dissolution of the federal Union between the free and the slave states. Disunionism provoked the hottest of passions and most flamboyant of gestures, including William Lloyd Garrison's incineration of a copy of the United States Constitution as part of a Fourth of July celebration. But there was calculation as well as emotion behind this, and loyalty to the United States as well as contempt for its Federal government.[1] Disunionism is the exception proving the nationalistic rule among abolitionists.

Garrison's own disunion sentiment emerged early in 1842 and received much impetus from an event in Congress. Among the antislavery petitions presented to the House by John Quincy Adams was one from various citizens of Haverhill, Massachusetts. It urged peaceful dissolution of the Union. For some time Southern delegates had threatened this if Northerners like Adams insisted upon agitating the question of slavery; now the tables were turned, and rather than greeting Haverhill's suggestion with glee, proslavery representatives tried to censure Adams. The importance of their outrage was not lost on Garrison, who informed a correspondent that the petition "has resulted in frightening the boastful South almost out of her wits, driving the slaveholding representatives to the wall." The result, he felt, was "a signal victory for the cause of liberty and its advocates." Shortly afterward disunion resolutions began appearing in local antislavery meetings. The first ones were presented by Garrison and generally included an expression of approval for the Haverhill petition.[2]

Although it called the South's bluff, disunionism also played to an abolitionist desire to preserve personal moral purity, to escape contamination from an evil institution. Always imprecise about how dissolution might come about, Garrison often put it in terms which were not at all political. "It is for each individual to withdraw his sanction from that compact [the Constitution], in order to keep his garments clear of innocent blood," he wrote in 1845, seemingly holding out the possibility that a human being, not just a state, might secede from the Union. Somewhat earlier he explicitly repudiated the notion that disunionists aimed at a "geographical secession." It was a moral secession he sought: those who perceived the sin of slavery should deny their consent to anything which might be considered to sanction it.[3]

Still, disunionist abolitionists did not feel they were buying personal righteousness at the expense of political effectiveness. They justified the strategy as a perfectly reasonable one to employ while seeking an end to slavery; the South itself confirmed their opinion by its violent reaction against Haverhill's petition. Dissolution, Garrisonians thought, would doom slavery by withdrawing Northern protection. It would eliminate economic privileges needed for the system's survival, and it would take away the military presence required to insure survival of the slaveholder himself: without the Union he would have to face insurrections alone, with no Yankee arms behind him.

There were additional bits of political wisdom concealed in the lurid rhetoric of disunionism. For years opponents of abolitionism had insisted that slavery should not be made an issue, because discussion would jeopardize the Union or because the Constitution stood as a barrier to emancipation. Garrisonians took the offensive after 1842, charging that both Union and Constitution ought to be overthrown if they helped uphold an immoral institution, as critics of abolitionism would have it. On a much less self-conscious level disunionism answered a nagging problem for abolitionists: how to justify aiming their propaganda at the North, where slavery did not exist, rather than at the South, where a friendly audience did not exist—at least among whites. The difficulty was answered by insisting that the North could abolish slavery unilaterally once it ceased to support the institution through the federal government. Conversion of the slaveholder became virtually irrelevant. The South, through its response to Haverhill's petition, its search for a refuge behind the Constitution and the Union, and its blockade against emancipation literature, helped formulate what appears to have been the most radical of all the tactics employed by abolitionists.[4]

Disunion, however, was not inherently radical. The Garrisonians themselves argued that nonresistance, their most extreme doctrine, was not a prerequisite of disunionism; they maintained that disunionism was a rejection of a specific government's involvement with slavery, not necessarily a rejection of all governments.[5] Phrased in such a way, it only applied so long as the United States, or its Constitution, upheld slavery. Oliver Johnson, a disunionist until the Civil War, reconciled his earlier position with his later national pride by pointing out that the Constitution had, in fact, been amended to eliminate slavery and that this met the objections of his fellow Garrisonians. "The Constitution under which we are now living is not that which [Garrison] publicly burned a certain Fourth of July in Framingham; nor is the Union which he sought to dissolve any longer in existence," Johnson wrote in 1880. "The Union of today is a Union 'redeemed, regenerated, and disenthralled by the Genius of Universal Emancipation.' "[6] And so, forty years after its emergence and fifteen years after a bloody war of secession, antislavery disunionism came to nothing more extreme than endorsement of the Thirteenth, Fourteenth, and Fifteenth Amendments.

Important as disunion sentiment was to the Garrisonians after 1844, they had no monopoly on it within the antislavery movement. Abolitionists far more respectable than the Garrisonians either advocated it, flirted with it, or shared its assumptions while not being able to bring themselves to reject things so sacred as the Union and the Constitution.[7] Judge William Jay, careful and moderate in most matters, gave cautious sympathy to disunionism, believing it was doomed to failure but feeling, as he wrote in 1857, that the Union "is at present a most grievous moral curse to the American people."[8] Abolitionists and antislavery organizations hostile to Garrison made similar pronouncements throughout the 1840s. In 1847 the American and Foreign Anti-Slavery Society, dominated by evangelical abolitionists, responded with heavy irony to resolutions from Virginia and South Carolina. The resolutions asserted that the federal government had no control over slavery, and the society urged Congress to accept the logic of that position. Congress, the society declared, ought to cooperate with Virginia and South Carolina "in terminating at once and for ever all the connexion heretofore supposed to exist between the Federal Government and the peculiar institutions of the South."[9] This was not full-blown disunionism like Garrison's, but it rested on the same desire to cut the North off from slavery and on the same sense that such action would doom the institution.

Events brought other non-Garrisonians near or actually into disunionism. Congressmen opposed to the expansion of slavery argued that the devious annexation of Texas in 1845 was "identical with dissolution," a position Garrison noted with satisfaction. Politicians like Henry Wilson of Massachusetts usually drew back at the last second, arguing "it is wise to remain in the Union, so as to operate more effectually against the system which has introduced Texas into it; to abolish slavery." But in such times of crisis Garrison found himself much closer than usual to moderate political figures and to rejected allies from early antislavery days. Joshua Giddings and the patrician Charles Francis Adams might decline a Garrisonian invitation to attend a disunionist convention, and William Jay might have his doubts, but all united with Garrisonians to denounce federal complicity with a hated institution. Disunion sentiment even filtered into the Republican Party and managed, by the 1850s, to touch a one-time anti-abolitionist like Francis Wayland.[10]

In reality, the assumptions necessary for disunionism were exclusive property of no particular sect of abolitionists, and they can be traced back to before 1840. On the eve of his break with Garrison in 1838, A. A. Phelps made the common point that "two such discordant elements as slavery and freedom never can be united in one political fabric. . . . While these two elements are incorporated in our system, [we cannot] be one people in point of fact." This placed the onus for sectional animosity on the South and its institution, as Garrison himself inevitably did. When Southerners made such assaults on Northern liberty as censorship of the mails in the 1830s, there were assertions like Alvan Stewart's that "slaveholders have dissolved the Union so far as the 100,000 abolitionists are concerned." This was precisely how Garrisonians later justified rejection of the Union.[11]

Non-Garrisonians, even non-disunionists, similarly agreed with Garrisonians that "a dissolution of the Union would be a death blow to slavery." "Let southern men dissolve this Union if they *dare*," Stewart challenged in 1835; "*slavery* would *then* take care of itself, and its masters too;—in one *little month* both would become extinct." By 1850 James G. Birney believed that the Union protected masters from their slaves and from poor whites, who, he felt, would turn against slaveholders once they were forced to defend a system that exploited them as well as the black man.[12] Birney's argument conceded the strategic logic behind disunion—it promised slaveholders extermination without the Union.

Non-disunionists also accepted the principles behind disunionism. In the summer of 1833 the *Emancipator* confessed "there is nothing sacred to us in a compact which binds me to do a moral wrong." Two years before Garrisonian disunionism emerged, James G. Birney told a British audience that George Washington and Benjamin Franklin "erred . . . in preferring *union* to [slavery's] abolition." Gamaliel Bailey repudiated disunionism but acknowledged "whenever we shall become convinced, that there is no other alternative than Union and perpetual slavery, or Disunion and Liberty, our choice would be made up in the instant."[13] Abolitionists like Bailey who kept their faith in the federal government did not believe its continued existence mattered more than antislavery—they simply refused to think there was an irreconcilable conflict between the two.

Disunionist assumptions made abolitionists appear antinationalistic —an appearance encouraged by other instances in which they placed conscience above patriotism. John Greenleaf Whittier blasted "the detestable maxim of 'Our country, right or wrong.'" Believing his country to be engaged in an immoral war in 1847, Garrison claimed "to desire the overwhelming defeat of the American troops, and the success of the injured Mexicans." The Norfolk County Anti-Slavery Society, meeting in Dedham, Massachusetts, in 1847, resolved that "we sympathize heartily with Mexico and wish her all success in her attempt to defend her liberty against the slaveholding tyranny of the United States."[14]

Surely men and women who wanted to break up the federal union and who hoped for their native land's defeat at the hands of a foreign enemy were exceptions to the nineteenth-century rule of romantic nationalism. That is misleading; disillusion and nationalism are quite compatible. Disillusion may even be inevitable among people who imagine their country to be chosen by God for high purposes—and more than anything, abolitionists were disillusioned by the United States. There was, they saw, a terrible gap between what America promised to be and what America was.

John Greenleaf Whittier explained the task engaging his creative energies in 1832. It was "a work of fiction, which shall have for its object the reconciliation of the North and the South—being simply an endeavor to do away with some of the prejudices which have produced enmity between the Southron and the Yankee." This was an appropriate theme for an admirer of Henry Clay's American System. In the post Civil War period James G. Birney's son stressed his father's nationalistic credentials, in part to separate him from Garrisonian disunionism, which the younger Birney thought treasonous. But Birney's early career bore his son out. In 1833 Birney urged the American Colonization Society to conciliate his native South, adding "this *Union* is precious to me—if it be destroyed, the world may mourn, for its liberty is lost." Half a decade later, having rejected colonization in favor of genuine antislavery, Birney informed a Southern congressman that abolitionists "*are* friends of *the* Union that was intended by the Constitution." By this time he had to add, "it is against the distortion of the glorious Union our fathers left us into one bound with despotic bands that the abolitionists are contending." Whittier eventually made this same qualification and preserved it in the uncertain months of early 1861. Anxiously watching the secession of Southern States, he wished "to maintain the Union if it could be *the* Union of our fathers."[15]

Garrison arrived at his despair with the Union much sooner, and with more fanfare than Whittier and Birney, but he too came from a background of patriotic pride and nationalistic politics. In a teenage effusion for the *Newburyport Herald,* Garrison advised South American nations to "take the United States as a fair and beautiful model by which to govern the affairs of their country—a model which no other nation under heaven can boast its equal, for correctness of sound republican principles and wise and judicious administration." In 1826 he chose an old Federalist slogan for the motto of the *Newburyport Free Press, "Our Country—Our Whole Country—And Nothing But Our Country,"* and he put his talent to work for the American System and for John Quincy Adams. In 1828 he read a poem of his own composition before Newburyport's Artillery Company, assuring his undoubtedly enchanted audience that:

> The Plots of division, though artfully done,
> Will fail on a people *whose hearts are but one!*

Thus disposing of sectional conflict, he said of America:

> Our march must keep pace with the *march of the mind,*
> Progressing in grandeur for ever and ever;
> Our deeds and example are laws to mankind.

When the Massachusetts Anti-Slavery Society published a statement of principles, signed and quite probably authored by Garrison, it acknowledged "to a union of these States we feel a deep attachment." By 1835, however, the sentiment was less than absolute. "No price can be paid too great for its preservation, but the sacrifice of honor and principle."[16]

Nationalism was not a mere shadow in the background of abolitionists like Garrison, Whittier and Birney. The rise of nationalistic sentiment following the War of 1812 formed an essential precondition of post-1830 antislavery. Although generally depicting sin and regeneration in terms of the individual, abolitionists could not have justified their course of action without arguing, as Lydia Maria Child did, that "slavery is certainly a *national* evil." Had this kind of assertion been made only after 1840, after abolitionists had virtually given up hope of reaching the slaveholder, it might well have been merely a rationalization for continuing to propagandize Northerners rather than those directly involved with the institution. But it appeared in Mrs. Child's first major piece of antislavery propaganda in the mid-1830s (when abolitionists still believed the South might be reasoned with), and it appeared elsewhere in the first decade. In 1836 Frances Harriet Whipple, making an "Appeal to American Women," wrote that "the unity of our national character is such that every individual who does not lift up his voice against a national crime, becomes a partaker, and an adherent of that crime." A year later Wendell Phillips, in one of his earliest addresses before an antislavery gathering, similarly emphasized national complicity in all moral things. "Our fate is bound up with that of the South," he said, "so that they cannot be corrupt and we sound; they cannot fail, and we stand."[17]

The very act of achieving nationhood made the guilt of all Americans unmistakable. "It is [a] matter of history," John Greenleaf Whittier told the Middlesex Anti-Slavery convention in 1834, "that this kind of Robbery against which we are contending, was not, and could not be legalized in our country until we had cast off the authority of Great Britain." In 1833 Garrison claimed "the first moment the people of the United States published their Declaration of Independence to the world, from that moment they became exclusively accountable for the existence and continuance of negro slavery." A decade later this interpretation of the Revolutionary era had soured into Stephen Foster's belief that "protection of the slave system was one of the objects for which the Union was formed."[18] To Foster's way of thinking, national responsibility, incurred with the Constitution, implied a need to dissolve the Union or purge it of slavery. But even such disunionism depended on a sense that from 1776 onward Americans were knit in moral destiny and moral responsibility, just as from 1789 onward they were knit together by political obligations.[19]

So strong was the sense of national complicity that it exerted a tempering influence on abolitionist feelings toward the white South. Gerrit Smith in the 1850s argued for a plan to end slavery by compensating masters for loss of their human chattel. If slavery were a national crime, it required sacrifices on the part of every American before its effects could be erased, and Smith saw no reason why the slaveholder should have to bear the whole financial burden. When the Civil War arrived, Smith urged Union soldiers to love the South while they conquered her. "But does it not ill become us to talk of punishing her?" he asked. "Slavery, which has infatuated her, is the crime of the north as well as of the south." This was more than mere rhetoric. Although Smith later supported such aims of radical Reconstruction as land redistribution in the South and suffrage for blacks, he nevertheless felt that the North should acknowledge its involvement in slavery, perhaps by giving the South exemption from taxation. In a gesture of conciliation he offered to sign a bail bond for Jefferson Davis when the ex-Confederate President was confined to a Union prison. Samuel J. May likewise came to support compensated emancipation in the winter of 1860, largely because he too felt the North must take responsibility for having upheld slavery. May, also a proponent of most radical Reconstruction measures, believed in 1869 that "it was right that our Federal Government should be forbearing in their treatment of the Southern Rebels, because the people of the North had been, to so great an extent, their partners in the enslavement of our fellow-men that it would have ill become us to have punished them condignly."[20]

Naturally enough, this sense of national responsibility found its way into the very texture of antislavery propaganda. Calls for individual repentance and commitment mingled with shameless plays upon symbols of the common past, reminders that Americans had a collective history as well as personal duties. Garrisonians, least overtly patriotic of the abolitionists, still hearkened back to the time of George Washington and John Adams. Eliza Lee Follen, in common with most of her colleagues mourned that

Those grand, historic days are gone,
Those heroes and their sons are dead.

Garrison, after burning his copy of the Constitution, set one document of the Revolution against the other by asking his audience "what is an abolitionist but a sincere believer in the Declaration of '76?" In his most disunionist phase Samuel J. May took pride in the fact that the New England Anti-Slavery Convention was to meet in Faneuil Hall, with its rich tradition of defiance to authority and advocacy of liberty. Abolitionists may even have contributed a patriotic phrase to the national pantheon: apparently they were the first to christen the bell atop the Philadelphia statehouse the "Liberty Bell."[21]

The glories of the Revolution, a favorite theme in antebellum oratory, were troublesome for abolitionists like May and Garrison, who repudiated the Constitution and who renounced use of arms. Yet Garrisonians often felt compelled to appropriate the sacred mantle of the Revolution while denouncing its flaws. Samuel J. May saw abolitionists striving to "complete, by moral and religious means and instruments, the great work which the American revolutionists commenced; to do what they left undone." Garrison at his bitterest still believed the Declaration of Independence to be "the most radical political instrument in the world," and he thought "its practical enforcement will be the redemption of the world." Antislavery would be fulfillment and perfection of the Revolution. It was no mere flourish of the pen when Garrison informed the public that he was beginning the *Liberator* in order to "lift up the standard of emancipation in the eyes of the nation, *within sight of Bunker Hill and in the birthplace of liberty.*"[22] This was perfectly consistent with Garrison's earlier nationalistic editorial ventures, with his later disunionism, and even with his relative conservatism during Reconstruction. All hinged on a deeply concealed feeling—a precondition as much as a feeling—that there were noble aspects to America and that the United States had a common fate, for better or worse.

Nationalistic utterances were the language of the day. But for abolitionists they served to reinforce a self-image, to express certain ideals, and at times to render serious social criticism unnecessary.

Like Henry Clay and Daniel Webster, their more famous and opportunistic contemporaries, abolitionists cast themselves in the role of national statesmen, as people who cared about the Revolutionary meaning of America and about erasing the division between North and South.[23] The root of the national problem, they were sure, was slavery, and the implication was clear: if slavery jeopardized the Union, then the Union's saviors were those who preached abolition.

Justifying many years of involvement with the cause, authors of the report of the Boston Anti-Slavery bazaar of 1858 proudly recalled "we saw that, but for slavery, our people would be united and happy." Like the ladies of the Boston bazaar, the gentlemen of the Liberty Party saw bondage as the source of discord. Their platform of 1844 declared that it was essential to break the Slave Power's hold upon the government in order to secure, among other things, "the salvation of the union of the States." That meant "the Liberty party is not a Sectional party, but a National party—has not originated in a desire to accomplish a single object, but in a comprehensive regard to the great interests of the whole country." Seven years earlier the *Anti-Slavery Almanac,* listing abolitionist goals, concluded that "we hope to bury *sectional jealousy* in the grave of the only deamon that, in our country, has ever engendered it:—we mean Slavery."[24]

Abolitionists relished their self-cast role of redeemer of the South, the Union, and the Nation. In the second issue of the *Liberator* Garrison noted the South's "miserable aspect." "We wish to relieve her, by endeavoring to remove the cause of the evil," he wrote. "We wish to see her as happy and flourishing as her more fortunate sisters." Eight years later, Charles Lester remarked upon how much anti-slavery had taught its advocates about the real task before them. "We commenced the struggle for the emancipation of the slave," Lester said, "and we have prosecuted it to liberate ourselves and our country."[25]

The redeemed nation abolitionists envisioned meant the spread southward of Northern ideals of morality and social order. After emancipation, Gilbert Haven imagined "the free and happy, busy and populous, wealthy and cultivated North, shall cover the whole land."[26] In picturing the perfect Union as a Yankee one abolitionists were more naïve than culpable. Theirs was not the first, not the last, and certainly not the worst example of middle-class Northern cultural imperialism and it was no special malevolence for them to want a nation of hardworking, educated, prosperous, freedom-loving independent farmers, artisans, merchants, and mechanics.

More unfortunate was the way nationalistic assumptions allowed abolitionists to avoid systematic analysis of that Northern ideal. If slavery was a national sin, then in slavery they had an explanation for national ills, even for Northern ones. In 1838 James G. Birney thought slavery was "improverishing our country, breaking up our schools—effeminating our men, converting female amiableness into ungovernable fury, and bringing the judgments of God upon our churches, whose members and whose ministers live, and are supported in their ministry, by the fruits of unrighteous exaction." Almost a quarter century later Samuel May, Jr., similarly placed the depravity of his day upon slavery. It, he told an Irish correspondent, "has corrupted our people fearfully—down deep the rottenness extends."[27]

May and his comrades did not realize that slavery was not in itself the sole disturber of American society and was far from being the only threat to the virtue, security, success, and harmony of the United States. Increasingly anachronistic and morally disturbing, the peculiar institution functioned to explain to abolitionists what was wrong with a nation expanding and diversifying with hopeful and fearful rapidity. Slavery and the South symbolized the ills of the day; but removal of slavery, contrary to what antislavery propaganda assumed, was not the beginning of a millennium of peace and brotherhood. It was not even much of a first step.

By their logic abolitionists were bound to accept the Union if it was on their own terms, that is, on what they conceived to be the terms of morality and justice.[28] After the firing on Fort Sumter abolitionists began an agonizing and complicated reassessment, through which they came to accept fighting to maintain a Union many of them believed protected slavery.[29] Garrisonians had the hardest time of it, especially the nonresistants, since they deplored both war and the sinfulness of the Union. Yet for once the federal government (what was left of it) seemed on the right side, or at least potentially so. Never having phrased their opposition to the Union in absolute terms, having made a number of nationalistic presuppositions, and having made antislavery commitment the test of morality, abolitionists could eventually support the war—with enthusiasm when it seemed definitely to be waged for freedom. Wendell Phillips, still advocating disunion in February 1861, nevertheless believed that "the people of the States between the Gulf and the great Lakes, yes, between the Gulf and the Pole, are essentially one. We are one in blood, trade, thought, religion, history; nothing can long divide us." It was disconcerting for Phillips and others to acknowledge the righteousness of a war being fought to preserve a Union they had spent two decades trying to smash; but the impulse for Union had been there all along.[30]

Gilbert Haven brought the ancient antislavery themes together in 1863 and foreshadowed their variations in post-war America. Upon hearing of the Emancipation Proclamation, he foretold "unification of the Republic." "We have never been, in reality, one people. Blood has not separated us. . . . Natural boundaries have not separated us. . . . There has been only one distinction, and that was slavery." The American Anti-Slavery Society, meeting the same year, made a smooth transition from disunionism to rejoicing at America's prospects. The convention was held in a hall that captured the new mood. "In the rear of the platform," the society's *Proceedings* reported, "the American flag, now at length the symbol of Liberty, hung in beautiful festoons, extending each way from an Eagle and a National Shield in the center, and surmounted by a white banner or band, on which were inscribed, in conspicuous black letters, the words 'UNION AND LIBERTY.'" Some abolitionists clung too long to a sense that only slavery had impeded genuine Union. Denying good evidence to the contrary, James Freeman Clarke in 1883 exalted that "the North and South are truly one; the American Union, this single root of bitterness having been taken away, is vastly more powerful and more united, than ever."[31]

Nationalism and desire for a stable Union had lurked in antislavery from the beginning. The war and its outcome simply made obvious what sectional animosity had hidden.

Abolitionists saw themselves as much more than prophets of national unity. They placed their own mission and America's in terms that were broadly international. The effect, however, was curious. By linking the United States to the world as they did, they heightened the importance of America.

Antislavery, abolitionists often argued, was part of a general war of antagonistic principles, temporarily embodied in the North and the South or in friends of the cause and opponents of the cause, but abstractions nonetheless. "The slave question in America is only one phase of the more comprehensive question that now begins to agitate the civilized world," William Goodell claimed in 1852, "and that presents the grand problem of the present age." Some saw abolitionism as an attempt to remove "an incongruity with the spirit of the age—the overlapping of the period of barbarism on the era of civilization." A bit more specific, James G. Birney declared that "the final conflict between Popular liberty and Aristocratic slavery has come; that one or the other must fall; and they [abolitionists] have made up their minds, with the blessings of God on their efforts, that their adversary shall die."[32]

Such feelings aligned abolitionism with then current European struggles for national independence and for republican forms of government. In 1835 the New York Young Men's Anti-Slavery Society characterized "love of liberty" as the spirit of the times, behind rebellion in Poland as well as antislavery in Britain and America. In 1852 the American Anti-Slavery Society resolved that "the cause of the American slave, and the cause of the oppressed and plundered people of Europe, are one: and that, in laboring for the abolition of American slavery, we are contributing to the emancipation of man in every part of the globe."[33]

Despite occasional disillusionment with European revolutionaries, abolitionists maintained on through the Civil War the idea that theirs was an important engagement in a universal struggle.[34] As her native South Carolina embarked on its fatal course in December 1860, Angelina Grimké Weld interpreted events in America and abroad in the fashion of past decades. "It is very clear that two great parties are being formed in Europe as well as America," she told her son, "—the lovers of the higher law—or Truth & Progress—& the Conservatives who love wealth & Power, Slavery & Despotism & they must meet in the terrible conflict, before the reign of Liberty & Love can be established."[35]

Although the struggle for freedom was international, abolitionists believed God had a special place for America, above all other nations, in that struggle. Like many of their contemporaries, abolitionists had faith in an American mission. Unlike most of their contemporaries, they felt slavery prevented its fulfillment. Slavery "neutralizes the power of our example upon other nations of the earth, and checks the progress of republican principles," a New York antislavery organization complained. It "hinders the conversion of the world," William Goodell echoed. In 1862 Gilbert Haven referred to America's part in world redemption to impress his hearers with the dreadful urgency of the Union cause. "To save this land to universal liberty and universal brotherhood, supported by universal law and sanctified by universal piety, is to save all lands," he exclaimed.[36]

Belief in American destiny served important functions for abolitionists. It infused antislavery with urgency but, at the same time, made the sinner more abstract and less human: abolitionists were fighting for divine history rather than against real people. The rhetoric of American mission, furthermore, provided a culturally acceptable vocabulary for expressing the moods of hope and despair that inevitably afflict committed individuals.[37] On the one hand, if God loved America so much and blessed it so greatly, then surely His anger would fall more heavily upon it for its sins. "Have we not reason . . . to think," asked William Goodell in 1834, "that if, in modern times, there should be found a highly favored nation which God has made the theatre of the most remarkable displays of his grace and mercy— but the great bulk of whom should still go on in sin—with their GREAT NATIONAL SINS UNREPENTED OF AND UNFORSAKEN—that such a nation would be probably marked for signal and sudden judgments?"[38] On the other hand, if repentence came soon enough to avoid the chastizing event, the future would be glorious; it would be the time of peace, plenty and brotherhood abolitionists predicted after the end of slavery.

Even when a chastizing event arrived, in the form of Civil War, abolitionists saw redemption and progress (its secular equivalent) flowing from it. Noting in 1863 the "Dismal Swamp of inhumanity" in the South, Thomas Wentworth Higginson nonetheless believed that "the triumph of Civilization over Barbarism is the only Manifest Destiny of America." The same year Sarah Grimké told the American Anti-Slavery Society that the nation was engaged in "God's War" from which would come the "salvation of the Anglo-Saxon as well as the African race."[39] Faith in American destiny buoyed up Sarah Grimké's confidence about the war just as it earlier darkly shaped her perception of slavery and of the sinfulness of Americans.

Miss Grimké's remarks and countless similar ones by abolitionists placed antislavery on a continuum stretching from past to present to future battles for freedom. Phrasing arguments in terms of American mission allowed abolitionists like Miss Grimké to reconcile nationalistic impulses with belief in human unity, with submission to God's will, and with their own controversial and sectional activities. Concern for the fate of mankind was the highest kind of American nationalism—a conviction that the United States (and abolitionism) were at the center of God's moral drama.

The temperament of patriotic Americans has always been of a peculiar sort, compromised by state and local attachments, yet often able to bound across national borders to shake hands with the races of the world. At its best it produces good-hearted assertions of universal brotherhood of the sort made so frequently and passionately by abolitionists.[40] At its worst it seeks to make the rest of the world American. Abolitionists were too much a part of antebellum culture to avoid the worst as well as the best.

Antislavery men and women generally were immune to the excitement of Manifest Destiny, especially since it meant aquisition of possible slave territory in the west. But their acceptance of the idea of America's mission and their yearning to bring mankind together in moral fellowship, were not far removed from the most idealistic excuses used to justify national expansion.

Bitterly as abolitionists felt about the annexation of Texas in 1845 and the subsequent war with Mexico, some of them still appreciated the spread of American influence to the Southwest. Stephen S. Foster, normally one of the purest of the Garrisonians, was equivocal about annexation in 1844. Gamaliel Bailey turned his eyes toward the whole of Mexico, urging a plan that would have allowed it to join the United States. This it would do willingly, he thought, and before long America's effect on Mexicans would prove "no race of mankind is so degenerate as to be beyond the influences of the agencies which a kind Providence has arranged in these latter days, for the redemption of all his children." Undaunted by the outrage his plan created, Bailey was looking forward by 1849 to taking up the burden of civilizing Canada. Shortly after Bailey's death in 1860, his editorial successor reprinted his suggestions for the annexation of Mexico as still worth consideration.[41]

Like Bailey, Gerrit Smith managed to encompass half the continent. "Poor Mexico needs to be brought under radically transforming influences," he told Congress in 1854. Canada and Cuba likewise caught Smith's fancy. "To bring the various people of North America into a nation with ourselves," he argued, "would be to bring them under a rapid process of enlightenment, civilization, and a homogenousness with each other and with us. I trust, that we shall be a better people, by that day. But bad, as we now are, even in that case, few of our neighbors would become worse, and most of them would become better, by becoming like us." Gilbert Haven's dreams spanned the Atlantic. He argued that "*Europe must become a Union of Democratic States,* in league, if not one with America." Haven's vision was sharp enough to detect Ulysses S. Grant as a divinely appointed agent who had "insured the essential extension of America over the world."[42]

At its most benign the American mission has been carried by example rather than conquest, and so the majority of abolitionists felt it should be. The prewar thirstings for territory of Gamaliel Bailey and Gerrit Smith—as well as Gilbert Haven's postwar anticipation of an American world—while not necessarily typical, are reminders that the difference between antislavery and antebellum Manifest Destiny and between antislavery and later imperialistic ventures was not absolute and sometimes was not even very great. Again the assumptions of antislavery blend with those of the general culture, and the world of 1831 flows into that of 1877. The antislavery movement looked beyond a divided land to future days of national glory and to the Progress of Civilization; after 1865 the nation itself shook off the effects of a war of division and marched toward the same goal, or so Americans thought.

In accepting national responsibility for sin, and in accepting the idea of a national destiny, antislavery built upon American traditions and upon the common ground of its day. Abolitionists similarly were not unique in their feelings about other matters: about political and religious institutions, mankind, race, sexuality, progress, civilization, and even to a degree, about slavery. Any number of their uncommitted or hostile contemporaries accepted many of the same assumptions. The difference lay in how abolitionists connected all the points together, in how they formed them into a shell of feeling encompass-

ing the South, slavery, and Northern society. Abolitionists mistrusted
the brawling and amoral political system of Jacksonian America yet
could be lured back to a righteous version of it. They lost their faith
in American Protestantism, splintered and self-absorbed; but they
were loyal to it in their moralism and they were searchers for its
equivalent in a Christian community of reform. They wished to liberate mankind and still control Man. They lusted after Progress while
feeling that the unrestrained economic individualism driving it was
wrong. Deeply disturbed by the effects of change, they nevertheless
judged the South by its inability to become a commercial and industrial society. They sought national unity and human brotherhood
while preaching from a pulpit which was resolutely sectional.

Caught in social and economic processes they did not fully understand, they fashioned what they could from the materials of the time.
Abolitionism became for them a cause in which to find personal meaning and direction; it provided solidarity and moral certainty no longer
available from the state, the churches, or conventional social relationships, all fragmented and seemingly corrupted by fearsome and promising America. Slavery and the South, for abolitionists, became reference points by which to organize a general, yet emotionally com-
elling pattern of perception; in slavery and the South were markers

of what might happen if restraints were taken off human nature; in slavery and South moral men and women could see the negation of their progress, their ideals, and their hopes. And so reform always is: as much for the reformer as for the reformed—an interplay between widely-held values, social conditions, events, and the mystery of personality. It is also, we should not forget, a noble glimpse of the disparity between common ideals and reality.

In the spring of 1865, after the Civil War's close, William Lloyd Garrison took the happiest sea voyage of his life, from New England to South Carolina. Once the epitome of fanaticism, he had been made respectable by the triumph of the Union Army. He was invited to speak at Fort Sumter, his words to help close the war against slavery on the very spot the fighting had begun.

While in Charleston the old abolitionist accepted a chance to address a group of newly freed slaves gathered at the Zion Church. Having spent thirty-five years reviling the United States for the sin of slavery, Garrison offered a belated acknowledgement of his patriotism. "Once I could not feel any gladness at the sight of the American flag because it was stained with your blood," he told the freedmen, "and under it four millions of slaves were daily driven to unrequited labor." Times had changed, Garrison conceded. "Now it floats purged of its gory stains, it symbolizes freedom for all, without distinction of race [or] color."[43] As was often the case, Garrison's sentiment proved better than his gift of prophesy. A divisive man seeking harmony, he could not foresee that sins were not easily washed away and that between sections and races there would be lingering and tragic divisions.

AFTERWORD
Discontinuity and Uniqueness

ANTISLAVERY did not suddenly end with the death of slavery in 1865. If we are to believe historians, the spirit of abolitionism lived well into the twentieth century. In the 1960s in particular there were numerous books and articles pointing out parallels between the anti-slavery movement and the civil rights struggles of the 1950s and 1960s.[1] The parallels existed. Abolitionists used many of the tactics and engaged in many of the tactical debates that characterized radicalism in the middle of this century. Sit-ins, boycotts, advocacy of non-violence, advocacy of violence, formation of inter-racial alliances, destruction of inter-racial alliances, and many other things were common to abolitionism and to the civil rights and anti-war movements of the 1960s. Indeed, those who wrote in the 1960s were able to see abolitionism so perceptively because they were engaged in righting the very real wrongs of their own day. Yet what is most distinctive about reform and radical activity in the United States is its lack of tradition and lack of continuity. Reformers and radicals in the 1950s and 1960s rediscovered abolitionism rather than built upon a vital abolitionist legacy.

That is appropriate. Antebellum reform, although part of a nineteenth-century continuum, had its own world. William Lloyd Garrison and the twentieth-century freedom rider each focused his moral perceptions upon the evil of racism, but how each saw it and how each responded to it differed. The millennialistic, deeply Protestant religious seeking of Garrison, his excitement at the advent of progress, his belief that civilization required the utmost measure of control—these all belong to his day and mark the distance between Garrison's activism and that of our times. Yet these also mark some of the many things abolitionists shared with their contemporaries.[2]

Initially it is frustrating to discover that abolitionists had as much or more in common with those who attacked them as with latter-day reformers and radicals. The problem, however, is with us, not with them. It comes from an unrequited desire to unravel motivation. We assume that the job of history is to find out what made members of distinct groups, like abolitionists and modern radicals, different from their peers. That is a legitimate line of inquiry, but it should not be the only one.

We will, of course, have new studies of abolitionism locating with greater clarity the kinds of social perspective that encouraged antislavery commitment—the economic and religious backgrounds, the regional factors, and the general life-experiences characteristic of the majority of antislavery men and women. Already we know a great deal and surely we can know more of the sociology of antislavery. But there will be hundreds of exceptions to each rule, and all we ever truly will have will be rough correlations. We will discover that such-and-such a life-history seems to have predisposed people to accept antislavery. We will not know why others with the same life-histories, so far as we can tell, did not become abolitionists or why still others with radically different life-histories did. We will never learn why there were some Southern-born abolitionists—James G. Birney and the Grimké sisters, most notably—and not more of them, or, for that matter, fewer of them. We will never find out why numerous evangelical Protestants of New England stock disdained an antislavery crusade in which evangelical Protestants of New England stock played such a large role.

There is another approach, more anthropological than sociological. It is to analyze the relationship between abolitionist thought and feeling and the social environment of antislavery. The question, in other words, need not be "who became an abolitionist?" It is equally valid to ask why the antislavery commitment took a particular shape at a particular moment in time—to ask what was antebellum and American about antislavery rather than to ask what was peculiar about abolitionists. That is contextual rather than causal history; it is the history of commonality and structure rather than of distinctiveness and movement, but it is a legitimate endeavor nonetheless.

There are risks. Chief among them is the danger that everybody will end up looking the same. To argue, as I have, for consideration of a general cultural matrix within which a reform movement operates, is purposely to obscure the boundaries between reformers and non-reformers. It is to say more about limits imposed by society and culture than about differences within those limits. That is proper—but only up to a point. There were, after all, differences between abolitionists and Northern anti-abolitionists and between both groups and Southern defenders of slavery. Some of those are obvious now and were serious enough at the time to lead to invective and, in the case of anti-abolition mobs, to violence.

Less obvious is the manner in which antebellum society and culture circumscribed the debate over slavery, as society and culture

circumscribe all public discourse. More than they recognized, abolitionists, Northern anti-abolitionists, and defenders of slavery expressed
similar concerns, occasionally in similar language (as when they all
used family as a metaphor for social harmony). The abolitionist desire to impose moral direction upon a changing society, for instance,
was exactly the desire of Northern anti-abolitionists. On one level,
the issue between the two groups was slavery. But on a less clearly
articulated level the issue for both sides was how best to insure that
change proceeded in an orderly fashion, whether by attacking evil
or by suppressing disruptive dissent. And on that level abolitionists
and anti-abolitionists alike worked out a dominating tension in antebellum America. In exactly the same manner the antislavery and
Southern proslavery arguments often bore deep similarities to each
other. The plantation ideal of defenders of slavery had much in common with the Christian utopia of Garrisonian nonresistants. Each
was a counterimage, a form of protest against an emerging society
in which relationships between humans seemed dictated more by the
market-place than by bonds of morality and feeling.

Still, there were those differences and it would be foolish to deny
them. The proslavery utopia—to continue that example—rested on
social, racial, and sexual heirarchy. It had little room for industrialization. The abolitionist utopia was relatively egalitarian and reconciled industry with order and morality. Those and other differences
are striking. But the matter comes to this: whether to trace the
boundaries between groups or to deal with the larger debate in which
they participated. By the latter way of going about things, abolitionists belong more with their contemporaries (even the ones who hated
them) than with twentieth-century reformers and radicals. That is
where I have tried to place them.

The fact that apparently diverse groups wind up having much in
common seems an unforgivable mystery in the past, but we accept
it without thought in our own time. In 1968 there was a major political movement, symbolized by George Wallace, largely Southern,
largely appealing to blue-collar workers. There was discontent among
the black poor and rebellion among white, middle-class college students. All lashed out at a government they perceived to be uncaring
and unrepresentative, all believed the American Dream had faded
for them, but all lived within its terms. Yet each group badly mis-
understood the others, perhaps despised the others. Few Americans
then stopped to ask why people sharing so many frustrations took
them out in such different fashions. Nor did Americans bother to
think much about why the majority of each group, although presum-

ably suffering under the same grievances, remained inactive. When we expect history to devote its energies to such problems we send it on an errand we are too lazy to run with our own recent past.

Perhaps it is a false errand. The beginning ought to be with the cultural and social forms that humans operate within and that individuals can only slightly reshape. As we ought to expect from men and women belonging to a larger culture, defenders of slavery, Northern anti-abolitionists and abolitionists frequently played in an identical key, yet disharmoniously. We should be as intrigued by that particular key as by why some chose to play it one way, others another, and the majority not at all.

NOTES

INTRODUCTION

1. [James G. Birney], *Correspondence, between the Hon. F. H. Elmore, One of the South Carolina Delegation in Congress, and James G. Birney* . . . (New York, 1838), p. 8. The American Anti-Slavery Society admonished its agents not to be drawn into discussing specific plans for immediate emancipation but simply to stick to the general principle (Gilbert H. Barnes and Dwight L. Dumond, eds., *Letters of Theodore Dwight Weld, Angelina Grimké Weld and Sarah Grimké, 1822-1844,* 2 vols. [New York, 1934], 1: 126). The crucial thing was the call for immediate and irrevocable commitment to end slavery. The process of actually ending it might take time and perhaps a transitional period.

2. David B. Davis, "The Emergence of Immediatism in British and American Antislavery Thought," *Mississippi Valley Historical Review* 49 (September 1962): 209-30. John L. Thomas, *The Liberator: William Lloyd Garrison* (Boston, 1963), pp. 104-5. Merton L. Dillon, *Benjamin Lundy and the Struggle for Negro Freedom* (Urbana, 1966), argues against a sharp break with the 1820s. See also Gordon E. Finnie, "The Antislavery Movement in the Upper South before 1840," *Journal of Southern History* 35 (August 1969): 319-42.

3. Willie Lee Rose, *Rehearsal for Reconstruction: The Port Royal Experiment* (New York, 1967), pp. 37-39, suggests ways in which a generational difference among abolitionists might have resulted in behavioral differences.

4. For example, Gilbert Hobbs Barnes, *The Antislavery Impulse, 1830-1844* (New York, 1964), and Aileen S. Kraditor, *Means and Ends in American Abolitionism: Garrison and His Critics on Strategy and Tactics, 1834-1850* (New York, 1967).

5. Leavitt to Birney, April 10, 1855, in Dwight L. Dumond, ed., *Letters of James Gillespie Birney, 1831-1857,* 2 vols. New York, 1938), 2:1173. The *Liberator,* February 27, 1857.

6. This definition is quite close to that given by James McPherson, *The Struggle for Equality: Abolitionists and the Negro in the Civil War and Reconstruction* (Princeton, 1964), p. 3, and Kraditor, *Means and Ends,* p. 8. Kraditor adds the provision of belonging to an antislavery society. Because of the fragmentation described in chapter 1 below, I think that it is wiser to avoid an institutional definition and to substitute a provision that an abolitionist must have made a public commitment to immediate emancipation.

7. Those who wish to pursue the charge of racism further can find evidence in Leon F. Litwack, "The Abolitionist Dilemma: The Antislavery Movement and the Northern Negro," *New England Quarterly* 34 (March 1961): 50-73; and in William H. Pease and Jane H. Pease, "Antislavery Ambivalence: Immediatism, Expediency, Race," *American Quarterly* 42 (Winter 1965): 682-95. There is something of a summary and commentary in Richard O. Curry, "The Abolitionists and Reconstruction: A Critical Appraisal," *Journal of Southern History* 34 (November 1968): 529-32.

8. Especially good are Benjamin Quarles, *Black Abolitionists* (New York, 1969); Leon F. Litwack, *North of Slavery: The Negro in the Free States, 1790-1860* (Chicago, 1961) and "The Emancipation of the Negro Abolitionist," in *The Anti-*

slavery Vanguard: New Essays on the Abolitionists, Martin Duberman (Princeton, 1965) pp. 137-55; and William H. Pease and Jane H. Pease, *They Who Would Be Free: Black's Search for Freedom* (New York, 1974).

9. Historians who stress underlying themes, as I do, often fall back upon grandly vague abstractions such as "climate of opinion," a phrase mercifully gone into remission. What we generally mean to discuss are "values" (or shared value systems) and "culture," two equally vague but extremely important concepts. I have tried to defend "values" as a useful, if limited, analytic category in "Sexual Matters as Historical Problems: Toward a Framework of Analysis," *Societas* (in press). I recognize the problem in defining values (illustrated in Pat Duffy Hutcheon, "Value Theory: Toward Conceptual Clarification," *The British Journal of Sociology* 23 [June 1972]: 172-87). I also realize that many sociologists minimize the importance of values or question the utility of the concept itself. Much of the criticism of values as an analytic category seems valid. I do, for instance, accept some of the argument of Charles E. Bidwell, who disputes the Parsonian contention that integrated social systems depend upon shared value systems (Bidwell, "Values, Norms, and the Integration of Complex Social Systems," *The Sociological Quarterly* 7 [Spring 1966]: 119-36). But to throw out the concept of values entirely seems to me to deny the rough consensus of thought, feeling, and response we know exists among groups of people at particular moments in time. As I use "values," the term refers to the most general and comprehensive evaluative judgments people pass upon themselves, others, and the external world. Thus "self-control" or "restraint" is the value central to chapter 5 of this work, even though the specific manifestations of it have to do with sexuality. Also of interest on values are the works of Fred Weinstein and Gerald Platt, *The Wish to Be Free: Society, Psyche, and Value Change* (Berkeley, 1969), and *Psychoanalytic Sociology* (Baltimore, 1973).

That leaves "culture," the other vague but important concept. Helpful are the essays by James A. Boon, Talcott Parsons, and Robert F. Berkhofer, in *The Idea of Culture in the Social Sciences,* ed. Louis Schneider and Charles M. Bonjean (Cambridge, England, 1973); also the treatment in Paul Bohannan, "Rethinking Culture: A Project for Current Anthropologists," *Current Anthropology* 14 (October 1973): 357-72. Bohannan conceives of culture as "a mode of encoding information." The encoding takes place both within the individual (it is what he or she learns) and in such aspects of the external world as in the social structure. When I speak of a "cultural matrix," I mean the latter: the pressures exerted by external reinforcements and communicators of culture. When I speak of "culture," I refer to widely shared modes of assessing and responding to the world. Behind this line of reasoning lies a particular sense of what cultural history is about: the cultural historian's job is, first, to explicate the assumptions embodied in culture and, second, to place those assumptions in relation to their "matrix," which includes their history, the society within which they function, and the individual and group needs they meet or fail to meet.

10. Two rather different kinds of contemporary social science help historians see just how much goes on beneath the surface of social interaction. I am thinking of the debate over "labeling theories" of deviance and of Clifford Geertz's style of anthropology. Useful introductions are Edwin M. Schur, *Labeling Deviant Behavior: Its Sociological Implications* (New York, 1971); Nanette Davis, "Labeling Theory in Deviance Research: A Critique and Reconsideration," *Sociological Quarterly* 13 (1972): 447-74; and Clifford Geertz, *The Interpretation of Cultures: Selected Essays* (New York, 1973).

11. For a perceptive—and somewhat different—interpretation of the abolitionist impulse after the Civil War, see McPherson, *Struggle for Equality,* and James M. McPherson, *The Abolitionist Legacy: From Reconstruction to the NAACP* (Princeton, 1975).

CHAPTER 1

1. Wendell Phillips Garrison and Francis Jackson Garrison, *William Lloyd Garrison, 1805-1879: The Story of His Life as Told by His Children*, 4 vols. (New York, 1885-89), 2: 346-48.

2. Two historians with very different political perspectives have done the most to reinforce the idea of deep divisions within the antislavery movement: Gilbert Hobbs Barnes, *The Anti-Slavery Impulse, 1830-1844* (1933; rpt., New York, 1964); and Aileen Kraditor, *Means and Ends in American Abolitionism: Garrison and His Critics on Strategy and Tactics, 1834-1850* (New York, 1967). Barnes wished to make a case for the "moderate" and allegedly more political approach of abolitionists who separated from Garrison in 1840. Kraditor accepted the moderate-radical dichotomy (developing it skillfully, in fact), but came down on the side of Garrison's "radicalism," which she saw as more flexible, rational, and productive than previous historians had granted. My reasons from dissenting from her view—much as I admire her work—are documented verbosely in Ronald Gordon Walters, "The Antislavery Appeal: American Abolitionism after 1830" (Ph.D. diss., Berkeley, 1971), chapters 1 and 2.

3. Bailey to James G. Birney, November 28, 1839, in *Letters of James Gillespie Birney, 1831-1857*, ed. Dwight L. Dumond, 2 vols. (New York, 1934), 1: 510. On the agency system see: Dwight L. Dumond, *Antislavery: The Crusade for Freedom in America* (Ann Arbor, 1961), pp. 183-96; and several articles by John L. Myres, the most accessible of which is "The Organization of 'The Seventy': To Arouse the North Against Slavery," *Mid-America* 48 (January 1966): 29-46.

4. William Goodell, *Slavery and Anti-Slavery: A History of the Great Struggle in Both Hemispheres, with a View of the Slavery Question in the United States* (New York, 1852), p. 466.

5. Stanley Elkins, *Slavery: A Problem in American Intellectual and Institutional Life* (Chicago, 1959), leveled the charge of anti-institutionalism against abolitionists. Elkins' selection of abolitionists was curious and his logic was a bit twisted —he argued that America lacked an institutional structure capable of mitigating slavery but faulted abolitionists for not working through existing institutions. In recent years books and articles by Aileen Kraditor, Robert Marcus, James Mc-Pherson, James B. Stewart, and Bertram Wyatt-Brown, among others, have attacked Elkins or significantly qualified his argument.

6. Thomas Wentworth Higginson, *Contemporaries* (Boston, 1899), pp. 249-50. For divisions during and just after the Civil War see: James M. McPherson, *The Struggle for Equality: Abolitionists and the Negro in the Civil War and Reconstruction* (Princeton, 1964), pp. 260-307.

7. Correspondence between Goodell and Spooner may be found in the Spooner Collection, New York Historical Society (hereafter cited as NYHS). For other examples of feuding among political abolitionists see: *National Era*, July 15, 1847; and Phillip Green Wright and Elizabeth Q. Wright, *Elizur Wright: The Father of Life Insurance* (Chicago, 1937), p. 122.

8. Kraditor, *Means and Ends*, makes a strong case for Garrison's willingness to tolerate dissent. Her argument is impressive, and she is on to something significant: the factions were not at all homogeneous, with the Garrisons in particular comprehending men and women with every sort of antislavery opinion. That lack of homogeneity indicates to me that friendship and local ties were as significant as—perhaps more significant than—ideology in formation of factions. Kraditor, it seems to me, underestimates those factors and does not take into account the degree to which Garrison's invective made life miserable for New York abolitionists. He could tolerate dissent—Kraditor is correct on that—but he also desired professions of loyalty and craved vindication. Neither was forthcoming from New York abolitionists in the late 1830s. I have treated these and other matters relating to the division in mind-numbing detail in chapter 1 of "Antislavery Appeal."

9. See note 2 above. For an example of an abolitionist (and son of an abolitionist) who emphasized differences between the factions see: William Birney,
*James G. Birney and His Times: The Genesis of the Republican Party with Some
Account of Abolition Movements in the South before 1828* (New York, 1890),
pp. ix-x. For an attempt to smooth over old differences by a key figure in the
division see: Elizur Wright, *Myron Holley: And What He Did for Liberty and
True Religion* (Boston, 1882), p. 232. There are signs that a more sensible approach to the division is emerging. Bertram Wyatt-Brown, *Lewis Tappan and the
Evangelical War Against Slavery* (Cleveland, 1969), is critical of Tappan's role
and refuses to see the schism as crippling to abolitionism. Lewis Perry, *Radical
Abolitionism: Anarchy and the Government of God in Antislavery Thought* (Ithaca, 1973), seeks patterns of thought common to all abolitionist factions.

10. Useful accounts of female participation in antislavery are: Alma Lutz, *Cru-
sade for Freedom: Women of the Antislavery Movement* (Boston, 1968); Keith
E. Melder, "The Beginnings of the Women's Rights Movement in the United
States, 1800-1840" (Ph.D. diss., Yale, 1963), pp. 209-69, 302-3; and Kraditor,
Means and Ends, 39-77.

11. The *Liberator*, October 5, 1849; Tappan to Weld, May 26, 1840, in *Letters
of Theodore Dwight Weld, Angelina Grimké Weld, and Sarah Grimké, 1822-1844*,
ed. Gilbert H. Barnes and Dwight L. Dumond, 2 vols. (New York, 1934), 2: 836.

12. F. Julius LeMoyne to James G. Birney, March 24, 1840, in Dumond,
Birney Letters, 1: 545.

13. Wright to Beriah Green, October 17, 1837, Wright Mss, Library of Congress
(hereafter cited as LC). See also Wright to A. A. Phelps, October 29, 1837,
Wright Mss, LC; Wright to Garrison, November 6, 1837, Ms Am 1.2, v.6, no. 96,
Boston Public Library (hereafter cited as BPL).

14. Perry, *Radical Abolitionism*, is a superb account of nonresistance. The best
treatment of Garrison's intellectual development—although somewhat unsympathetic—is John L. Thomas, *The Liberator: William Lloyd Garrison* (Boston,
1963). Kraditor's more favorable treatment in *Means and Ends* is an important
corrective.

15. James G. Birney, *A Letter on the Political Obligations of Abolitionists, By
James G. Birney: With a Reply by William Lloyd Garrison* (Boston, 1839), p. 32;
the *Liberator*, September 12, 1856. Garrisonians, of course, were critical of the
moral failings of the Free Soil and Republican positions and not all Garrisonians
were enthusiastic about either party. "The difference between the anti-slavery
movement and the Republican party is one of principle and is heaven-wide," declared the Pennsylvania Anti-Slavery Society (The *Liberator*, November 7, 1856).
For divisions among Garrisonians over the Republican Party in the election of
1860, see McPherson, *Struggle for Equality*, pp. 13-14.

16. The *Liberator*, March 13, 1840.

17. The *Philanthropist*, June 15, 1842; Joshua Leavitt to James G. Birney,
January 18, 1842, in Dumond, *Birney Letters*, 2: 726, 659. Betty Fladeland, *James
G. Birney: Slaveholder to Abolitionist* (Ithaca, 1955), pp. 215-16, 219.

18. The *Philanthropist*, July 9, 1842; letter of Gerrit Smith, reprinted in the
Daily Chronotype, September 25, 1848; the *Radical Abolitionist* 1 (June 1856):
102, 103. See also Arthur Henry Rice, "Henry B. Stanton as a Political Abolitionist" (Ph.D. diss., Columbia University, 1968), pp. 2, 113.

19. Green to James G. Birney, April 6, 1853; November 23, 1847, in Dumond,
Birney Letters, 2: 1143, 1087. See also Perry, *Radical Abolitionism* and "Versions
of Anarchism in the Antislavery Movement," *American Quarterly* 20 (Winter
1968): 779. A plank in the party's 1844 platform took it as "a principle of
universal morality, that the moral laws of the Creator are paramount to all
human laws" (Kirk H. Porter, *National Party Platforms* [New York, 1924]
p. 13).

20. The *Philanthropist*, January 6, 1841; Porter, *National Party Platforms*, p. 7. Birney and his colleagues were quite aware of their drift toward Jacksonian democracy—an odd drift, considering Birney's earlier career in the South, which had been adamantly anti-Jackson (Theodore Foster to Birney, September 12, 1845, in Dumond, *Birney Letters*, 2: 970; Birney Ms Diary, March 3, 1840, Birney Mss, LC). For an example of the Democratic and libertarian tendencies of the Liberty Party, see the "Call for a Nominating Convention" (1847) in Dumond, *Birney Letters*, 2: 1047-57.

21. The most interesting criticisms of Garrison's position by Garrisonians came from Stephen S. Foster, Abby Kelley Foster, A. Brooke, Sidney Howard Gay, Lydia Maria Child (who thought Garrison was *too* political), and J. Miller McKim. These can best be followed through the pages of the *Liberator* and the *National Anti-Slavery Standard* as well as in private correspondence, notably in the correspondence to Maria Weston Chapman and her sisters, BPL, and in the Gay Mss, Columbia University. I have treated these debates, as well as the important goings-on in Ohio, in "The Antislavery Appeal."

22. Charles W. Denison to Garrison, quoted in McPherson, *Struggle for Equality*, p. 104.

CHAPTER 2

1. As I wrote these words, more and more books appeared that were less preoccupied with quarrels and with antislavery organizations than older works. Leonard L. Richards, *"Gentlemen of Property and Standing": Anti-Abolition Mobs in Jacksonian America* (New York, 1970), and Gerald Sorin, *The New York Abolitionists: A Case Study of Political Radicalism* (Westport, Conn., 1971), seek the social bases of abolitionism and anti-abolitionism. Lewis Perry, *Radical Abolitionism: Anarchy and the Government of God in Antislavery Thought* (Ithaca, 1973), is a fine study of abolitionist assumptions. Even Aileen S. Kraditor, *Means and Ends in American Abolitionism: Garrison and His Critics on Strategy and Tactics, 1834-1850* (New York, 1967), although dealing largely with institutions, does so in a sensitive fashion, with awareness that reform commitments are only partly expressed through them. Carlton Mabee, *Black Freedom: The Nonviolent Abolitionists from 1830 through the Civil War* (New York, 1970), is a discussion of many abolitionist tactics. Jane H. Pease and William H. Pease, *Bound With Them in Chains: A Biographical History of the Antislavery Movement* (Westport, Conn., 1972), likewise gives a reader a sense of the variety of methods pursued by antislavery men and women. The interpretation embodied in this book took shape well before I read Clifford Geertz's essays, most conveniently collected in *The Interpretation of Cultures: Selected Essays* (New York, 1973). Geertz, however, is extremely helpful for historians, particularly in giving rather more precise content to problems of "deep meaning" such as mentioned in this chapter.

2. Phillips, "Philisophy of the Abolition Movement" (1853), in *Speeches, Lectures, and Letters*, first ser., ed., James Redpath (Boston, 1902), p. 135. This speech and "Public Opinion" in the same volume give succinct statements of Phillips' ideas.

3. Richard Hofstadter, *The American Political Tradition and the Men Who Made It* (New York, 1948). See also Robert D. Marcus, "Wendell Phillips and American Institutions," *Journal of American History* 56 (June 1969): 41-58.

4. The best biography of Phillips is Irving H. Bartlett, *Wendell Phillips: Brahmin Radical* (Boston, 1961). Kraditor, *Means and Ends*, pp. 217-20, has an excellent brief discussion of the "free produce question" among Garrisonians.

5. Green to James G. Birney, April 23, 1847; April 6, 1852, in *Letters of James Gillespie Birney, 1831-1857*, ed. Dwight L. Dumond, 2 vols. (New York, 1938), 2: 1067, 1143-44; Phillips, "Mobs and Education" (1860) and "Public Opinion" (1852), in *Speeches*, first ser., pp. 338-39, 45.

6. The *Liberator*, November 19, 1836; Thomas Wentworth Higginson, *Contemporaries* (Boston, 1899), p. 123.

7. I have in mind factionalization of the Socialist and Communist left as well as the interminable debates over tactics among student radicals in the 1960s.

8. The quotes from Goodell in this and the previous paragraph are taken from Goodell, *Slavery and Anti-Slavery: A History of the Great Struggle in Both Hemispheres: With a View of the Slavery Question in the United States* (New York, 1853), pp. 388-89.

9. The *Liberator*, October 19, 1855; October 8, 1852; and various issues throughout the years for August 1st and July 4th gatherings. See also Robert Samuel Fletcher, *A History of Oberlin College from Its Foundation through the Civil War*, 2 vols. (Oberlin, 1943), 1: 249-50. Kraditor, *Means and Ends*, pp. 236, 261 fn. 2, mentions the "therapeutic" function of conventions.

10. Keith E. Melder, "The Beginnings of the Women's Rights Movement in the United States, 1800-1840" (Ph.D. diss., Yale, 1963), pp. 164-65. The *Liberator*, November 24, 1843; September 18, 1840; November 12, 1852; November 29, 1839; January 14, 1842; November 8, 1839. Mary Grew, "Annals of Women's Anti-Slavery Societies," in American Anti-Slavery Society, *Proceedings of the American Anti-Slavery Society at Its Third Decade* . . . (New York, 1854), p. 128.

11. The *Emancipator*, May 5, 1835; [Maria Weston Chapman], *Right and Wrong in Boston* . . . . 2nd ed. (Boston, 1836), p. 77; Catherine H. Birney, *The Grimké Sisters: Sarah and Angelina Grimké, The First Women Advocates of Abolition and Women's Rights* (Boston, 1885), pp. 132-33 fn. (a similar motto is in the *Liberator*, January 2, 1837); the *Liberator*, October 26, 1838. Antislavery stationery appears in various manuscript collections. Dwight Lowell Dumond, *A Bibliography of Antislavery in America* (Ann Arbor, 1961), pp. 18-19, gives examples of slogans on wafers.

12. William Lloyd Garrison, *Thoughts on African Colonization* (1832; rpt., New York, 1969), p. xix; the *Liberator*, November 12, 1831; Bayard Tuckerman, *William Jay and the Constitutional Movement for Abolition of Slavery* (New York, 1893), p. 37. Robert H. Abzug, "The Influence of Garrisonian Abolitionists' Fear of Slave Violence on the Antislavery Argument," *Journal of Negro History* 55 (January 1970): 15-28, sees fear of slave insurrection as one factor impelling Garrisonians to immediate emancipation. In that I think he is correct. He also argues that western abolitionists did not share the Garrisonians' fears and that the issue of violence died down after 1840. Those points seem doubtful to me.

13. For examples see Moncure D. Conway, *The Rejected Stone; Or, Insurrection vs. Resurrection in America. By a native of Virginia*, 2nd ed. (Boston, 1862), pp. 122-24; Elizur Wright, "The Horrors of St. Domingo," *Quarterly Anti-Slavery Magazine*, 1 (May 1834): 67; (August 1834), 116-22; the *Emancipator*, November 30, 1833; the *Philanthropist*, April 7, 1841.

14. Garrison to R. D. Webb, February 27, 1842, Ms Am 1.1, v. 3, no. 85, BPL; the *Liberator*, October 17, 1856, and June 2, 1843; *Disunion. Address of The American Anti-Slavery Society; and F. Jackson's Letter on the Pro-Slavery Character of the Constitution* (New York, 1845), pp. 21-22.

15. The *Emancipator*, May 31, 1838; the *Radical Abolitionist* 2 (March 1857): 69. See also a protest by New England abolitionists in the *Liberator*, June 7, 1844; and the letter of "O" to the *National Anti-Slavery Standard*, April 25, 1844.

16. The *Liberator*, January 8, 1831. See also Gerda Lerner, *The Grimké Sisters from South Carolina: Rebels Against Slavery* (Boston, 1967), pp. 119-20, 123-27.

17. Chapman to Bell [?], December 10, 1850, Ms Am 9.2, v. 5, no. 70, BPL; Stewart to Gamaliel Bailey, April, 1842, in Luther R. Marsh, *Writings and Speeches of Alvan Stewart, on Slavery* (New York, 1860), p. 266 (also, pp. 113-14, 251, 260); report from the *Friend of Man*, reprinted in the *Liberator*, February 11, 1842.

18. The *Liberator*, February 4, 1842; August 25, September 22, December 8, 1843.

19. The *National Era*, January 8, 1857; October 27, 1859.

20. The *Liberator*, January 21, 1842; March 5, 1858. See also Perry, *Radical Abolitionism*, and Mabee, *Black Freedom*.

21. The *Emancipator*, June 7, 1838; the *Liberator*, December 22, 1837. Also see George Perkins, "Can Slaves Rightfully Resist and Fight?" in Julia Griffiths, *Autographs for Freedom*, 2 vols. (1853; rpt., Miami, Florida, 1969), 1: 33-4.

22. Birney to Thomas Wentworth Higginson, October 27, 1856, quoted in Tilden G. Edelstein, *Strange Enthusiasm: A Life of Thomas Wentworth Higginson* (New Haven, 1968), p. 192 (also pp. 197-200). See also Bertram Wyatt-Brown, "William Lloyd Garrison and Antislavery Unity: A Reappraisal," *Civil War History* 13 (March 1967): 17-18.

23. [Gerrit Smith], *Speeches of Gerrit Smith in Congress* (New York, 1855), pp. 401-2; Octavius Brooks Frothingham, *Gerrit Smith: A Biography*, 2nd ed. (New York, 1879), p. 240. See also Smith to the Liberty Party Convention, in the *Principia*, September 15, 1860. The standard biography of Smith is Ralph Volney Harlow, *Gerrit Smith: Philanthropist and Reformer* (New York, 1939)—useful but out-dated.

24. The *Liberator*, January 23, February 6, February 13, 1857 (c.f. June 4, 1858, in which Garrison deplored the rising spirit of violence).

25. American Anti-Slavery Society, *Anti-Slavery History of the John Brown Year* (New York, 1860), p. 130; Phillips, "Harper's Ferry" (1859), in *Speeches*, first ser., p. 263; the *National Anti-Slavery Standard*, October 29, 1859. Wyatt-Brown, "William Lloyd Garrison and Antislavery Unity," shows Garrison and the Tappans trying to stem the tide of violent sentiment. John Demos, "The Antislavery Movement and the Problem of Violent Means," *New England Quarterly* 37 (December 1964): 522-4, speaks of the breakdown of the nonviolent consensus (although he places it earlier than I would) and gives examples of nonresistants renouncing the faith.

26. Stephen B. Oates, *To Purge This Land with Blood: A Biography of John Brown* (New York, 1970), p. 240.

27. Mabee, *Black Freedom*, pp. 333-70. Cf. Lydia Maria Child's remarks in Philadelphia Female Anti-Slavery Society Minute Book, November 12, 1863, Pennsylvania Abolition Society Papers, Pennsylvania Historical Society.

CHAPTER 3

1. [Lyman Beecher], *The Autobiography of Lyman Beecher*, ed. Barbara Cross, 2 vols. (Boston, 1961), 1: 252-53; Bernard Weisberger, *They Gathered at the River: The Story of the Great Revivalists and Their Impact on Religion in America* (Chicago, 1966), 77-8.

2. The classic account of the connection between the revival and antislavery, first published in 1933, is Gilbert Hobbs Barnes, *The Anti-Slavery Impulse: 1830-1844* (New York, 1964). Other deservedly well-known monographs on the relationship between evangelical Protestantism and reform are: Whitney R. Cross, *The Burned-Over District: The Social and Intellectual History of Enthusiastic Religion in Western New York, 1800-1850* (New York, 1950); Timothy L. Smith, *Revivalism and Social Reform: American Protestantism on the Eve of the Civil War* (New York, 1965); Clifford S. Griffin, *Their Brother's Keepers: Moral Stewardship in the United States, 1800-1865* (New Brunswick, New Jersey, 1960); David B. Davis, "The Emergence of Immediatism in British and American Antislavery Thought," *Mississippi Valley Historical Review* 49 (September 1962), 209-30; and Anne C. Loveland, "Evangelicalism and Immediate Emancipation' in American Antislavery Thought," *Journal of Southern History* 32 (May 1966): 172-88. Recent efforts of special significance are: Lewis Perry, *Radical Abolitionism: Anarchy and the Government of God in Antislavery Thought*

(Ithaca, 1973); Lois W. Banner, "Religious Benevolence as Social Control: A Critique of an Interpretation," *Journal of American History* 60 (June 1973): 23-42; and John L. Hammond, "Revival Religion and Antislavery Politics," *American Sociological Review* 39 (April 1974): 175-86, the latter of which attempts to relate evangelical Protestantism to political behavior. Also see Perry Miller, *The Life of the Mind in America* (New York, 1965); and Ernest Lee Tuveson, *Redeemer Nation: The Idea of America's Millennial Role* (Chicago, 1968).

3. The most complicated and carefully qualified statement of this argument is Davis, "The Emergence of Immediatism," pp. 209-30. Davis's perspective is much wider than that of those who merely stress the revival, but his attempt is to show that immediate emancipation was "an appropriate doctrine for a romantic and evangelical age." See also Loveland, "Evangelicalism and 'Immediate Emancipation,'" pp. 172-88.

4. Hammond, "Revival Religion and Antislavery Politics;" and Cross, *Burned-Over District*, p. 226.

5. William T. Allan, Sereno W. Streeter, J. W. Alvord, and James A. Thome, to Theodore Dwight Weld, August 9, 1836, in *Letters of Theodore Dwight Weld, Angelina Grimké and Sarah Grimké: 1822-1844*, ed. Gilbert H. Barnes and Dwight L. Dumond, 2 vols. (New York, 1934), 1: 323-29. Leonard L. Richards, *"Gentlemen of Property and Standing": Anti-Abolition Mobs in Jacksonian America* (New York, 1970), p. 146 fn. 16, notes that his analysis of abolitionists and anti-abolitionist rioters shows a significantly greater identification of the former with New Light Presbyterianism, although the correlation between it and anti-slavery was far from perfect. Finney's influence is an important (and over-drawn) part of Barnes, *Anti-Slavery Impulse*. There is a superior, but misguidedly anti-Garrisonian, history of Oberlin: Robert Samuel Fletcher, *A History of Oberlin College from Its Foundation through the Civil War*, 2 vols. (Oberlin, 1943). Donald G. Matthews, *Slavery and Methodism: A Chapter in American Morality, 1780-1845* (Princeton, 1965), is a significant work on the fate of abolitionism in an evangelical sect. There is a good short sketch of Leavitt's activities in Charles C. Cole, Jr., *The Social Ideas of the Northern Evangelists, 1826-1860* (New York, 1954), pp. 34-43.

6. Irving H. Bartlett, *Wendell Phillips: Brahmin Radical* (Boston, 1961), p. 58. Samuel J. May, *Some Recollections of Our Antislavery Conflict* (Boston, 1869), p. 337, lists prominent Unitarians in the Massachusetts branch of the movement, including some names I do not mention here and omitting others.

7. Mathews, *Slavery and Methodism*, pp. 12-13, 109, 144-45, 166-67. Smith, *Revivalism*, 184-85; Lucius C. Matlack, *The History of American Slavery and Methodism, from 1780 to 1849: And History of the Wesleyan Connection of America; In Two Parts* (New York, 1849); and Lewis M. Purifoy, "The Southern Methodist Church and the Proslavery Argument," *Journal of Southern History* 32 (August 1966): 325-41, also provide useful information.

8. Russel B. Nye, "Marius Robinson, A Forgotten Abolitionist Leader," *The Ohio State Archaeological and Historical Quarterly* 55 (April-June 1946): 138-39.

9. The autobiographical fragment is in Cross, *Autobiography of Lyman Beecher*, 2: 232. Benjamin P. Thomas, *Theodore Weld, Crusader for Freedom* (New Brunswich, New Jersey, 1950), 37-38, dates Weld's commitment (I think correctly) from late 1832. In September of that year Weld still pinned hope on the Colonization Society. Weld to Birney, September 27, 1832, in *Letters of James Gillespie Birney, 1831-1857*, ed. Dwight L. Dumond, 2 vols. (New York, 1938), 1: 27.

10. Birney dated his conversion in a letter to Robert H. Folger, July 24, 1844 (from which the quote above is taken), and in Birney to Ralph R. Gurley, July 12, 1832, in Dumond, *Birney Letters*, 2: 826, 1: 9; see also 1: 242 fn 4. Betty Fladeland, *James Gillespie Birney: Slaveholder to Abolitionist* (Ithaca, 1955),

pp. 78-82, traces Birney's path from Colonization to Abolitionism.

11. American Anti-Slavery Society, *Proceedings of the American Anti-Slavery Society at Its Third Decade* . . . (New York, 1864), p. 32; Ira V. Brown, "Miller McKim and Pennsylvania Abolitionism," *Pennsylvania History* 30 (January 1963): 59. Much of McKim's questioning came out in letters to Lucretia Mott; see Anna Davis Hallowell, ed., *James and Lucretia Mott. Life and Letters* (Boston, 1884), pp. 120, 193, 261, 281; and Otelia Cromwell, *Lucretia Mott* (Cambridge, Mass., 1958), pp. 38-40. Loveland, "Evangelicalism and 'Immediate Emancipation,'" p. 179, notes that the "failure of evangelicalism as a reform of religion also impelled converts into abolitionism."

12. *Anti-Slavery Record* 1 (April, 1835): 46; Birney to Lewis Tappan, August 23, 1837, in Dumond, *Birney Letters*, 1: 419; the *Liberator*, December 10, 1841 (see also issue of January 10, 1840, and September 23, 1842, for mention of Southern revivals); and American Anti-Slavery Society, *The Anti-Slavery History of the John Brown Year; Being the Twenty-Seventh Annual Report of the American Anti-Slavery Society* (New York, 1861; rpt., New York, 1969), p. 34. A letter to the *Philanthropist*, June 23, 1840, argued that revivals were the same North and South and concluded (inconclusively) that they produced some antislavery sentiment sometimes.

13. Smith, *Revivalism*, pp. 149-50; Weld to Lewis Tappan, November 17, 1835, and Finney to Weld, July 21, 1836, in Barnes and Dumond, *Weld-Grimké Letters*, 1: 244, 319.

14. Fletcher, *History of Oberlin*, 1, 252-53, 267; William T. Allan, Sereno W. Streeter, J. W. Alvord, and James A. Thome to Weld, August 9, 1836, in Barnes and Dumond, *Weld-Grimké Letters*, 1: 323-29; the *Liberator*, March 27, 1846 (quoting and commenting on an article in the *Oberlin Evangelist*), the *Philanthropist*, April 14, 1840.

15. James C. Birney Ms Diary, March 15, March 29, 1840, Birney Mss, LC; Elizur Wright to James Wright, October 10, 1837, Wright Mss, LC. Also Bertram Wyatt-Brown, *Lewis Tappan and the Evangelical War Against Slavery* (Cleveland, 1969), p. 185; the *Liberator*, January 9, 1846; and Oliver Johnson, *William Lloyd Garrison and His Times* . . . (Boston, 1880), p. 68.

16. William Goodell, *Slavery and Anti-Slavery; A History of the Great Struggle in Both Hemispheres; With a View of the Slavery Question in the United States* (New York, 1853), pp. 388-89, 402ff, 425, 435.

17. The *Liberator*, April 9, 1831; *Proceedings of the General Anti-Slavery Convention, Called by the Committee of the British and Foreign Anti-Slavery Society, and Held in London, from Friday, June 12th, to Tuesday, June 23rd, 1840* (London, 1841), pp. 270, 140.

18. Spooner to George Bradburn, January 30, 1847, Spooner Papers, NYHS; the *Liberator*, June 4, 1852. Wyatt-Brown (*Lewis Tappan*, p. 249), argues that in 1840 Christian antislavery was growing old, losing its grip, and becoming more narrowly sectarian.

19. Goodell to Phelps, November 25, 1845, Phelps Mss, v. 15, no. 82, BPL; William Goodell, *The American Slave Code in Theory and Practice: Its Distinctive Features Shown by its Statutes, Judicial Decisions and Illustrative Facts*, 4th ed. (New York, 1853), pp. 15-18; *The Principia*, January 21, 1860; the *National Anti-Slavery Standard*, December 18, 1858; the *Liberator*, April 9, 1831.

20. Louis Filler, *The Crusade Against Slavery: 1830-1860* (New York, 1963), p. 24 fn 34, cites John A. Collins, who repudiated religion when he left the movement. Elizur Wright referred to himself as an atheist long after the Civil War, but he may have been closer to being an agnostic. See Philip Green Wright and Elizabeth Q. Wright, *Elizur Wright: The Father of Life Insurance* (Chicago, 1937), pp. 308-9.

21. Goodell to A. A. Phelps, April 24, 1837, Phelps Mss, v. 7, no. 6, BPL.

Beriah Green to James G. Birney, August 2, 1847, in Dumond, *Birney Letters*, 2: 1078: "I know of no men among us, whose influence is every way so pernicious as that of the clergy." These were strong words for a minister.

22. Weld to Birney, May 23, 1842, in Dumond, *Birney Letters*, 2: 693; the *Liberator*, August 11, 1837; August 9, 1839. See also Phelps to E. G. Howe, September 8, September 2, 1837, Ms Am 21.7, nos. 49 and 45, BPL.

23. Phelps, *Lectures on Slavery*, pp. 17, 18; May, *Recollections*, p. 329; "An Appeal to the Philanthropists of Great Britain on Behalf of Oberlin College" (1839), in Barnes and Dumond, *Weld-Grimké Letters*, 2: 743. There were occasional opposing statements. A. A. Phelps to Samuel J. May (November 15, 1837, Phelps Mss, v. 7, no. 84, BPL) argued that "the ministry are in advance of the people on this subject." But Phelps was, at the time, upset with the Garrisonians for their anticlericalism. Phelps himself had been quite critical of the clergy in the early stages of controversies over the Pastoral Letter and the Clerical Appeal.

24. The *Liberator*, July 1, July 22, 1853; June 25, 1847; Charles K. Whipple, *Relations of Anti-Slavery to Religion* (New York, [1856]), p. 13; the *Liberator*, August 20, 1858. Green's discourse appears in the *Liberator*, April 23, and April 30, 1841. Although Green had parted company with the Garrisonians, his comments were in line with their beliefs. The *Liberator*, April 30, April 2, 1858. See also Weisberger, *They Gathered at the River*, p. 139, on the increasing formalism of the revival.

25. Smith to Weld, July 11, 1840, in Barnes and Dumond, *Weld-Grimké Letters*, 2: 850 (see also Smith to Garrison, printed in the *Liberator*, February 22, 1839: "Blessed be God, that, in proportion as men are abolitionized, sectarianism loses its iron hold upon them!"); Goodell to Phelps, September 12, 1839, Phelps Mss, BPL; *National Principia*, November 19, 1859.

26. Joshua Leavitt to Roger Leavitt, January 5, 1825, Leavitt Mss, LC; Phelps to Lewis Tappan, March 1, March 19, 1838, Tappan Mss, LC; Phelps, *Lectures on Slavery*, p. xi; the *Liberator*, June 17, 1853. Birney's son delicately passed over the more peculiar turnings by saying "his nature was too broad for sectarianism." William Birney, *James G. Birney and His Times: The Genesis of the Republican Party with Some Account of Abolition Movements in the South Before 1820* (New York, 1890), p. 54. Birney attacked sectarianism in his Ms Diary, October 23, October 24, 1850, Birney Mss, LC.

27. On McKim see note 11 above; Gerda Lerner, *The Grimké Sisters from South Carolina: Rebels Against Slavery* (Boston, 1967), pp. 40-41, 58; Wright and Wright, *Elizur Wright*, pp. 9, 87-89; Child to Convers Francis, May 31, 1840; Child to Anne Whitney, June 1879, in [Child], *Letters of Lydia Maria Child. With a Biographical Introduction by John Greenleaf Whittier and an Appendix by Wendell Phillips* (Boston, 1883), pp. 7, 255.

28. Lerner, *Grimké Sisters*, pp. 306-8; Wright and Wright, *Elizur Wright*, pp. 288-309; Child to Convers Francis, February 27, 1856, in [Child], *Letters of Lydia Maria Child*, p. 74.

29. Pillsbury and Foster recount their spiritual journeys in the *Liberator*, July 23, 1858; September 1, 1843; on Himes and Fitch see the *Liberator*, February 10, 1843; on Storrs and Wilson see Mathews, *Slavery and Methodism*, p. 230; on Sunderland see the *Liberator*, January 4, 1850, and Filler, *Crusade*, p. 115. There is also information on Storrs, Himes, and Fitch (as Millerites) in Cross, *Burned-Over District*, pp. 292-93, 296. Except for Foster, Pillsbury, and Henry C. Wright, these men were non-Garrisonians, representatives of the wing of antislavery presumed by historians to have been more conservative and less given to heterodoxy.

30. Weld to Angelina Grimké Weld and Sarah M. Grimké, February 17, 1842; Weld to Angelina Grimké Weld; February 24, 1842, in Barnes and Dumond, *Weld-Grimké Letters*, 2: 924, 933; Weld to Birney, December 16, 1848, in Du-

mond, *Birney Letters*, 2: 1121. See also: Sallie Holley to Caroline Putman, December 19, 1852, in John White Chadwick, ed., *A Life for Liberty: Anti-Slavery and Other Letters of Sallie Holley* (1899; reprint, New York, 1969), pp. 107-8; Fladeland, *Birney*, pp. 285ff; and Lerner, *Grimké Sisters*, p. 328.

31. Birney Ms Diary, February 4, 1840 (also entries of February 28, March 2, May 2, 1850), Birney Mss LC; Fladeland, *Birney*, pp. 271-72, 285ff.

32. The *Emancipator Extra* June 25, 1833; Fletcher, *History of Oberlin*, 1: 254. On come-outerism see Perry, *Radical Abolitionism*, pp. 92-128; and Carleton Mabee, *Black Freedom: The Nonviolent Abolitionists from 1830 Through the Civil War* (New York, 1970), pp. 216-43.

33. The *Emancipator*, December 6, 1838. See also a letter of 1854 by William Jay, quoted in Bayard Tuckerman, *William Jay and the Constitutional Movement for the Abolition of Slavery* (New York, 1893), p. 148.

34. Birney to Tappan, July 4, 1836, Tappan Mss, LC; Birney to Gerrit Smith, June 1, 1846, in Dumond, *Birney Letters*, 2: 1023; Wyatt-Brown, *Lewis Tappan*, p. 322, argued that "in some ways, Lewis was not very far from Garrison's 'come-outer' position." See Tappan, "Fellowshipping Slaveholders," in Griffiths, *Autographs for Freedom*, 2: 163-64.

35. The *Liberator*, April 21, 1843, reprinted and commented on the essay, which originally appeared in *The Christian Investigator;* May to J. B. Estlin, December 29, 1845, Ms B, 1.6, v. 2, no. 10, BPL. See also the *Liberator* February 25, 1842; October 22, 1847; and William Goodell, *Slavery and Anti-Slavery* . . . (New York, 1853), pp. 473, 488-89.

36. Gerald Sorin, *The New York Abolitionists: A Case Study of Political Radicalism* (Westport, Connecticut, 1971), p. 61; Frothingham, *Gerrit Smith*, pp. 53-67.

37. The *Liberator*, October 1, 1841; the *Philanthropist*, July 5, 1843; the *Liberator*, July 7, 1843; Matlack, *Slavery and Methodism*, p. 320. See also Goodell, *Slavery and Anti-Slavery*, pp. 488-89.

38. Child to Eliza Scudder, 1864, in [Child], *Letters of Lydia Maria Child*, p. 185; Green to James G. Birney, August 2, 1847, in Dumond, *Birney Letters*, 2: 1078-89; Fletcher, *History of Oberlin*, 1: 234.

39. The *Liberator*, May 23, 1850; June 14, 1850; September 29, 1848, Henry C. Wright, *Anthropology; Or, the Science of Man* . . . (Cincinnati, 1850), p. 11; the *Liberator*, May 14, 1852. Note also Garrison's commentary on Wright in the *Liberator*, November 24, 1848. Garrison denied that the Bible was the sole judge of morality, asserting that he thought highly of it but "as a human composition."

40. Samuel Crothers, *Strictures on African Slavery* (Rossville, Ohio, 1833), p. 40; Birney to Gerrit Smith, October 29, 1857, in Dumond, *Birney Letters*, 2: 1175.

41. The *Liberator*, December 30, 1842.

42. Whittier to Ann E. Wendell, August 19, 1842, in Samuel T. Pickard, *Life and Letters of John Greenleaf Whittier*, 2 vols. (Boston, 1894), 1: 281; Mott to Richard and Hannah Webb, February 25, 1842, in Hallowell, *James and Lucretia Mott*, p. 225.

43. Green to James G. Birney, August 2, 1847, in Dumond, *Birney Letters*, 2: 1078. See also Child to [Mrs. F. G. Shaw], April 2, and May 25, 1873, Shaw Coll., NYPL.

44. Chadwick, *Life for Liberty*, p. 32; Wright, *Myron Holley*, pp. 39, 207-8, 310-15; Tilden G. Edelstein, *Strange Enthusiasm: A Life of Thomas Wentworth Higginson* (New Haven, 1968), pp. 66-67, 82, 310; Frothingham, *Gerrit Smith*, pp. 73-74, 90; Cromwell, *Lucretia Mott*, pp. 180-81; Hallowell, *James and Lucretia Mott*, pp. 424-27. Wyatt-Brown, *Lewis Tappan*, p. 311, notes many abolitionists who adopted some form of the religion of humanity. Garrison even criticized Finney—of all people—for being "too much given to metaphysics, to logic, to legal niceties, to theological speculations," which says more about Garrison's tol-

erance for theology than it does about Finney (*Liberator*, September 17, 1841).

45. Goodell to A. A. Phelps, September 12, 1839, Phelps Mss, BPL. The *Liberator*, January 1, 1847; Conway, *Autobiography, Memories, and Experiences of Moncure Daniel Conway*, 2 vols. (Boston, 1904), 1: 184.

46. American Anti-Slavery Society, *Proceedings . . . Third Decade*, p. 53. Also Cushing Strout, *The New Heavens and New Earth: Political Religion in America* (New York, 1974), pp. 159-72; and Loveland, "Evangelicalism and 'Immediate Emancipation,'" pp. 179-80.

CHAPTER 4

1. On Rogers see the *Liberator*, February 21, 1845. On Andrews' views see Stephen Pearl Andrews, ed., *Love, Marriage, and Divorce, and the Sovereignty of the Individual . . .* (New York, 1853); volume 2 of Joseph Dorfman, *The Economic Mind in American Civilization: 1606-1865* (New York, 1953), pp. 671-78; and Madeline B. Stern, *The Pantarch: A Biography of Stephen Pearl Andrews* (Austin, Texas, 1968).

2. The *Liberator*, December 17, 1831; Angelina Grimké to L. L. Dodge, July 14, 1836, Weld Mss, LC. Garrison tried to reconcile individual regeneration and organizational efforts in the *Liberator*, August 9, 1844. See also [Maria Weston Chapman], *Right and Wrong in Boston . . .*, 2nd ed. (Boston, 1836), pp. 41, 43-45; and articles by Maria Weston Chapman and Edmund Quincy in the *Liberator*, December 23, 1845.

3. Weld to James G. Birney, May 23, 1842, in Dwight L. Dumond, ed., *Letters of James Gillespie Birney, 1831-1857*, 2 vols. (New York, 1938), 2: 693; the *Philanthropist*, July 23, 1842.

4. [Theodore Dwight Weld], *The Bible Against Slavery. An Inquiry into the Patriarchal and Mosaic Systems on the Subject of Human Rights*, 4th ed. (New York, 1838), p. 10; the *Liberator*, May 23, 1835.

5. Amos A. Phelps, *Lectures on Slavery and Its Remedy* (Boston, 1834), pp. 177-79. This kind of reasoning had other applications besides to slavery. Wendell Phillips argued that increased freedom for women would be a means of controlling sensuality and vice among them. (Phillips, "Woman's Rights" (1851), in *Speeches, Lectures, and Letters*, first ser., ed. James Redpath (Boston, 1902), pp. 32-34.

6. The *Liberator*, September 4, 1840; June 9, 1837; October 26, 1838; October 3, 1845. Lewis Curtis Perry, "Aantislavery and Anarchy: A Study of the Ideas of Abolitionism before the Civil War" (Ph.D. diss., Cornell University, 1967), pp. 34-36, 51-52, comments on the paradox of assuming that order will arise out of anarchy. Professor Perry's analysis also appears in "Versions of Anarchism in the Antislavery Movement," *American Quarterly* 22 (Winter 1968), p. 771; and in fullest form in *Radical Abolitionism: Anarchy and the Government of God in Antislavery Thought* (Ithaca, 1973).

7. Phillips, "The Metropolitan Police" (1863), in *Speeches*, first ser., p. 501; Tappan, *The Life of Arthur Tappan* (New York, 1870), pp. 106-7.

8. James McPherson, *The Struggle for Equality: Abolitionists and the Negro in the Civil War and Reconstruction* (Princeton, 1964), pp. 172-73, argues that abolitionists published reports from the South during the war which differed from sentiments expressed in personal documents.

9. Parker's speech before the Massachusetts Anti-Slavery Society, January 29, 1858, is in the *Liberator*, February 18, 1858; Phillips, "Harper's Ferry" (1859), in *Speeches*, first ser., p. 281. See also Mary Thacher Higginson, ed., *Letters and Journals of Thomas Wentworth Higginson, 1846-1906* (Boston, 1921), p. 213 (in which Higginson congratulates himself for his "constitutional affinity for undeveloped races"); and George M. Frederickson, *The Black Image in the White Mind: The Debate on Afro-American Character and Destiny, 1817-1914* (New York, 1971), pp. 97-164. Much of the material in this section falls within Fred-

rickson's aptly-named category of "romantic racialism."

10. Whittier, "Justice and Expediency," in the *Emancipator*, October 12, 1833. There are other early statements of this latter position in the *American Anti-Slavery Reporter* 1 (February 1834): 1; the *Anti-Slavery Record* 1 (March 1835): 25-8; and L. Maria Child, *The Patriarchical Institution, as Described by Members of Its Own Family* (New York, 1860), pp. 10-18.

11. The *Anti-Slavery Record* 2 (March 1836): 2; William Allen in the *Liberator*, November 26, 1852; Parker in the *Liberator*, February 19, 1858.

12. Phelps, *Lectures on Slavery*, p. 223.

13. Originally in the *Liberty Bell* (1841), also reprinted in the *Liberator*, January 8, 1841.

14. The *Liberator*, March 12, 1858.

15. The *Anti-Slavery Record* 2 (March 1836): 2.

16. Quincy, April 13, 1840, in "An Anti-Slavery Album," p. 165, in Western Anti-Slavery Society Mss, LC. Abolitionists were not the only people to believe in the peculiar religiosity of black people.

17. Angelina Grimké to Sarah Douglass, February 22, 1837, in *Letters of Theodore Dwight Weld, Angelina Grimké Weld, and Sarah Grimké, 1822-1844, Gilbert H. Barnes and Dwight L. Dumond, eds., 2 vols. (New York, 1934), 1: 364-65.

18. Winthrop D. Jordan, *White Over Black: American Attitudes Toward the Negro, 1550-1812* (Chapel Hill, 1968); for a similar process, revolving around the Indian, see Roy Harvey Pearce, *Savagism and Civilization: A Study of the Indian and the American Mind*, rev. ed. (Baltimore, 1965).

19. Child, "African Inventors," the *Liberty Bell* (1852), p. 22; the *Emancipator*, November 18, 1834.

20. Quotes are from [Chapman], *Right and Wrong in Boston*, p. 79; the *Philanthropist*, September 29, 1840; and Parker, "The Nature of Man," in *Lessons from the World of Matter and the World of Man*, ed. Rufus Leighton (Boston, n.d.), p. 69.

21. The *Emancipator*, December 22, 1836. On the early origins of the idea of a "moral sense" see Ernest Tuveson, "The Origins of the 'Moral Sense,'" *The Huntington Library Quarterly* 11 (May 1948): 241-59. For its place in Jefferson's thoughts see Jordan, *White Over Black*, pp. 439-41, 452.

22. For a statement of the radical potential in the moral sense, see Staughton Lynd, *Intellectual Origins of American Radicalism* (New York, 1968), pp. 27-37.

23. American Anti-Slavery Society, *Proceedings of the American Anti-Slavery Society at its Third Decade . . .* (New York, 1864), p. 24; the *Emancipator*, April 8, 1834; Gilbert Haven, *National Sermons. Sermons, Speeches and Letters on Slavery and Its War . . .* (Boston, 1869), p. 9; the *Liberator*, January 26, 1833. See also William Goodell, "Human Rights," part 2, in the *Emancipator*, October, 1835; and Lydia Maria Child to Convers Francis, December 19, 1835, in [Lydia Maria Child], *Letters of Lydia Maria Child. With a Biographical Introduction by John G. Whittier and an Appendix by Wendell Phillips* (Boston, 1883), p. 18. Lynd, *Intellectual Origins*, pp. 110-11, sees Garrison's emphasis on the conscience as a faith in the common man. This emphasis, however, was shared by men who did not measure up to Lynd's standards of radicalism. Garrison's own faith was balanced by a conscience which would not bend to majority will unless convinced of its rectitude. Lynd glosses over this antidemocratic feature of a set of attitudes he himself shares. Abolitionists could only believe that the people were potentially right, not that their voice was God's.

24. [George Bourne], *Picture of Slavery in the United States of America* (Middletown, Connecticut, 1834), p. 36. See also James G. Birney Ms Diary, February 27, 1850, Birney Mss, LC. Birney referred to slavery as "a condition in which men make no improvement of those faculties which God has given them." The idea did not originate in the 1830s. Green, in *The Chattel Principle*, p. 4,

quoted the Presbyterian General Assembly Minutes of 1818 to much the same effect.

25. Stanton speaking before a Ladies Anti-Slavery Meeting in Boston, quoted in the *Liberator*, February 11, 1837; the *Liberator*, July 16, 1841. See also: Weld in a reply to James Hall, editor of *The Western Monthly Magazine*, March, 1834, in Barnes and Dumond, *The Weld-Grimké Letters*, 1: 143; Child to Lucy Osgood, 1870 (see also Child to Convers Francis, July 27, 1834, in [Child], *Letters of Lydia Maria Child*, pp. 209, 15).

26. Smith, *Revivalism*, p. 95. Leo Marx, *The Machine in the Garden: Technology and the Pastoral Ideal in America* (New York, 1964), pp. 266, 274, contains interesting remarks about use of the head and heart dichotomy by Hawthorne and Melville.

27. Jordan, *White Over Black*, pp. 440-57. Clearly the difference between generations of abolitionists was not absolute. The *Emancipator*, November 18, 1834, quoted one of the earlier antislavery propagandists in confirmation of its own sentiments on the subject: "The disparagers of the colored race make *intellect* the test. . . . But *moral feeling* is far better than that."

28. A. E. Grimké, *Letters to Catherine E. Beecher in Reply to an Essay on Slavery and Abolitionism, Addressed to A. E. Grimké*, rev. ed. (Boston, 1838), p. 114.

29. Henry C. Wright, *Marriage and Parentage: Or, the Reproductive Element in Man, as a Means to His Elevation and Happiness*, 5th ed. (Boston, 1866), p. 249. This was first published in 1854.

30. Adin Ballou, *History of the Hopedale Community, From Its Inception to Its Virtual Submergence in the Hopedale Parish*, ed. William S. Heywood (Lowell, Massachusetts, 1897), pp. 17, 21-22.

31. William Birney, *James G. Birney and His Times: The Genesis of the Republican Party with Some Account of Abolition Movements in the South before 1820* (New York, 1890), pp. 26-27.

32. "The Diversities of Men," *Quarterly Anti-Slavery Magazine* 2 (January 1837): 208; the *National Anti-Slavery Standard*, February 1, 1849 (the author of the statement was probably James Russell Lowell).

33. L. Maria Child, *Letters from New York*, 1st ser. (New York, 1843), pp. 250-51.

34. L. Maria Child, *An Appeal in Favor of Americans Called Africans* (Boston, 1836; rpt., New York, 1968), pp. 188-89; "M.B.C." to the *National Era*, June 3, 1847. For a strong statement on the effects of the institution of slavery upon the slave's behavior see Richard Hildreth, *Despotism in America: An Inquiry into the Nature, Results, and Legal Basis of the Slave-Holding System in the United States* (Boston, 1840), pp. 48-56.

35. [Bourne], *Picture of Slavery*, pp. 83, 86, 87, 98, 104, 122, 131; George Thompson, *Prison Life and Reflections* . . . (Hartford, 1849), p. 38; the *Liberator*, February 5, 1841. Abolitionists were aware that Southerners also worried over the effects of slavery upon whites. LaRoy Sunderland, *Anti-Slavery Manual, Containing a Collection of Facts and Arguments on American Slavery*, 2nd ed. (New York, 1837), pp. 30-32, for example, quoted Jefferson on the subject, as did Child, *Appeal*, pp. 22-23. For statements of the idea that prejudice is "unnatural" and a product of slavery see the *Liberator*, March 12, 1831 (letter to Garrison); October 16, 1840; January 13, 1843 (Maria Weston Chapman); March 5, 1852 (Gerrit Smith). Lewis Tappan, *The Life of Arthur Tappan* (New York, 1870), p. 131, makes the common argument that prejudice was confined to America. Haven, *National Sermons*, p. 134, apparently thinking of caste prejudice in India, claimed that prejudice could stem from religion or from social condition. For an early statement of the belief that prejudice stemmed from oppression, expressed in a private communication, see Samuel J. May to Garrison, March 20, 1831, Ms

Am 1.2, v. 1, nos. 20-21, BPL.

36. *American Anti-Slavery Reporter* 1 (March 1834): 40; Hildreth, *Despotism in America*, pp. 301-2. The idea that Northerners going South became quickly brutalized did not originate with Mrs. Stowe; for early statements see comments by Amos Dresser in the *Liberator*, February 11, 1837, and the *Liberator*, March 4, 1837. Child, *Appeal*, p. 28, gave the example of a Northerner going to the West Indies.

37. Hildreth, *Despotism in America*, pp. 165-66.

38. "A Review—The Elements of Moral Science," *Quarterly Anti-Slavery Magazine* 1 (January 1836): 144-45; Garrison to Henry C. Wright, April 1, 1843; October 1, 1844, Ms Am 1.1, v. 3, no. 106; v. 4, no. 10, BPL; the *Liberator*, January 5, 1844. Also see Child to Lucy Osgood, January 16, 1859, in [Child], *Letters of Lydia Maria Child*, p. 99.

39. Child, *The Patriarchical Institution*, p. 49; [George Bourne], *Slavery Illustrated in Its Effects Upon Woman and Domestic Society* (Boston, 1837), pp. 9-13. For a statement of the idea that there was a reciprocal relationship between environment and conscience, see "The Influence of Slavery on Slaveholders," *Quarterly Anti-Slavery Magazine* 1 (July 1836): 315.

40. It is tempting to attribute another failing to environmentalism: the relaxation of reform zeal once slavery ended. One could believe that all black people needed was a simple liberation from the oppressive atmosphere of slavery and then human nature would assert itself—"to be set up erect on their feet with full liberty to use their faculties of whatever kind, as others do, for their own improvement" (James G. Birney to William Wright, June 20, 1845, in Dumond, *Birney Letters*, 2: 945). I am not entirely persuaded that abolitionists did renounce reform after the Civil War any more than could reasonably be expected for aging men and women who had been at a thankless task for decades. Other factors besides environmentalist assumptions (and fatigue) also figure into abolitionist behavior during Reconstruction: the lack of a real belief that government might serve as an active agent of reform; a basic optimism concerning America; and a feeling that work brought inevitable reward.

CHAPTER 5

1. Charles K. Whipple, *The Family Relation, as Affected by Slavery* (Cincinnati, [1858], p. 17; [Theodore Dwight Weld], *American Slavery As It Is: Testimony of a Thousand Witnesses* (New York, 1839), p. 117; the *Philanthropist*, April 14, 1840.

2. Amos A. Phelps, *Lectures on Slavery and Its Remedy* (Boston, 1834), p. 60; the *Liberator*, March 1, 1850; A. E. Grimké, *Letters to Catherine E. Beecher in Reply to an Essay on Slavery and Abolitionism, Addressed to A. E. Grimké*, rev. ed. (Boston, 1838), p. 8.

3. Angelina Grimké Weld to Anna R. Frost, [August, 1839], in *Letters of Theodore Dwight Weld, Angelina Grimké Weld, and Sarah Grimké, 1822-1844*, ed. Gilbert H. Barnes and Dwight L. Dumond, 2 vols. (New York, 1934), 2: 789; Goodell, "Lectures on Anti-Slavery," part 5 (most conveniently reprinted in the *Liberator*, June 21, 1839).

4. J. Elizabeth Jones, *The Young Abolitionists, Or Conversations on Slavery* (Boston, 1848), p. 54; [Beriah Green], *The Chattel Principle the Abhorrence of Jesus Christ and the Apostles; Or, No Refuge for American Slavery in the New Testament* (New York, 1839), p. 17.

5. Whipple, *Family Relations*, p. 23; [Weld], *American Slavery As It Is*, p. 115.

6. John White Chadwick, ed., *A Life for Liberty: Anti-Slavery and Other Letters of Sallie Holley* (1899; reprint, New York, 1969), p. 123.

7. Even abolitionists who were not nonresistants had difficulty determining

where authority and power should be used. See, for example, Weld's *American Slavery As It Is* and the speech of Nathaniel Colver, as reported in *Proceedings of the General Anti-Slavery Convention . . . Held in London, from Friday, June 12th, to Tuesday, June 23rd, 1840* (London, 1841), pp. 278-79. Lewis Perry, *Radical Abolitionism: Anarchy and the Government of God in Antislavery Thought* (Ithaca, 1973), shows how attacks on slavery easily became attacks upon authority. John L. Thomas, *The Liberator: William Lloyd Garrison* (Boston, 1963), pp. 327, 45, argued that "Garrison distrusted politics not simply because he feared power but because he wanted it." This seems to me to brush past the very real—and diverse—concern of Garrison and other abolitionists about power. Lewis Perry, "Versions of Anarchism in the Antislavery Movement," *American Quarterly* 22 (Winter 1968): 772, seems more nearly correct in giving it as the goal of the Garrisonians "to renounce all authoritarian relationships among men."

8. The *Emancipator*, July 21, 1836; January 28, 1834. Also L. Maria Child, *An Appeal in Favor of Americans Called Africans* (1836; reprint, New York, 1968), p. 101.

9. Bernard Bailyn, *The Origin of American Politics* (New York, 1968), p. 56; Woolman conveniently quoted in *The Antislavery Argument,* ed. William H. Pease and Jane H. Pease (Indianapolis, 1965), p. 7; Adams quoted in Ernest Lee Tuveson, *Redeemer Nation: The Idea of America's Millennial Role* (Chicago, 1968), p. 21.

10. The *Liberator*, February 5, 1831. For another early example see LaRoy Sunderland, *Anti-Slavery Manual, Containing a Collection of Facts and Arguments on American Slavery,* 2nd ed. (New York, 1837), pp. 132-33.

11. Gerrit Smith to the Jerry Rescue Committee, August 27, 1859, in Octavius Brooks Frothingham, *Gerrit Smith: A Biography,* 2nd ed. (New York, 1879), p. 240; [George Bourne], *Slavery Illustrated in Its Effects upon Woman and Domestic Society* (Boston, 1837), p. 73. Cf. Thomas Wentworth Higginson, *Black Rebellion* (New York, 1969), pp. 126-27, 175-76.

12. [Mrs. Louisa J. Barker], *Influence of Slavery upon the White Population* (American Anti-Slavery Tracts no. 9, 1855-56), p. 6; [Bourne], *Slavery Illustrated,* p. 71; John Rankin, *Letters on American Slavery, Addressed to Mr. Thomas Rankin, Merchant at Middlebrook, Augusta Co., Va.* (1838; reprint, New York: 1969), xi.

13. Abolitionists seldom assaulted the image of the pure Southern white woman so directly, although they often blamed the women of the South for cruelty, idleness, and for maintaining the system. For one of the few open (and vicious) attacks on the image see [Bourne], *Slavery Illustrated,* p. 77, in which a young slaveholder explains why he will not marry any Southern lady: "Do you think that I am going to marry a young woman with a vitiated constitution, the remains of her attachment for her father's niggers?"

14. Whipple, *Family Relation,* p. 8; "Influence of Slavery on Slaveholders," *Quarterly Anti-Slavery Magazine* 1 (July 1836): 326; Rankin, *Letters on Slavery,* pp. 62-63; Puritan, *The Abrogation of the Seventh Commandment by the American Churches* (New York, 1835), p. 5; Thome quoted in the *Liberator,* May 17, 1834. Thomas F. Harwood, "The Abolitionist Image of Louisiana and Mississippi," *Louisiana History* 7 (Fall 1966): 298, 299-300, notes abolitionist concern for Southern sexuality.

15. The *Liberator*, May 10, 1834 (comments on Thome's address by "G. B.," undoubtedly George Bourne); January 29, 1858; the *Pennsylvania Freeman,* July 4, 1834; Higginson quoted in Tilden G. Edelstein, *Strange Enthusiasm: A Life of Thomas Wentworth Higginson* (New Haven, 1968), p. 100; the *Liberator,* October 8, 1858. Also see Parker Pillsbury, *Acts of the Anti-Slavery Apostles* (Boston, 1884), p. 491; and Sarah M. Grimké, *Letters on the Equality of the Sexes, and the Condition of Woman: Addressed to Mary S. Parker, President of*

the Boston Female Anti-Slavery Society (Boston, 1838), p. 51.

16. [Barker], *Influence of Slavery*, p. 6. William R. Taylor, *Cavalier and Yankee: The Old South and American National Character* (New York, 1961), p. 139, notes that the planter, as a literary figure, was often depicted as lacking vitality and manliness. Taylor felt (I think correctly) that this may reflect the image of John Randolph as well as a nineteenth-century fascination with Hamlet. In the case of Mrs. Barker's planter—and perhaps in the case of the languid and erratic and unstable Southerner of other antislavery writings—the implications are sexual: the worn-out, enfeebled planter is not Hamlet but the age's concept of the man who has committed sexual excesses.

17. Birney to R. R. Gurley, December 3, 1833 (also, Birney to Gurley, September 24, 1833), in *Letters of James Gillespie Birney, 1831-1857*, ed. Dwight L. Dumond, 2 vols. (New York, 1938), 1: 97, 90; James G. Birney, *Letter on Colonization, Addressed to the Rev. Thornton J. Mills, Corresponding Secretary of the Kentucky Colonization Society* (New York, 1834), p. 44; Rankin, *Letters on Slavery*, p. 108; Sunderland, *Anti-Slavery Manual*, pp. 11-12. The *Liberator*, August 13, 1841, noted that by the Census of 1840 blacks showed less than "a fair rate of increase." It was then impossible to maintain that the South was in danger of being overwhelmed. The *Liberator*, alert to an argument, explained that the new figures now proved that slavery had murdered a quarter of a million people who might otherwise have lived.

18. The *Emancipator*, September 14, 1833; August 1837. See also "Humanitas," in *The National Era*, September 7, 1854; and George Thompson, *Prison Life and Reflection* . . . (Hartford, Connecticut, 1849), p. 251. Leonard L. Richards, *"Gentlemen of Property and Standing": Anti-Abolition Mobs in Jacksonian America* (New York, 1970), pp. 31-32, notes the intense fear of miscegenation which anti-abolitionists fastened onto antislavery men and women.

19. Sunderland, *Anti-Slavery Manual*, p. 132; the *Liberator*, May 7, 1831 (also, November 17, 1832); see also Child, *Appeal*, p. 133; Phelps, *Lectures on Slavery*, p. 236; and Gerrit Smith, *Letter of Gerrit Smith to Hon. Henry Clay* (New York, 1839), p. 36. Bertram Wyatt-Brown, *Lewis Tappan and the Evangelical War Against Slavery* (Cleveland, 1969), p. 177, quotes a passage which he interprets as showing a belief on the part of Tappan that miscegenation was inevitable. I suspect that Tappan may instead have been assuming the climatic theory of race. But under either interpretation it is obvious that Tappan believed that in several generations Americans would all be the same skin color—and that that color would be dark.

20. Winthrop D. Jordan, *White Over Black: American Attitudes Toward the Negro, 1550-1812* (Chapel Hill, 1968), p. 137. Also Robert W. Fogel and Stanley L. Engerman, *Time on the Cross*, 2 vols. (Boston, 1974).

21. Anonymous, *The Lustful Turk* . . . (1893 ed.; reprint, New York, 1967), p. 71; Bernard Wishy, *The Child and the Republic: The Dawn of Modern American Child Nurture* (Philadelphia, 1968), p. 40, notes the belief that servants were corruptors, and he cites George Combe, an author respected and personally known by many abolitionists; Philip Rieff, *Freud: The Mind of the Moralist* (New York, 1959), p. 166. On Victorian pornography generally, see Steven Marcus, *The Other Victorians: A Study of Sexuality and Pornography in Mid-Nineteenth Century England*, rev. ed. (New York, 1967). Marcus relates the cult of sensibility to sexuality, which certainly appeared among antislavery writers (*Other Victorians*, p. 211). *The Lustful Turk* seems to have been written sometime around 1828.

22. Bourne, letter to the Rhode Island Anti-Slavery Society, in the *Liberator*, February 6, 1836. [Bourne], *Lorette, The History of Louise, Daughter of a Canadian Nun, Exhibiting the Interior of Female Convents*, 3rd ed. (New York, 1834), pp. 37-40, 45, stresses the absolute power of the priest—a theme, actually,

of the whole novel. Bourne was also a supporter of the notorious Maria Monk. This aspect of his career is brushed by in what is otherwise the best work on him, the introduction to John W. Christie and Dwight L. Dumond, *George Bourne and the Book and Slavery Irreconcilable* (Wilmington, Del., 1969), pp. 1-101.

23. The *Philanthropist*, quoted in the *Emancipator*, December 6, 1838.

24. [Theodore Dwight Weld], *The Bible Against Slavery. An Inquiry into the Patriarchal and Mosaic Systems on the Subject of Human Rights*, 4th ed. (New York, 1838), p. 7; James G. Birney Ms Diary, May 9, 1850, Birney Mss, LC; Gilbert Haven, *National Sermons. Sermons, Speeches and Letters on Slavery and Its War . . .* (Boston, 1869), p. 3. Daniel Walker Howe, *The Unitarian Conscience: Harvard Moral Philosophy, 1805-1861* (Cambridge, Massachusetts, 1970), p. 60 observes that "Unitarians were led to espouse the view that sin consisted of a breakdown in the internal harmony, an abdication by the higher faculties of their dominion over the lower." The theme of control clearly was not confined to antislavery. Wishy, *Child and the Republic*, p. 17 sees an attempt to balance individualism and control in nineteenth-century child-raising. Clifford S. Griffin, *Their Brother's Keepers: Moral Stewardship in the United States, 1800-1865* (New Brunswick, New Jersey, 1960), sees this as an impulse behind "moral stewardship," but is overly unsympathetic and covers too broad a range of people really to be able to get at its roots. J. A. Banks, *Prosperity and Parenthood: A Study of Family Planning among the Victorian Middle Classes* (London, 1954), p. 198, notes that about 1830 the English middle class began "applying the theme of control to their own way of life." They did this, in part, by advocating sexual self-restraint. I am aware that the word "passions" had a rather technical, psychological sense which lingered on into the nineteenth century. But both the context of comments and a check of the *Oxford English Dictionary* have convinced me that the abolitionists generally used the word in its more modern sense of "intense emotions," largely sexual. There is information on topics discussed on following pages, as well as on Victorian sexuality, in John R. Betts, "Mind and Body in Early American Thought," *Journal of American History* 54 (March 1968): 787-805; and in Charles E. Rosenberg, "Sexuality, Class and Role in 19th-Century America," *American Quarterly* 25 (May 1973): 131-53. John C. Burnham, "American Historians and the Subject of Sex," *Societas* 2 (Autumn 1972): 307-16, is a good bibliographical essay. See also Ronald G. Walters, ed., *Primers for Prudery: Sexual Advice to Victorian America* (Englewood Cliffs, N.J., 1974).

25. Henry C. Wright, *Marriage and Parentage: Or, the Reproductive Element in Man, as a Means to His Elevation and Happiness*, 5th ed. (Boston, 1866), p. 271; Parker to Robert White, October 7, 1849, in John Weiss, *Life and Correspondence of Theodore Parker, Minister of the Twenty-Eighth Congregational Society, Boston*, 2 vols. (New York, 1864), 1: 386; the *Liberator*, January 12, 1838. I realize that Miss Grimké could have simply been referring to distinctions based on sex, but in the antebellum period attempts to deny social distinctions based on sex were often coupled with attempts to deny sexuality itself. Miss Grimké's views, parts of which will appear below, were strongly pointed toward subduing erotic impulses.

26. Green to Weld, July 11, 1841, in Dumond, *Weld-Grimké Letters*, 2: 868. On the religious meaning of slavery, sin, and bondage see David Brion Davis, *The Problem of Slavery in Western Culture* (Ithaca, 1966), and Jordan, *White Over Black*.

27. The *Radical Abolitionist* 1 (July 1856): 101; Goodell quoted in the *Graham Journal, of Health and Longevity* 2 (1838): 214; the *Emancipator*, August 24, 1833. Bertram Wyatt-Brown, "Prophets Outside Zion: Career and Commitment in the Abolitionist Movement," unpublished paper, delivered at the American Historical Association annual convention, December 30, 1970, notes many abolitionists recalled childhood struggles with self-control. Professor Wyatt-Brown

has recast his ideas in slightly different form in "The New Left and the Abolitionists: Romantic Radicalism in America," *Soundings* 44 (Summer 1971): 147-63; and in "New Leftists and Abolitionists: A Comparison of American Radical Styles," *Wisconsin Magazine of History* 53 (Summer 1970): 256-68.

28. Weld to Angelina Grimké, March 12, 1838; Angelina Grimké to Weld, February 21, March 4, 1838 (see also Weld to Angelina and Sarah M. Grimké, February 16, 1838; and Weld to Angelina Grimké, February 18, 1838), in Barnes and Dumond, *Weld-Grimké Letters*, 2: 602, 565, 587, 556, 560; Birney Ms Diary, March 14, 1840, Birney Mss, LC. Katherine Du Pre Lumpkin's *The Emancipation of Angelina Grimké* (Chapel Hill, 1974) is a very good account of Miss Grimké and her marriage to Weld. It appeared after I had written these passages.

29. Higginson, "Holiness Unto the Lord," the *Harbinger* 3 (1847): 28; the *Liberator*, September 17, 1836; Garrison to Helen Garrison, May 28, 1840, Ms Am 1.1, v. 3, no. 46, BPL; the *Emancipator*, January 14, 1834; Stephen Pearl Andrews, *Love, Marriage and Divorce, and the Sovereignty of the Individual* . . . (New York, 1853), p. 17.

30. Parker, "The Public Function of Woman" (1853), in *Sins and Safeguards of Society*, ed. Samuel B. Steward (Boston, n.d.), p. 203. Keith E. Melder, "The Beginnings of the Women's Rights Movement in the United States, 1800-1840" (Ph.D. diss., Yale University, 1963), p. 88, notes the coincidence of moral reform and antislavery in time. Robert Samuel Fletcher, *A History of Oberlin College from Its Foundation through the Civil War*, 2 vols. (Oberlin, 1943), 1: 296-308, gives material on the appeal of moral reform at Oberlin and Western Reserve. The Magdalen Society episode is recounted in Wyatt-Brown, *Lewis Tappan*, 68-70; Lewis Tappan, *The Life of Arthur Tappan* (New York, 1870), pp. 110-20; and Charles C. Cole, Jr., *The Social Ideas of the Northern Evangelists, 1826-1860* (New York, 1954), pp. 125-30. Data on abolitionist connections with the American Society for Promoting the Observance of the Seventh Commandment can be found in Fletcher, *History of Oberlin*, 1: 297, 305; the *Emancipator*, February 18, 1834; Barnes and Dumond, *Weld-Grimké Letters*, 1: 130-31, 136. Otelia Cromwell, *Lucretia Mott* (Cambridge, Massachusetts, 1958), p. 106, recounts the story of Lucretia Mott and the moral reform society. Also see William Goodell's *Friend of Man*, particularly the issues of January 12, 1837, and December 1, 1836; and Garrison to Helen Benson, December 17, 1836, Ms Am 1.1, v. 2, no. 47, BPL.

31. Stanton to Susan B. Anthony, March 1, 1853, in *Elizabeth Cady Stanton As Revealed in Her Letters, Diary and Reminiscences*, ed. Theodore Stanton and Harriet Stanton Blatch, 2 vols. (New York, [1922?]), 2: 48-49. "Woman's degradation is in man's idea of his sexual rights" (Stanton to Anthony, June 14, 1860, in ibid., 2: 82). This theme appeared in the woman's rights movement, of which Mrs. Stanton was such a notable part. For interesting parallels with English experience see J. A. and Olive Banks, *Femininism and Family Planning in Victorian England* (Liverpool, 1964).

32. Wright, *Marriage and Parentage*, pp. 265, 100; Andrews, *Love, Marriage and Divorce*, p. 20. Wright's book received a generally favorable review by C. K. Whipple in the *Liberator*, September 29, 1854. Perry, *Radical Abolitionism*, pp. 222-29, discusses Wright's views on marriage and the family. Professor Perry plans to analyze Wright's complicated personal attitudes in his forthcoming biography of Wright.

33. Tappan, *Life of Arthur Tappan*, p. 121; the *Liberator*, January 16, 1846.

34. Weld to Theodore Grimké Weld, July 26, 1860, Weld Mss, Clements Library. The episode also appears in Gerda Lerner, *The Grimké Sisters from South Carolina: Rebels Against Slavery* (Boston, 1967), pp. 345-49.

35. William B. Walker "The Health Reform Movement in the United States: 1830-1870" (Ph.D. diss., The Johns Hopkins University, 1955), p. 124; H. B.

Stanton and others to Theodore Dwight Weld, August 2, 1832, in Barnes and Dumond, *Weld-Grimké Letters,* 1: 85; Fletcher, *History of Oberlin,* 1: 318-39; *Graham Journal, of Health and Longevity* 3 (1839): 185; 1 (1837): 5; and 2 (1838): 209. Thomas H. LeDuc, "Grahamites and Garrisonites," *New York History* 22 (April 1939): 189-91, reprints (with commentary) an amusing document about abolitionists who believed in Graham's system.

36. Walker, "Health Reform Movement," p. 276; Benjamin P. Thomas, *Theodore Dwight Weld, Crusader for Freedom* (New Brunswick, New Jersey, 1950), p. 39; Henry Villard, *The Memoirs of Henry Villard, Journalist and Financier: 1835-1900,* 2 vols. (Boston, 1904), 2: 52.

37. Thomas Wentworth Higginson, *Out-Door Papers* (Boston, 1863), p. 142; Sallie Holley to Mrs. Samuel Porter, February 28, 1859, in *A Life for Liberty: Anti-Slavery and Other Letters of Sallie Holley,* ed. John White Chadwick (1899; reprint, New York, 1969), pp. 166-67. Edelstein, *Strange Enthusiasm,* pp. 25-26, writes of Higginson: "The issue of manliness would be very close to many of the social causes he would champion." Walker, "Health Reform Movement," pp. 285-87, notes the "vigorous life" as an outgrowth of health reform.

38. Higginson, *Out-Door Papers,* p. 139.

39. "First Annual Report of the Oneida Community" (1848), in Norman E. Himes, *Medical History of Contraception* (1936; reprint, New York, 1963), pp. 269-74.

40. Wright, *Marriage and Parentage,* pp. 18, 227.

41. Stanton to Susan B. Anthony, March 1, 1853, and Stanton to Elizabeth Smith Miller, September 11, 1862, in Stanton and Blatch, *Elizabeth Cady Stanton,* 2: 48-9, 91; Elizabeth Cady Stanton, S. B. Anthony, and M. J. Gage, eds., *History of Woman Suffrage,* 2 vols. (New York, 1881-82 [later volumes were added, with different combinations of editors]), 1: 51, 89.

42. Andrews, *Love, Marriage, and Divorce,* p. 20.

43. Birney Ms Diary, December 10, 1850, Birney Mss, LC. Anne L. Kuhn, *The Mother's Role in Childhood Education: New England Concepts, 1830-1860* (New Haven, 1947), pp. 114-18, and Walker, "Health Reform Movement," pp. 27-29, see phrenology coupled with interest in progress and improvement. On phrenology see John D. Davis, *Phrenology, Fad and Science: A Nineteenth Century American Crusade* (New Haven, 1955).

44. Henry C. Wright, for instance, advocated a form of birth control when he advised abstinence and the conception of children at intervals of no less than three years. Yet Wright railed against physicians who promoted artificial birth control instead of telling couples to control their passions (Wright, *Marriage and Parentage,* pp. 126, 132-33). The birthrate was declining even before 1831, particularly in New England and in urban areas, suggesting that contraception may have been practiced before the first pamphlets on it appeared in America in the 1830s (J. Potter, "The Growth of Population in America, 1700-1860," in *Population in History: Essays in Historical Demography,* ed. D. V. Glass and D. E. C. Eversley [London, 1965], pp. 672-73, 677-78). Recent works in European historical demography have also uncovered evidence that contraception was practiced with some effect in the eighteenth century, before the prevalence of birth control literature, and in preindustrial communities. It seems to me, however, no accident that birth control became a public issue at the same time as other reform movements, likewise concerned with man's physical nature; and it further seems that this sort of concern interacted nicely with economic and cultural changes brought about by industrialization. These changes, of course, primarily affected the family, and some of them appear in the following chapter. I have dealt with these themes in a slightly broader context in "The Family and Ante-bellum Reform: An Interepretation," *Societas* 4 (Summer 1973): 221-32, and in *Primers for Prudery.*

45. Parker, "The Three Chief Safeguards of Society" (1851), *Sins and Safe-guards*, p. 53; Stowe, "Bodily Religion," *Atlantic Monthly* 18 (July 1866): 92. LaRoy Sunderland, at the time a Methodist minister, argued that religious duty required people to preserve health, in *The Graham Journal, of Health and Long-evity* 3 (1839): 186-87. For a similar feeling, expressed in a different reform, see Charles E. Rosenberg and Carroll S. Rosenberg, "Pietism and the Origins of the American Public Health Movement: A Note on John H. Garrison and Robert M. Hartley," *Journal of the History of Medicine and Allied Sciences* 23 (January 1968): 16-35.

46. Moncure Daniel Conway, *Autobiography, Memories, and Experiences of Moncure Daniel Conway*, 2 vols. (Boston, 1904), 2: 350; Stanton to Robert Dale Owen, April 10, 1866, in Stanton and Blatch, *Elizabeth Cady Stanton*, 2: 113; Parker Pillsbury, *Acts of the Anti-Slavery Apostles* (Boston, 1884), pp. 489-90. Among the subscribers to an early publication of Spencer's philosophical works were such antislavery stalwarts as Wendell Phillips, Theodore Dwight Weld, and O. B. Frothingham (Herbert Spencer, *Education: Intellectual, Moral, and Physical* [New York, 1861], pp. viii-ix).

CHAPTER 6

1. James A. Thome, *Address to the Females of Ohio, Delivered at the State Anti-Slavery Anniversary* (Cincinnati, 1836), p. 10; Theodore Parker, "Home and Its Moral Influence" (1843), in *Sins and Safeguards of Society*, ed. Samuel B. Stewart (Boston, n.d.), p. 208.

2. *The Family and Slavery, by a Native of the Southwest* (Cincinnati, n.d.), pp. 13, 1; the *National Principia*, November 26, 1859. John L. Thomas, "Romantic Reform in America, 1815-1865," reprinted in *Ante-Bellum Reform*, ed. David Brion Davis (New York, 1967), pp. 163-64, 173, notes the importance of the family in the calculations of reformers. Also see Christopher Lasch, *The New Radicalism in America, 1889-1963: The Intellectual as a Social Type* (New York, 1967), p. xiii.

3. Whittier to Sarah and Angelina Grimké, August 14, 1837, in *Letters of Theo-dore Dwight Weld, Angelina Grimké Weld, and Sarah Grimké: 1822-1844*, ed. Gil-bert H. Barnes and Dwight L. Dumond, 2 vols. (New York, 1934), 1: 423; [Theo-dore Dwight Weld], *The Bible Against Slavery. An Inquiry into the Patriarchal and Mosaic Systems on the Subject of Human Rights*, 4th ed. (New York, 1838), p. 6; quotations from Wright in Henry C. Wright, *Marriage and Parentage: Or, the Re-productive Element in Man, As a Means to His Elevation and Happiness*, 5th ed. (Boston, 1866), p. 276; the *Liberator*, December 1, 1837; March 12, 1841. Wright discussed the problem of authority in the family in the *Liberator*, July 21, 1837; March 7, 1838.

4. See William R. Taylor, *Cavalier and Yankee: The Old South and American National Character* (New York, 1961), especially p. 104; and Bernard Wishy, *The Child and the Republic: The Dawn of Modern American Child Nurture* (Philadelphia, 1968). The best introduction to literature about the family in nineteenth-century America is Edward N. Saveth "The Problem of American Family History," *American Quarterly* 21 (Summer 1969): 311-29. J. A. Banks, *Prosperity and Parenthood: A Study of Family Planning Among the Victorian Middle Classes* (London, 1954), p. 32, sees a change in British attitudes toward marriage around 1830. Cf. Martin Duberman, "The Northern Response to Slavery," in *The Antislavery Vanguard: New Essays on the Abolitionists*, ed. Martin Duber-man (Princeton, 1965), p. 407 fn.

5. J. Potter, "The Growth of Population in America, 1700-1860," in *Population in History: Essays in Historical Demography*, ed. D. V. Glass and D. E. C. Evers-ley (London, 1965), pp. 672-73, 677-78. On English practices see Banks, *Pros-perity and Parenthood*. Norman E. Himes, *Medical History of Contraception*

(1936; reprint, New York, 1963), traces the growth of contraceptive information. The first trace on birth control written by an American came from a Massachusetts physician in the 1830s.

6. Stuart Bruchey, *The Roots of American Economic Growth, 1607-1861: An Essay in Social Causation* (New York, 1968), pp. 30, 85-86; Richard C. Wade *The Urban Frontier: Pioneer Life in Early Pittsburgh, Cincinnati, Lexington, Louisville, and St. Louis* (Chicago, 1964), pp. 304-10.

7. Weld to Angelina Grimké, April 15, 1838; also Lydia Maria Child to Angelina and Theodore Weld, December 26, 1838, in Barnes and Dumond, *Weld-Grimké Letters*, 2: 637, 731; the *Liberator*, December 19, 1851. Miss Holley never married on earth.

8. Stephen Pearl Andrews, *Love, Marriage, and Divorce, and the Sovereignty of the Individual . . .* (New York, 1853), p. 85.

9. Birney to Theodore Parker, July 5, 1848, in *Letters of James Gillespie Birney, 1831-1857*, ed. Dwight L. Dumond, 2 vols. (New York, 1938), 2: 1106.

10. Noyes quoted in Alice Felt Tyler, *Freedom's Ferment. Phases of American Social History from the Colonial Period to the Outbreak of the Civil War* (New York, 1962), p. 194. See Anne L. Kuhn, *The Mother's Role in Childhood Education: New England Concepts, 1830-1860* (New Haven, 1947), pp. 36-68, for much descriptive material on domestic reform, including mention of Adams. David Donald, "The Proslavery Argument Reconsidered," *Journal of Southern History* 37 (February 1971): 3-18, gives both an analysis of defenses of slavery and makes the point that such writings bear similarity to those of the abolitionists, among others.

11. *The Family and Slavery*, p. 6; Stephen S. Foster, *The Brotherhood of Thieves; Or, A True Picture of the American Church and Clergy: A Letter to Nathaniel Barney, of Nantucket* (Boston, 1844), p. 9.

12. [George Bourne], *Picture of Slavery in the United States of America* (Middletown, Connecticut, 1834), p. 87.

13. *The Family and Slavery*, p. 23; Harriet Beecher Stowe, *Uncle Tom's Cabin: Or, Life Among the Lowly and A Key to Uncle Tom's Cabin*, 2 vols. (Boston, 1896), 2: 371; the *Anti-Slavery Record* 2 (March 1836): 10.

14. Phillipe Ariès, *Centuries of Childhood: A Social History of Family Life*, trans., Robert Baldick (New York, 1962).

15. Potter, "Growth of the Population in America," in Glass and Eversley, *Population in History*, pp. 660, 663, 668-71, 673. E. J. Hobsbawm, *The Age of Revolution: 1789-1848* (New York, n.d.), p. 204, notes that world populations generally were younger in the nineteenth century.

16. P. J. Staudenraus, *The African Colonization Movement, 1816-1865* (New York, 1961), p. 127; Bernard A. Weisberger, *They Gathered at the River: The Story of the Great Revivalists and Their Impact upon Religion in America* (Chicago, 1966), pp. 142-43; Timothy L. Smith, *Revivalism and Social Reform: American Protestantism on the Eve of the Civil War* (New York, 1965), p. 40; the *Boston Evening Transcript*, January 18, 1855. In general see Wishy, *Child and the Republic*; Kuhn, *Mother's Role*; and the selections discussed in Saveth, "Problem of American Family History," pp. 311-29.

17. Garrison to Elizabeth Pease, July 2, 1842, Ms Am 1.1, v. 3, no. 93, BPL; the *Liberator*, February 25, 1837.

18. The *Slave's Friend*, vol. 1, no. 6; the *Child's Newspaper*, January 7, 1834; Parker, "Phases of Domestic Life," in *Lessons from the World of Matter and the World of Man*, ed. Rufus Leighton (Boston, n.d.), p. 198; the *Anti-Slavery Alphabet* (Philadelphia, 1847).

19. Wright to Garrison, in the *Liberator*, December 24, 1836; J. Elizabeth Jones, *The Young Abolitionists, Or Conversations on Slavery* (Boston, 1848), pp. 7-8. For an example of assertions of juvenile depravity see the item from the

Child's Newspaper, cited in note 18 above, and the *Slave's Friend,* vol. 1, no. 3, p. 12.

20. Jones, *The Young Abolitionists,* p. 21; Mrs. Eliza Lee Follen, *The Liberty Cap* (Boston, 1846), p. 17; the *Philanthropist,* quoted in the *Slave's Friend,* vol. 1, no. 11, p. 16.

21. Parker, "Home and Its Moral Influence" (1843), in *Sins and Safeguards,* p. 208; Wright, *Marriage and Parentage,* p. 134; Sarah Grimké to Gerrit Smith, June 28, 1837, in Barnes and Dumond, *Weld-Grimké Letters,* 1: 408.

22. Thomas Wentworth Higginson, *Out-Door Papers* (Boston, 1863), p. 174; Harriet Beecher Stowe, "Bodily Religion: A Sermon on Good Health," *Atlantic Monthly* 18 (July 1866): 93.

23. Sarah M. Grimké, *Letters on the Equality of the Sexes, and the Condition of Woman; Addressed to Mary S. Parker, President of the Boston Female Anti-Slavery Society* (Boston, 1838), p. 54; Parker, "The Public Function of Woman" (1853), in *Sins and Safeguards,* pp. 182-83; Keith E. Melder, "The Beginnings of the Women's Rights Movement in the United States, 1800-1840" (Ph.D. diss., Yale University, 1963), pp. 13-14, 19, 34, notes the changing economic role of women as well as the importance of Irish servant labor in the 1840s.

24. *Elizabeth Cady Stanton As Revealed in Her Letters, Diary, and Reminiscences,* eds. Theodore Stanton and Harriot Stanton Blatch, 2 vols. (New York, [1922?]), 1: 144; also, Elizabeth Cady Stanton to Susan B. Anthony, April 2, 1852, in Stanton and Blatch, *Elizabeth Cady Stanton,* 2: 41-2.

25. Lucretia Mott, "Discourse on Woman," delivered March 17, 1849, in *James and Lucretia Mott. Life and Letters,* ed. Anna Davis Hallowell (Boston, 1884), p. 493; L. Maria Child, *Letters from New York,* first ser. (New York, 1843), p. 282. See also Barbara Welter, "The Cult of True Womanhood: 1820-1860," *American Quarterly* 18 (Summer 1966): 151-74; and Mary Patricia Ryan, "American Society and The Cult of Domesticity, 1830-1860" (Ph.D. diss., University of California, Santa Barbara, 1972).

26. A. E. Grimké, *Letters to Catherine E. Beecher in Reply to an Essay on Slavery and Abolitionism, Addressed to A. E. Grimké,* rev. ed. (Boston, 1838), pp. 114-15; Gerritt Smith to Miss Pellet, October 25, 1852, in Octavius Brooks Frothingham, *Gerrit Smith: A Biography,* 2nd ed. (New York, 1879), pp. 123-24; see also Sarah M. Grimké in the *Liberator,* February 16, 1838.

27. This was A. Hawley's repetition of a resolution which passed unanimously at a meeting of the Massachusetts Anti-Slavery Society in 1836. He recalled it, with the emphasis here reproduced, to remind anti-Garrisonians how much of woman's rights they had accepted before the schism (the *Liberator,* February 7, 1840).

28. Parker, "Public Function of Woman" (1853), in *Sins and Safeguards,* p. 190.

29. Child, *Letters from New York,* first ser., p. 240; the *Liberator,* January 29, 1847.

30. Reprinted in *History of Woman Suffrage,* ed. Elizabeth Cady Stanton, S. B. Anthony, and M. J. Gage, 2 vols. (New York, 1881-82), 1: 72.

31. Angelina Grimké, *Appeal to the Christian Women of the South,* 3rd ed. (New York, 1836), p. 27; the *Emancipator,* December 21, 1833; Thome, *Address to the Females of Ohio,* p. 4; Gilbert Haven, *National Sermons. Sermons, Speeches, and Letters on Slavery and Its War . . .* (Boston, 1869), p. 627; Thomas Wentworth Higginson, *Women and Men* (Boston, 1888), p. 17. Taylor, *Cavalier and Yankee,* pp. 124-25, notes in popular literature a "new moral authority assumed by American women, and [a] sentimental obsession with childhood innocence." He traces this to a breakdown of the family unit. The family, I suspect, was changing rather than breaking down, but I would add the "breakdown" of another institution: the church. No longer could a church serve as the moral locus for a

whole community. Of course, others besides abolitionists stressed woman's moral influence. In addition to examples given in *Cavalier and Yankee*, see Kuhn, *Mother's Role*, pp. 71-97. Cultural changes, moreover, do not take place independently of events. There were examples before abolitionists of women who had exerted social authority. Elizabeth Heyrick's influence on British antislavery was undeniable, and Victoria sat upon the throne of Great Britain. Not all abolitionists were advocates of woman's rights, but even abolitionists who were "conservative" on this issue in terms of the movement were often in advance of the times. Robert Samuel Fletcher, *A History of Oberlin College from Its Foundation through the Civil War*, 2 vols. (Oberlin, 1943), 1: 293-94, gives evidence in the cases of Asa Mahan and James A. Thome. Lewis Tappan, in 1849, took the position that a woman should be allowed to address the American Union Missionary Association. The *Liberator*, October 5, 1849, noted this change from Tappan's opposition to such things in 1840.

32. Puritan, *The Abrogation of the Seventh Commandment by the American Churches* (New York, 1835), p. 17; Parker, "Home and Its Moral Influence" (1843), *Sins and Safeguards*, p. 214; the *Liberator*, August 13, 1836.

33. Stowe, "Appeal to the Women of the Free States of America on the Present Crisis in Our Country," the *Liberator*, March 3, 1854; Ludlow quoted in the *Liberator*, November 5, 1836.

34. Welter, "Cult of True Womanhood," *American Quarterly*, vol. 18; [Lyman Beecher], *The Autobiography of Lyman Beecher*, ed. Barbara Cross, 2 vols. (Boston, 1961), 1: xxix; Grimké, *Letters to Catherine Beecher*, p. 104.

35. *The Daily Chronotype*, June 19, 1848.

36. See Parker, "Home and Its Moral Influence" (1843), in *Sins and Safeguards*, p. 210; Wright, *Marriage and Parentage*, p. 223; Sarah Grimké to [Elizabeth Smith Miller], June 1, 1873, Weld Mss., the Clements Library. Elizabeth Cady Stanton thought "the mother of mankind" had the prerogative "to set bounds to [man's] indulgence" in sex. Stanton to Susan B. Anthony, March 1, 1853, in Stanton and Blatch, *Elizabeth Cady Stanton*, 2: 49. For a good statement of woman's supposed freedom from excessive "animal propensities" (and thus her relation to higher civilization), see Sarah M. Grimké to Jeanne Deroin, in the *Liberator*, August 8, 1856.

37. Angelina Grimké to L. L. Dodge, July 14, 1836, Weld Mss, LC; the *Philanthropist*, September 17, 1842; the *National Era*, August 3, 1854.

38. Tilton quoted in James M. McPherson, *The Struggle for Equality: Abolitionists and the Negro in the Civil War and Reconstruction* (Princeton, 1964), p. 145; Haven, *National Sermons*, p. 149. Women and blacks were also linked in the "plantation novel," a genre which usually idealized slavery (Taylor, *Cavalier and Yankee*, p. 152).

39. The *Emancipator*, January 14, 1834; the *Liberator*, February 2, 1838. The comparison between women and slaves occurs time and again in the literature of the early woman's rights movement.

40. The *National Anti-Slavery Standard*, December 10, 1840; Grimké, *Letters to Catherine Beecher*, p. 118; the *Liberator*, January 5, 1838.

41. J. A. Banks, *Feminism and Family Planning in Victorian England* (Liverpool, 1964), pp. 110-13, 120-21, saw the campaign for sexual equality in Great Britain focusing on controlling male sexuality, bringing men up to the standard expected of women. There was, furthermore, much opposition to birth control on the ground that it was yet another attempt to victimize women by male sexuality.

42. Cf. Helen Waite Papashvily, *All the Happy Endings: A Study of the Domestic Novel in America, the Women Who Wrote It, the Women Who Read It, in the Nineteenth Century* (New York, 1956).

43. The *Slave's Friend*, vol. 1, no. 8, pp. 1-2; *Anti-Slavery Almanac* (1837), pp. 43-44.

44. Jones, *The Young Abolitionists*, pp. 13-15; *The Child's Anti-Slavery Book: Containing a Few Words About American Slave Children and Stories of Slave-Life* (New York, 1859), pp. 69-101.

45. Kindly fathers did appear. The *Slave's Friend* seemed particularly willing to use them as instructors to their children. But also frequent were characters like Mrs. Nelson's husband. For a prime example of a father utterly humiliated by the moral superiority of his little girl see Jones, *The Young Abolitionists*, pp. 90-91. Other antislavery fiction also presented depressing examples of masculine behavior. *Uncle Tom's Cabin* abounds in them. A fascinating instance is in L. Maria Child, "The Quadroons," in *Fact and Fiction: A Collection of Stories* (New York, 1846), pp. 61-76. Cf. Wishy, *Child and the Republic*, p. 56.

46. Grimké, *Letters to Catherine Beecher*, p. 114. The importance of abolitionism for woman's rights is acknowledged in Stanton, Anthony, and Gage, *History of Woman Suffrage*, 1: 52-53; Melder "Beginnings of the Women's Rights Movement;" and American Anti-Slavery Society, *Proceedings of the American Anti-Slavery Society at Its Third Decade* . . . (New York, 1864), p. 42.

47. The *National Anti-Slavery Standard*, April 27, 1843; Sarah M. Grimké to [Elizabeth Smith Miller?], June 1, 1873, Weld Mss, the Clements Library.

48. Grimké, *Appeal to the Christian Women of the South*, p. 26; [George Bourne], *Slavery Illustrated in Its Effects upon Woman and Domestic Society* (Boston, 1837), p. 22; Puritan, *Abrogation of the Seventh Commandment*, p. 3; Mrs. E. L. Follen, *To Mothers in the Free States* (New York, 1856), p. 1; Walker's letter to Garrison in the *Liberator*, February 23, 1849.

CHAPTER 7

1. Lewis Tappan, *Is It Right To Be Rich?* (New York, 1869).

2. For an example of lack of consistency on the subject of economic motivation see John Rankin, *Letters on American Slavery, Addressed to Mr. Thomas Rankin, Merchant at Middlebrook, Augusta Co., Va.* (1838; reprint, New York, 1969), pp. 12, 55. In the first instance he blames all the world's evils on the love of gain, which he sees as the motive behind slavery. He later admits that "the love of gain affords all the protection the poor slaves can have, and it is well known that this has but little influence on the violent passions of men—to the vicious heart revenge is gain."

3. George B. Cheever, *God Against Slavery: And the Freedom and Duty of the Pulpit to Rebuke It, As a Sin Against God* (1857; reprint, Miami, Florida, 1969), p. 57; the *Philanthropist*, January 19, 1842; Pierpont to Alvan Stewart, March 24, 1840, in *Writings and Speeches of Alvan Stewart, on Slavery*, ed. Luther Rawson Marsh (New York, 1860), p. 24.

4. I am aware that there is a considerable controversy over when industrialization began in America and when the results of the industrial revolution were first felt. An exceptionally good guide is Stuart Bruchey, *The Roots of American Economic Growth, 1607-1861: An Essay in Social Causation* (New York, 1968). For my purposes the findings of Paul A. David, "Growth of the Real Product in the United States before 1840: New Evidence, Controlled Conjectures," *Journal of Economic History* 27 (June 1967): 156, 167, are particularly important. David argues that there was a significant gain in the gross domestic product after 1820 and before the mid-1830s—the eve of abolitionism. He also notes the "instability of the rate of per capita real output growth during the ante-bellum era." David further remarks that "One cannot help but be impressed by the rapidity of the economy's structural transformation in the decades immediately preceeding 1840." This strikes me as a quantification of what contemporaries were saying—that there was a noticeable but erratic expansion and prosperity. The precise moment the "effects" of industrialization were felt is less important for this essay than the fact that by 1830 Americans perceived a remarkable prosperity and also realized that

it was fragile. The unevenness of the Jacksonian economy gave new meaning to old ideas and to ambivalences about luxury and economic acquisitiveness. William R. Taylor, *Cavalier and Yankee: The Old South and American National Character* (New York, 1961), p. 97, presents examples of nonabolitionists who similarly fretted over economic individualism and who saw a relationship between it and control. Leo Marx, *The Machine in the Garden: Technology and the Pastoral Ideal in America* (New York, 1964), p. 350, argues that in American literature around the time of abolitionism technology stood as a symbol for power. Again there seems to have been. a resonance between objective conditions and much deeper cultural and psychological catgories—and antislavery was only on manifstation among many. Peter Temin, *The Jacksonian Economy* (New York, 1969), also has much data on economic fluctuations of the late 1830s.

5. Fear of "luxury" among the Revolutionary generation has been commented upon by many scholars. See Gordon S. Wood, *The Creation of the American Republic, 1776-1787* (Chapel Hill, 1969), pp. 52, 65, 70; and Ernest L. Tuveson, *Millennium and Utopia: A Study in the Background of the Idea of Progress* (Berkeley, 1949), pp. 6-7, 16, 17, 57 (for earlier comments on luxury).

6. The *Emancipator*, September 28, 1833; Parker, "Moral Dangers of Prosperity" (1854), in *Sins and Safeguards of Society*, ed. Samuel B. Stewart (Boston, n.d.), p. 243. Robert B. Hall, speaking before the New England Anti-Slavery Society, argued that slavery breeds luxury, made the inevitable analogy to the fall of Rome, and asserted that luxury is inconsistent with a republic. He then argued that America's "prosperity and happiness" would be advanced by antislavery! (*Liberator*, April 14, 1832).

7. Phillips, speaking before the Massachusetts Anti-Slavery Society, quoted in the *Liberator*, March 5, 1858; Robinson quoted in Russel B. Nye, "Marius Robinson, a Forgotten Abolitionist Leader," *The Ohio State Archaeological and Historical Quarterly* 55 (April-June 1946): 152-53; Bayard Tuckerman, *William Jay and the Constitutional Movement for the Abolition of Slavery* (New York, 1893), p. 80.

8. See Eugene D. Genovese, *The World the Slaveholders Made: Two Essays in Interpretation* (New York, 1969), regarding defenders of slavery.

9. This material may be found in the standard biographical references, the *Dictionary of American Biography* and the *National Cyclopaedia of American Biography* in particular. Henry Villard's career can be traced in Villard, *The Memoirs of Henry Villard, Journalist and Financier: 1835-1900*, 2 vols. (Boston, 1904), and is treated briefly and sympathetically in Thomas C. Cochran, "The Legend of the Robber Barons," *Pennsylvania Magazine of History and Biography* 74 (July 1950): 310-15.

10. Again, see the standard biographical resources. Also, on Whittier see Wendell Phillips Garrison and Francis Jackson Garrison, *William Lloyd Garrison, 1805-1879: The Story of His Life as Told by His Children*, 4 vols. (New York, 1885-89), 1: 115; on Robinson see Nye, "Marius Robinson," *Ohio State Archaeological and Historical Quarterly*, vol. 55, and Dwight L. Dumond, ed., *Letters of James Gillespie Birney, 1831-1857*, 2 vols. (New York, 1938), 1: 38 fn 2; on Wright see Philip Green Wright and Elizabeth Q. Wright, *Elizur Wright: The Father of Life Insurance* (Chicago, 1937), pp. 220-39. The best source on the Tappans is Bertram Wyatt-Brown's fine biography, *Lewis Tappan and the Evangelical War Against Slavery* (Cleveland, 1969).

11. John White Chadwick, ed., *A Life for Liberty: Anti-Slavery and Other Letters of Sallie Holley* (1899; reprint, New York, 1969), p. 33; Samuel May, Jr., to Richard Webb, October 30, 1871, Ms B 1.6, v. 11, no. 19, BPL. Myron Holley had helped build the Erie Canal. Elizur Wright, his biographer, thought such activities "an incalculable blessing." Elizur Wright, *Myron Holley: And What He Did for Liberty and True Religion* (Boston, 1882), p. 143. Gerrit Smith invested

fair amounts of money in railroads—including $25,000 in a line which was never built. Ralph Volney Harlow, *Gerrit Smith: Philanthropist and Reformer* (New York, 1939), pp. 478-82.

12. *Herald of Freedom*, June 14, 1844, in [Nathaniel Peabody Rogers], *A Collection from the Newspaper Writings of Nathaniel Peabody Rogers* (Concord, New Hampshire, 1847), p. 272; Higginson, "The Railroad," the *Harbinger* 2 (1846): 269-70; Higginson, *Out-Door Papers* (Boston, 1863), pp. 35-36. The *Liberator*, April 19, 1844, also comments on "Get Off the Track." Tilden J. Edelstein, *Strange Enthusiasm: A Life of Thomas Wentworth Higginson* (New Haven, 1968), p. 60, mentions Higginson's attitudes toward the railroad.

13. Wright and Wright, *Elizur Wright*, pp. 168-69; the *Radical Abolitionist* 4 (September, 1858): 11; *National Era*, January 14, 1847; the *National Anti-Slavery Standard*, September 28, 1843.

14. The *Liberator*, October 26, 1849; November 25, 1853. Other enthusiastic comments from Garrison appear in the *Liberator*, January 12, 1844; March 19, November 11, 1852; and William Lloyd Garrison, *Thoughts on African Colonization* (1832, reprint, New York, 1969), part 1, p. 36. See Lucretia Mott on the telegraph, quoted in *James and Lucretia Mott. Life and Letters*, ed. Anna Davis Hallowell (Boston, 1884), p. 342.

15. *Journal of the Times*, October 3, 1828, reprinted in Garrison and Garrison, *William Lloyd Garrison*, 1: 103-4; Garrison to Helen Garrison, November 10, 1865, Ms Am 1.1, v. 9, no. 138, BPL.

16. Parker, "Thoughts on Labor," *Dial* 1 (April 1841): 497-519, cited in Marx, *Machine in the Garden*, p. 201; [Elizur Wright], "What Are We Going to Make?" *Atlantic Monthly* 2 (June 1858): 90-101; Phillips, "Lincoln's Election" (1860), *Speeches*, first ser., p. 315.

17. I am aware of the controversy sparked by David Donald, "Toward a Reconsideration of the Abolitionists," in *Lincoln Reconsidered: Essays on the Civil War Era* (New York, 1956), pp. 19-36. Donald presented the abolitionists as tending to come from occupations suffering declining status and as latching on to reform as a way of retaining moral authority. His interpretation represented a quantification, and a modification, of the thesis advanced by Avery O. Craven, "An Unorthodox Interpretation of the Abolition Movement," *Journal of Southern History* 7 (February 1941): 57-58. Craven argued that industrialization was the cause of abolitionism and that those who had trouble adjusting to it tended to become dissenters. Donald's thesis has been nibbled at through the years. The first assault was Robert Allen Skotheim, "A Note on Historical Method: David Donald's 'Toward a Reconsideration of the Abolitionists,'" *Journal of Southern History* 25 (August 1959): 356-65, which drew an angry rebuttal from Donald, in *Journal of Southern History* 26 (February 1960): 156-57. Later and more cautious challenges appear in many places. See Daniel Walker Howe, *The Unitarian Conscience: Harvard Moral Philosophy, 1805-1861* (Cambridge, Massachusetts, 1970), pp. 275-76; and Donald G. Mathews, *Slavery and Methodism: A Chapter in American Morality, 1780-1845* (Princeton, 1965), p. 175. No one has effectively joined the issue by seeking to re-do Donald's quantification or to set up different categories of analysis. There is some attempt along this line in Gerald Sorin, *The New York Abolitionists: A Case Study of Political Radicalism* (Westport, Connecticut, 1971), but I am not convinced that this is an adequate refutation of Donald, nor am I convinced that Sorin's categories represent an advance over Donald's. More successful is Leonard L. Richards, "*Gentlemen of Property and Standing*": *Anti-Abolition Mobs in Jacksonian America* (New York, 1970). Richards, however, examines a different kind of abolitionist from Donald's: followers rather than leaders. Richards does do what Donald did not—compare abolitionists with those who were not abolitionists—and thus has the advantage on that point. But few historians have sought to deal with the basic questions

posed quite explicitly by Donald: why did abolitionism begin in the 1830s, and what was its relation to Northern society? Furthermore, few critics of the "status revolution" thesis have noted that in one of its earliest and most sustained formulations it allowed for declining and rising status to produce the same results. See the treatment of teachers in Richard Hofstadter, *The Age of Reform: From Bryan to F.D.R.* (New York, 1960), pp. 152-53. Once that admission is made, the crucial thing would seem to be social change itself, not necessarily the direction of change. Very likely, we are back to the connection Craven and Donald tried to establish between industrialization and reform. What they did not adequately acknowledge is that one does not have to lose status to be concerned about change, and that it is possible for men to find positions other than simple opposition or endorsement of change. It is possible to wish to modify change, alter some aspects and not others, or to hope to impose an order upon change and thereby control it.

18. Richards, *"Gentlemen of Property and Standing."* For an interesting attack on the "aristocratic spirit" of slaveholders, see James G. Birney to F. T. Taylor and others, July 22, 1835, in Dumond, *Birney Letters*, 1: 207-8. E. J. Hobsbawm, *The Age of Revolution: 1789-1848* (New York, n.d.), p. 17, notes "aristocracy" as a word coined between 1789 and 1848, the linguistic product of levelling times.

19. *Liberator*, August 21, 1840; Birney to Ezekial Webb and others, October 6, 1836, in Dumond, *Birney Letters*, 1: 363. Particularly interesting are the comments of Richard Hildreth, *Despotism in America: An Inquiry into the Nature, Results, and Legal Basis of the Slave-Holding System in the United States*, rev. ed. (Boston, 1854), p. 96. Eric Foner, *Free Soil, Free Labor, Free Men: The Ideology of the Republican Party before the Civil War* (New York, 1970), pp. 19-21, noted much the same pattern among Republicans as I see in abolitionists: a mistrust of large accumulations of capital and a hope for harmony between capital and labor (but not a desire for destruction of capital). Aileen Kraditor, *Means and Ends in American Abolitionism: Garrison and His Critics on Strategy and Tactics, 1834-1850* (New York, 1967), pp. 244-55, deals with Garrisonians and the labor question, the subject of the next paragraphs.

20. The *Daily Chronotype*, June 1, 1848. See Beriah Green to A. A. Phelps, November 3, 1843, Phelps Mss, v. 13, no. 100, BPL.

21. Letter from a New York abolitionist, reprinted in the *Liberator*, January 9, 1836; the *National Anti-Slavery Standard*, April 20, 1843.

22. Kraditor, *Means and Ends*, pp. 244-45.

23. The *Liberator*, June 14, 1850.

24. Parker, "Chief Sins of the People" (1851), in *Sins and Safeguards*, p. 15. The *Liberator*, December 18, 1840, contains the exchange with the Chartists, which is also discussed in Kraditor, *Means and Ends*, pp. 244-46, and Lydia Maria Child, *The Frugal Housewife, Dedicated to Those Who Are Not Ashamed of Economy*, 2nd ed. (Boston, 1830), pp. 92-93.

25. Wright quoted in Wright and Wright, *Elizur Wright*, p. 187; the *Liberator*, March 26, 1847; Robinson quoted in Nye, "Marius Robinson," *Ohio State Archaeological and Historical Quarterly*, vol. 55, p. 154. Note that John A. Collins, who became disgusted with conditions endured by English workers, left antislavery. He did so for the utopian socialism of Robert Owen and his response was thus not revolution but rather to form his own communitarian organization. (John L. Thomas, *The Liberator: William Lloyd Garrison* [Boston, 1963], pp. 312-13).

26. L. Maria Child, *Letters from New York*, first ser. (New York, 1843), p. 1; Garrison to Helen Garrison, May 20, 1840, Ms Am 1.1, v. 3, no. 43, BPL.

27. The best work on urban reform impulses in this period is Carroll S. Rosenberg, *Religion and the Rise of the City: The New York City Mission Movement, 1812-1870* (Ithaca, 1971). Also see Timothy L. Smith, *Revivalism and Social*

Reform: American Protestantism on the Eve of the Civil War (New York, 1965), pp. 59-60, 72-73, 153, 170, 205.

28. Garrison to Helen Garrison, August 11, 1846, and May 24, 1867, Ms Am 1.1, v. 4, no. 24, and v. 7, no. 41, BPL. On New York see Lewis Tappan, *The Life of Arthur Tappan* (New York, 1870), p. 110; the *Friend of Man*, January 12, 1837.

29. Child, *Letters from New York*, first ser., pp. 2-3; Child, *Letters from New York*, second ser. (New York, 1845), p. 248; the *Liberator*, May 23, 1856; November 26, 1852; September 10, 1841; Garrison to Helen Garrison, July 23, 1848, Ms Am 1.1, v. 4, no. 84, BPL. Garrison, in a revealing slip of the pen, gave his address incorrectly as Boston on the letter from Northampton.

30. The *Liberator*, March 15, 1834, contains Garrison's railings against the Bank War.

31. The *National Era*, March 11, 1847; Theodore Foster to James G. Birney, September 29, 1845, in Dumond, *Birney Letters*, 2: 973-74; Phillips, "Woman's Rights" (October, 1851), "Idols" (1859), and "Harper's Ferry" (1859), in *Speeches, Lectures and Letters*, first series, ed. James Redpath (Boston, 1902), pp. 22, 249, 264. Richard O. Curry, "The Abolitionists and Reconstruction: A Critical Appraisal," *Journal of Southern History* 34 (November 1968): 532-34, suggests that post-War Darwinism weighed against a paternalistic approach to Reconstruction. I think that Curry's criticism of George M. Frederickson, *The Inner Civil War: Northern Intellectuals and the Crisis of the Union* (New York, 1968), is valid on this point—but also that the roots of antigovernment sentiment went deep into antebellum experience and that Darwinism marked less of a break with antebellum ideas than has often been assumed.

32. Gerrit Smith believed that government existed only to give "protection, not from competition, but from crimes" (Octavius Brooks Frothingham, *Gerrit Smith: A Biography*, 2nd ed. [New York, 1879], p. 181). During his brief congressional term Smith, a booster of railroads on most occasions, opposed the transcontinental railroad even though he felt a transcontinental line should be built. He reasoned that private enterprise was adequate to the job. Free Trade sentiment was also rife among abolitionists. (Louis Filler, *The Crusade Against Slavery: 1830-1860* [New York, 1963], p. 181).

33. The *Emancipator*, September, 1835; Gilbert Haven, *National Sermons. Sermons, Speeches and Letters on Slavery and Its War* . . . (Boston, 1869), p. 230; [Beriah Green], *The Chattel Principle the Abhorrence of Jesus Christ and the Apostles: Or, No Refuge for American Slavery in the New Testament* (New York, 1839), p. 65.

34. The *National Era*, March 25, 1847; manuscript prospectus cited in Garrison and Garrison, *William Lloyd Garrison*, 1: 200.

35. See C. B. Macpherson, *The Political Theory of Possessive Individualism, Hobbes to Locke* (Oxford, 1962), for an interpretation and analysis of these assumptions in British political theory. Also see Staughton Lynd, *Intellectual Origins of American Radicalism* (New York, 1968), p. 72.

36. Weld to Arthur Tappan and others, November 22, 1833, in Barnes and Dumond, *Weld-Grimké Letters*, 1: 120.

37. The *American Anti-Slavery Reporter* 1 (February 1834): 1; William Goodell, *The American Slave Code in Theory and Practice. . . .* , 4th ed. (New York, 1853), p. 373; the *Liberator*, February 9, 1838. See similar comments in Stephen S. Foster, *The Brotherhood of Thieves* . . . (Boston, 1844), pp. 8-10; L. Maria Child, *An Appeal in Favor of Americans Called Africans* (1836; reprint, New York, 1968), p. 99; Gerrit Smith, *Letters of Gerrit Smith to Hon. Henry Clay* (New York, 1839), pp. 21-23.

38. Amos A. Phelps, *Lectures on Slavery and Its Remedy* (Boston, 1834), p. 133; C. C. Burleigh in the *Liberator*, March 2, 1849; Child, *Letters from New*

York, second ser., pp. 144-50; Haven, *National Sermons*, p. 219.

39. Hildreth, *Despotism in America*, p. 138; Grandin to ."B.F.W." in the *Liberator*, January 12, 1849. J. A. Banks, *Prosperity and Parenthood: A Study of Family Planning among the Victorian Middle Classes* (London, 1954), p. 30, notes an increasing consciousness in the early nineteenth century of a "standard of living" as something at which people aimed. Although he writes only of England, his findings seem relevant to the American middle class of the time.

40. Birney to Lewis Tappan, February 5, 1841, in Dumond, *Birney Letters*, 2: 623-24; the *Liberator*, August 27, 1852; November 21, 1856. Thomas Davis used the conventional antislavery statistics and the conventional arguments in Congress —appropriate behavior for an old friend of the Garrison family (*Congressional Globe*, 33rd Cong., 1st sess., 23, appendix, pp. 639-42). Foner, *Free Soil*, pp. 43-45, notes Republicans making much the same sort of statistical comparison between North and South. There was an interesting sense here that inward states could be measured, even quantified, by outward things.

41. Leavitt's "The Financial Power of Slavery" was reprinted in the *Philanthropist*, December 30, 1840. Julian P. Bretz, "The Economic Background of the Liberty Party," *American Historical Review* 34 (January 1929): 250-64, makes much of the depression as a cause of the turn to political action. There may be a small measure of truth to this, but rhetoric about slavery's financial power was not confined to political abolitionists nor to the time of the formation of the Liberty Party.

42. Birney to Myron Holley and others, May 11, 1840, in Dumond, *Birney Letters*, 1: 572-73; Kirk H. Porter, *National Party Platforms* (New York, 1924), p. 11; Marsh, *Writings and Speeches of Alvan Stewart*, pp. 47-48, 115, 240-42.

43. Examples from Child in the *National Anti-Slavery Standard*, December 2, December 22, 1842; and the *Liberator*, May 22, 1846. Quotations from Quincy and Garrison in the *Liberator*, February 25, 1842; October 22, 1841.

44. The *Liberator*, November 19, 1841; October 23, 1857. See also the *Liberator*, November 21, 1856.

45. The *Liberator*, August 10, 1838; Haven, *National Sermons*, p. 211; Phillips, "The State of the Country," *Speeches*, first ser., p. 538.

46. Tappan, *Is It Right to Be Rich?*, pp. 5-6. Wyatt-Brown, *Lewis Tappan*, p. 229, 236, notes that the brothers' attitude toward credit was partly moral, partly a sense of the necessity for orderly and predictable business relations. Wyatt-Brown's comments on the replacement of older institutions by credit-rating are particularly perceptive and have a much wider application than he was able to give them in this biography. Howe, *Unitarian Conscience*, p. 255, writes of men who were (for the most part) not abolitionists: "While they welcomed America's industrial transformation, Boston's moral elite were anxious to keep its consequences under control."

47. Tappan, *Life of Arthur Tappan*, p. 388.

CHAPTER 8

1. E. J. Hobsbawm, *The Age of Revolution: 1789-1848* (New York, n.d.), p. 163, discusses European nationalism in the context of Revolutionary change. See Aileen S. Kraditor, *Means and Ends in American Abolitionism: Garrison and His Critics on Strategy and Tactics, 1834-1850* (New York, 1967), pp. 196-217, for a sympathetic account of Garrisonian disunionism. Contrast this to the disdainful virtual silence in Dwight Lowell Dumond, *Antislavery: The Crusade for Freedom in America* (Ann Arbor, 1961), and Gilbert Hobbs Barnes, *The Anti-Slavery Impulse: 1830-1844* (1933; reprint, New York, 1964).

2. Garrison to Richard D. Webb, February 27, 1842, Ms Am 1.1, v. 3, no. 85, BPL. For the Essex County resolutions—probably the first—see the *Liberator*, February 25, 1842. Other issues of the *Liberator* containing much important in-

formation on the development of disunionism are those of March 4, March 11, April 29, May 6, and May 13, 1842.

3. The *Liberator*, May 2, 1845; October 4, 1844.

4. For good, clear statements on disunion by disunionists see the summary of an address by the Massachusetts Anti-Slavery Society in the *Liberator*, January 25, February 2, 1844. Garrison gave a brief response to questions on the subject in the *Liberator*, May 7, 1847. Also see Garrison's *Disunion. Address of the American Anti-Slavery Society; and F. Jackson's Letter on the Pro-Slavery Character of the Constitution* (New York, 1845). James M. McPherson, *The Struggle for Equality: Abolitionists and the Negro in the Civil War and Reconstruction* (Princeton, 1964), pp. 35-36, notes the prevalence among non-Garrisonians of the idea that disunionism equalled the end of slavery.

5. The *Liberator*, September 20, September 27, October 4, 1844. Also Kraditor, *Means and Ends*, pp. 195-217.

6. Oliver Johnson, *William Lloyd Garrison and His Times* . . . (Boston, 1880), p. 348.

7. The idea of Union, and American attachment to it, is traced in Paul C. Nagel, *One Nation Indivisible: The Union in American Thought* (New York, 1964). See also Fred Somkin, *Unquiet Eagle: Memory and Desire in the Idea of American Freedom, 1815-1860* (Ithaca, 1967); and Yehoshua Arieli, *Individualism and Nationalism in American Ideology* (Baltimore, 1966).

8. Jay's letter to the National Disunion Convention is reprinted in Bayard Tuckerman, *William Jay and the Constitutional Movement for the Abolition of Slavery* (New York, 1893), pp. 154-55.

9. American and Foreign Anti-Slavery Society, *The Annual Report of the American and Foreign Anti-Slavery Society, Presented at the General Meeting, Held in Broadway Tabernacle, May 11, 1847* . . . (New York, 1847), p. 31. The resolution was adopted after some debate.

10. Documents and comments by Garrison on the reaction of congressmen, and on the collaboration of Garrisonians and moderates on the Texas question, can be followed in the *Liberator*, August 8, November 7, 1845; June 5, 1846. Also see James Brewer Stewart, *Joshua R. Giddings and the Tactics of Radical Politics* (Cleveland, 1970), pp. 115-16. Charles C. Cole, Jr., *The Social Ideas of the Northern Evangelists, 1826-1860* (New York, 1954), p. 216, cites Wayland; and Eric Foner, *Free Soil, Free Labor, Free Men: The Ideology of the Republican Party before the Civil War* (New York, 1970), pp. 138-41, deals with Republican disunionist sentiment. Benjamin P. Thomas, *Theodore Dwight Weld, Crusader for Freedom* (New Brunswick, New Jersey, 1950), p. 237, says that Sarah Grimké's views were "not dissimilar to Garrison's." Garrison himself felt that by 1854 William Goodell had come virtually to the position of the American Anti-Slavery Society's then current motto: "No Union with Slave-holders" (the *Liberator*, March 31, 1854).

11. The *Liberator*, February 2, 1838; Luther Rawson Marsh, ed., *Writings and Speeches of Alvan Stewart, on Slavery* (New York, 1860), p. 98. See also Wendell Phillips Garrison and Francis Jackson Garrison, *William Lloyd Garrison, 1805-1879: The Story of His Life as Told by His Children*, 4 vols. (New York, 1885-1889), 2: 104, and the *Liberator*, March 26, 1836. Johnson, *William Lloyd Garrison*, pp. 334-35, found it remarkable, from the perspective of the late 1870s, that abolitionists had taken so long to arrive at disunion, which he correctly felt had been implied all along.

12. LaRoy Sunderland, *Anti-Slavery Manual, Containing a Collection of Facts and Arguments on American Slavery*, 2nd ed. (New York, 1837), p. 135; Marsh, *Writings and Speeches of Alvan Stewart*, p. 56; James G. Birney Ms Diary, April 27, 1850, Birney Mss, LC; Birney to Theodore Parker, May 1, 1850, in *Letters of James Gillespie Birney, 1831-1857*, ed. Dwight L. Dumond, 2 vols. (New

York, 1938), 2: 1135.

13. The *Emancipator*, July 27, 1833; *Proceedings of the General Anti-Slavery Convention, Called by the Committee of the British and Foreign Anti-Slavery Society, and Held in London, from Friday, June 12th, to Tuesday, June 23rd, 1840* (London, 1841), p. 107; the *Philanthropist*, March 16, 1842. See also Gerrit Smith, *Letter of Gerrit Smith to Hon. Henry Clay* (New York, 1839), pp. 45-46; the *Emancipator*, May 25, 1837; December, 1835; and John Greenleaf Whittier to F. H. Underwood, February, 1861, in Samuel T. Pickard, *Life and Letters of John Greenleaf Whittier*, 2 vols. (Boston, 1894), 2: 436.

14. The *National Era*, July 22, 1847; Garrison to Elizabeth Pease, April 1, 1847, Ms Am 1.1, v. 4, no. 53, BPL; the *Liberator*, May 27, 1847. Also, Garrison to Richard Webb, July 1, 1847, Ms Am 1.1, v. 4, no. 54, BPL.

15. Whittier to Mrs. Sigourney, February 2, 1832; and Whittier to F. H. Underwood, February, 1861, in Pickard, *Life and Letters of Whittier*, 1: 101, and 2: 436; William Birney, *James G. Birney and His Times: The Genesis of the Republican Party with Some Account of Abolition Movements in the South before 1828* (New York, 1890), pp. 90-91; Birney to R. R. Gurley, June 29, 1833, in Dumond, *Birney Letters*, 1: 79; [James G. Birney], *Correspondence, between the Hon. F. H. Elmore, One of the South Carolina Delegation in Congress, and James G. Birney . . .* (New York, 1838), p. 34.

16. Garrison and Garrison, *William Lloyd Garrison*, 1: 45, 60, 96-97; the *Liberator*, August 22, 1835.

17. L. Maria Child, *An Appeal in Favor of Americans Called Africans* (1836; reprint, New York, 1968), p. 126; Whipple, "Appeal to American Women," the *Liberator*, May 21, 1836; Wendell Phillips, "The Right of Petition" (1837), *Speeches, Lectures, and Letters*, second ser., ed. Rev. Theodore C. Pease (Boston, 1900), p. 5.

18. The *Liberator*, October 11, 1834; Garrison and Garrison, *William Lloyd Garrison*, 1: 373; Stephen S. Foster, *The Brotherhood of Thieves; Or, A True Picture of the American Church and Clergy . . .* (Boston, 1844), p. 17.

19. *Proceedings of the Convention of Radical Political Abolitionists, Held at Syracuse, N.Y., June 26, 27th, and 28th, 1855* (New York, 1855), pp. 42-43.

20. Smith's opinions can be found in various places, but most conveniently and most significantly (because of his disagreements with Garrison) in the *Liberator*, May 12, 1854; October 9, 1857. His speech appears in Octavius Brooks Frothingham, *Gerrit Smith: A Biography*, 2nd ed. (New York, 1879), p. 260. It was given at a war meeting in Peterboro, New York, April 27, 1861. May's opinions can be found in Samuel J. May, *Some Recollections of Our Antislavery Conflict* (Boston, 1869), pp. 388-96. The quotation may be found on pp. 395-96.

21. E. L. Follen, "Lines," the *Liberty Bell* (1856), pp. 39-40; the *Liberator*, July 7, 1854; June 8, 1849. On the christening of the Liberty Bell see Daniel J. Boorstin, *The Americans: The National Experience* (New York, 1967), pp. 380-81.

22. May, *Recollections*, pp. 4-5; the *Liberator*, July 7, 1854; January 1, 1831.

23. Note the approximate coincidence in time between antislavery, defenses of slavery, and the rise of a body of literature about the plantation, literature concerned with depicting—and often with reconciling—a divided national character. William R. Taylor, *Cavalier and Yankee: The Old South and American National Character* (New York, 1961).

24. The *Liberator*, February 12, 1858; Kirk H. Porter, *National Party Platforms* (New York, 1924), p. 11; *Anti-Slavery Almanac* (1837), p. 31.

25. The *Liberator*, January 8, 1831; November 15, 1839.

26. Gilbert Haven, *National Sermons, Sermons, Speeches and Letters on Slavery and Its War . . .* (Boston, 1869), p. 212. See also Phelps, *Lectures on Slavery*, p. 140.

27. Birney to Lewis Tappan, February 3, 1835, in Dumond, *Birney Letters*, 1: 179; May, Jr., to Richard Webb, May 22, 1859, Ms B 1.6, v. 7, no. 46, BPL.

28. The *Radical Abolitionist* 1 (August 1855): 2 and 2 (December, 1856): 41; the *Liberator*, May 25, 1855; March 22, 1850.

29. Well traced in James M. McPherson, *The Struggle for Equality: Abolitionists and the Negro in the Civil War and Reconstruction* (Princeton, 1964), pp. 3-133.

30. Phillips, "Progress" (February, 1861), *Speeches, Lectures, and Letters*, first ser., ed. James Redpath (Boston, 1902), p. 375; Johnson, *William Lloyd Garrison*, p. 347. Phillips' basic nationalism is noted in Robert D. Marcus "Wendell Phillips and American Institutions," *Journal of American History*, 56 (June 1969): 43, 48-49. McPherson, *Struggle for Equality*, pp. 49-51, recounts Phillips' struggle over whether to support the war.

31. Haven, *National Sermons*, p. 282; American Anti-Slavery Society, *Proceedings of the American Anti-Slavery Society at Its Third Decade . . .* (New York, 1864), p. 4; James Freeman Clarke, *Antislavery Days. A Sketch of the Struggle which Ended in the Abolition of Slavery in the United States* (New York, 1883), p. 11.

32. William Goodell, *Slavery and Anti-Slavery . . .* (New York, 1852), p. 1; [Birney], *Correspondence . . . F. H. Elmore*, p. 47. Clifford S. Griffin, *Their Brother's Keepers: Moral Stewardship in the United States, 1800-1865* (New Brunswick, New Jersey, 1960), p. 64, noted that antebellum benevolent societies generally pictured themselves as part of a scheme of universal reform. "The Republicans saw their anti-slavery program as one part of a world-wide movement from absolutism to democracy, aristocracy to equality, backwardness to modernity" (Foner, *Free Soil*, p. 72). Again, part of the antislavery crusade (and antebellum reform as a whole) seems to have filtered into the much milder and more respectable Republican Party.

33. The *Emancipator*, June 30, 1835; the *Liberator*, May 21, 1852. Richard Hildreth, *Despotism in America: An Inquiry into the Nature, Results, and Legal Basis of the Slave-Holding System in the United States*, rev. ed. (Boston, 1854), pp. 7, 9, noted that it was common to regard America as "a great social experiment" on which hangs the future "of all mankind." He felt that principles, however, would not fail because of the sins of any one nation and that America's role thus might well be less special than Americans imagined. But he then cast the conflict between North and South as part of a general struggle between Aristocracy and Democracy in which America had a complicated and peculiar role.

34. The *Liberator*, December 19, 1851, and January 9, February 27, May 7, 1852, contains exchanges about Kossuth.

35. Angelina Weld to Theodore Grimké Weld, December 12, 1860, Weld Mss, the Clements Library.

36. The *Emancipator*, May 27, 1834; Weld to Birney, June 19, 1834, in Dumond, *Birney Letters*, 1: 120; Haven, *National Sermons*, pp. 358-59.

37. For example see the *Liberator*, March 24, 1854; Julia Griffiths, *Autographs for Freedom*, 2 vols. (1853-54; reprint, Miami Florida, 1969), 1: 68-70; Child to John Greenleaf Whittier, January 21, 1862, in [Lydia Maria Child], *Letters of Lydia Maria Child. With a Biographical Introduction by John G. Whittier and an Appendix by Wendell Phillips* (Boston, 1883), p. 160. On the idea of American mission see Ernest Lee Tuveson, *Redeemer Nation: The Idea of America's Millennial Role* (Chicago, 1968), and Frederick Merk, with the collaboration of Lois Bannister Merk, *Manifest Destiny and Mission in American History. A Reinterpretation* (New York, 1966).

38. The *Emancipator*, July 22, 1834; Weld to James G. Birney, December 22, 1835, in Dumond, *Birney Letters*, 1: 289. See also Garrison to George Thompson, May 24, 1836, Ms Am 1.1, v. 2, no. 19, BPL; Phelps *Lectures on Slavery*, p. 58;

and George B. Cheever, *God Against Slavery: And the Freedom and Duty of the Pulpit to Rebuke It, as a Sin Against God* (1857; reprint, Miami, Florida, 1969), pp. 162-65.

39. Higginson, *Out-Door Papers* (Boston, 1863), pp. 129-30; American Anti-Slavery Society, *Proceedings . . . Third Decade*, p. 145 (see also comments of Samuel J. May and Jehiel Clafflin, ibid., pp. 88-89, 144). For retrospective remarks along this line see May, *Recollections*, p. 384; Lewis Tappan, *The Life of Arthur Tappan* (New York, 1870), pp. 372-73; and Parker Pillsbury, *Acts of the Anti-Slavery Apostles* (Boston, 1884), pp. 70-71.

40. Samuel J. May, May 14, 1840, "Anti-Slavery Album . . . J. Elizabeth Jones and Benjamin S. Jones," p. 166½, Western Anti-Slavery Society Mss, LC; [Beriah Green], *The Chattel Principle the Abhorrence of Jesus Christ an dthe Apostles; Or, No Refuge for American Slavery in the New Testament* (New York, 1839), p. 23. On Garrison's internationalism see: the *Liberator*, December 15, 1837; January 7, 1848. For statements of commitment to human unity by the abolitionists see [Bourne], *Picture of Slavery*, p. 17; Garrison to Henry C. Wright, April 1, 1843, Ms Am 1.1, v. 3, no. 106, BPL; Birney to the Liberty Party, September 1, 1846, in Dumond, *Birney Letters*, 2: 1036; Haven, *National Sermons*, p. 150; Child to Francis G. Shaw, 1873, in [Child], *Letters of Lydia Maria Child*, p. 216; Gerrit Smith in the *Liberator*, August 25, 1843.

41. The *National Anti-Slavery Standard*, May 16, 1844; the *National Era*, August 19, October 1, 1847; February 3, 1848; July 26, 1849; January 26, 1860.

42. Speech of June 27, 1854, in the *Congressional Globe*, 33rd Cong., 1st sess., 23, appendix, pp. 1016-17; Haven, *National Sermons*, pp. 460, 614-15. Smith's attitude toward Cuba received support from Elihu Burritt, best known as a promoter of world peace. Burritt to Smith, October 6, 1856, in *The Learned Blacksmith: The Letters and Journals of Elihu Burritt*, ed. Merle, Curti (New York, 1937), p. 129. In the 1870s Smith supported efforts of revolutionary organizations to free Cuba from Spain. Frothingham, *Gerrit Smith*, pp. 311-12; Ralph Volney Harlow, *Gerrit Smith: Philanthropist and Reformer* (New York, 1939), pp. 487-88. Betty Fladeland, *James Gillespie Birney: Slaveholder to Abolitionist* (Ithaca, 1955), p. 291, remarks that Birney by 1857 seemed to have "caught the spirit of 'manifest destiny.'" Foner, *Free Soil*, p. 223, notes William Seward's belief that slavery was an obstacle to American imperial power—another example of the nearness of the ideas of abolitionists to those of mainstream politicians. This is not to argue that abolitionism inevitably led to Imperialism. A number of abolitionists and antislavery politicians opposed American expansion in the postwar period. Yet it was possible to be an anti-imperialist and still believe in American Mission. Theodore Parker, for instance, opposed the Mexican War. He felt that the United States would be able to take all of Mexico peacefully in half a century anyway. Tilden G. Edelstein, *Strange Enthusiasm: A Life of Thomas Wentworth Higginson* (New Haven, 1968), p. 62. The *Liberator* attacked the idea of American Destiny (as it grew with the Mexican War) and yet itself spoke of an "Anglo-Saxon destiny" of "liberty, not of license" (the *Liberator*, January 25, 1850). The point here is not the inevitability of Imperialism but that antislavery was less detached from the concerns of Jacksonian America than has been thought—and that there is a greater continuum from antebellum reform to the post war world than the usual emphasis on the Civil War as a transforming event would lead us to believe.

43. The *Liberator*, May 5, 1865.

AFTERWORD

1. For an example of an attempt to lin kthe two movements, see Howard Zinn, "Abolitionists, Freedom Riders, and the Tactics of Agitation," in *The Antislavery Vanguard: New Essays on the Abolitionists*, ed. Martin Duberman (Princeton,

1965), pp. 417-51. Staughton Lynd, *Intellectual Origins of American Radicalism* (New York, 1968), and Aileen S. Kraditor, *Means and Ends in American Abolitionism: Garrison and His Critics on Strategy and Tactics, 1834-1850* (New York, 1967), present the abolitionists as early advocates of participatory democracy and civil disobedience, the then-current tactics of the student movement—in those gentler days of Students for a Democratic Society. Bertram Wyatt-Brown sensitively explored similarities and differences between antislavery and the "New Left." Wyatt-Brown, "The New Left and the Abolitionists: Romantic Radicalism in America," *Soundings* 44 (Summer 1971): 147-63; "New Leftists and Abolitionists: A Comparison of American Radical Styles," *Wisconsin Magazine of History* 53 (Summer 1970): 256-68. Also see Carlton Mabee, *Black Freedom: the Nonviolent Abolitionists from 1830 through the Civil War* (New York, 1970).

2. For suggestive commentaries along this line see: David Brion Davis, "Some Themes of Counter-Subversion: An Analysis of Anti-Masonic, Anti-Catholic, and Anti-Mormon Literature," *Mississippi Valley Historical Review* 47 (September 1960): 205-24; and David Donald, "The Proslavery Argument Reconsidered," *Journal of Southern History* 37 (February 1971): 17-18.

BIBLIOGRAPHICAL
NOTE

THE APPEARANCE of yet another book on American antislavery does not imply a need for yet another antislavery bibliography. Few as the abolitionists were in number, they inspired a great quantity of scholarship, and I have tried to indicate the most significant titles in my notes, a task I will not duplicate here. Readers hoping for a more general and more chronological survey than this should turn to Dwight Lowell Dumond, *Antislavery: The Crusade for Freedom in America* (Ann Arbor, 1961); Louis Filler, *The Crusade Against Slavery, 1830-1860* (New York, 1963); Gerald Sorin, *Abolitionism: A New Perspective* (New York, 1972); Merton Dillon, *The Abolitionists: The Growth of a Dissenting Minority* (DeKalb, Illinois, 1974); or to a forthcoming study by James B. Stewart, as yet untitled. Dwight Lowell Dumond, *Bibliography of Antislavery in America* (Ann Arbor, 1964), remains the best introduction to source materials, although it is marred by omissions and surprising instances of carelessness.

Even if an exhaustive bibliography is not in order, a word of explanation is— at least regarding the relationship of this manuscript to the documents and to the work of other historians.

The Antislavery Appeal began as a straightforward assessment of attitudes (not quite ideas, not quite emotions, but attitudes). The more it progressed the less straightforward it became. My original emphasis on propaganda gave way before an obvious need to check public utterances against what abolitionists were willing to say in the privacy of letters and diaries. That meant examination of most of the published correspondence of abolitionists, archival work in the Library of Congress and the Boston Public Library, and shorter excursions to other antislavery repositories. The result was neither a study of propaganda nor an absolutely comprehensive exploration of antislavery artifacts: it was an attempt to recapture a cast of mind and comprehend what made that cast of mind viable at a particular historical moment.

The great difficulty was to make sense out of it all. Conversations with those listed in the preface were especially helpful and so were the secondary sources acknowledged in footnotes and acknowledged with even greater pedantry in the dissertation upon which this is based. Also valuable was an ecclectic and disorderly reading of works on values, perception, and on the structure of mind. I shall not list those titles—to do so would imply greater mastery of them than I have. Yet historians who look to quantitatively oriented disciplines for method and explanation run the risk of forgetting that cognition and culture (that slippery concept) are a vital, largely unmeasurable part of human experience. These are too important to be entirely abandoned to social theorists, anthropologists, linguists, art historians, and psychologists.

Whatever historians owe to their eccentric readings in other disciplines, they owe more to colleagues in the same field. Old and enduring studies like Gilbert Hobbs Barnes, *The Anti-Slavery Impulse: 1830-1844* (1933; rpt., New York, 1964), continue to influence everything written afterward. Newer works of significance materialize at an alarming rate. Between conception of this book in 1967 and its final revision in 1976 there appeared numerous articles and several good books. Even in related fields there were such striking works as David Brion Davis, *The Problem of Slavery in the Age of Revolution, 1770-1823* (Ithaca, 1975); Robert W. Fogel and Stanley L. Engerman, *Time on the Cross,* 2 vols. (Boston, 1974); and Eugene D. Genovese, *Roll, Jordan Roll: The World the Slaveholders Made* (New York, 1974).

Between 1967 and 1975 there were also three major contributions to post-1830 antislavery historiography: Aileen S. Kraditor, *Means and Ends in American Abolitionism: Garrison and His Critics on Strategy and Tactics, 1834-1850* (New York, 1967); Bertram Wyatt-Brown, *Lewis Tappan and the Evangelical War Against Slavery* (Cleveland, 1969); and Lewis Perry, *Radical Abolitionism: Anarchy and the Government of God in Antislavery Thought* (Cornell, 1973).

These recent books, fine as they are, mark both a beginning and an end in antislavery scholarship. The beginning is of an appreciation of reform in which serious analysis is improved, not warped, by moral commitment. The end is of an emphasis on divisions among abolitionists, a theme running through works from Barnes' assault upon the Garrisonians in the 1930s to Kraditor's defense of them in the 1960s. Also ending is a preoccupation with the connection between religion and antislavery, even though David Brion Davis is dealing with that connection brilliantly. Those who follow Barnes and Kraditor are right to point out diversity within the antislavery movement. But in Kraditor's work diversity is pushed to where there is little meaningful left to say, other than that the time has come to go back and find out what abolitionists shared.

Similarly, historians who emphasize the evangelical origins of antislavery are right, but only within limits. Davis, Wyatt-Brown, and Perry, in particular, treat religious impulses with a subtlety that was impossible in past decades; but the evangelical tradition is not enough to explain antislavery. Revivalistic Protestantism provided reformers with a mode of thought, a language, a way of perceiving the world; yet, as Perry and Wyatt-Brown help us see, evangelicalism was not a static thing. Some of its branches grew old and brittle; others remained vital; still others flowered with strange and exotic growths. Why that occurred is what we understand least well. These unanswered questions relate to the general antebellum culture and society that provided the soil within which evangelicalism and reform functioned, flourished, and eventually died. This is where scholarship has brought us and this is where scholars must now go—to the social and cultural matrix of reform.

SOURCES FOR ILLUSTRATIONS

Section divisions: *The Legion of Liberty!* and *Force of Truth* (New York, 1857), p. 18. P. 17: *The Child's Anti-Slavery Book* (New York, 1859), p. 156. P. 21: *Harper's Monthly Magazine,* March 1860, p. 576. P. 31: Alexander Milton Ross, *Recollections of an Abolitionist, from 1855 to 1865,* (Toronto, 1875), frontispiece. P. 51: *Child's Anti-Slavery Book,* p. 62; P. 65: *Harper's Monthly Magazine,* July 1857, p. 158. P. 67: *Legion of Liberty,* p. 198. P. 79: Will Carleton, *Farm Ballads* (Chicago, 1876), p. 31. P. 85: *Harper's Monthly Magazine,* January 1856, p. 155. P. 94: *Child's Anti-Slavery Book,* frontispiece. P. 107: *Ballou's Pictorial Drawing-Room Companion,* February 10, 1855, p. 85. P. 113: *Ballou's Pictorial Drawing-Room Companion,* February 3, 1855, p. 73. P. 126: *Ballou's Pictorial Drawin-Room Companion,* January 20, 1855, p. 40. P. 144: *Gleason's Pictorial Drawing-Room Companion,* March 20, 1852, p. 192.

INDEX